PALESTINE
REBORN

D1524946

PALESTINE REBORN

WALID KHALIDI

I.B.Tauris & Co Ltd
Publishers
London · New York

Published in 1992 by
I.B.Tauris & Co Ltd
45 Bloomsbury Square
London WC1A 2HY

175 Fifth Avenue
New York
NY 10010

In the United States of America
and Canada distributed by
St Martin's Press
175 Fifth Avenue
New York
NY 10010

A full CIP record for this book is available from the British Library

Library of Congress catalog card number available:
A full CIP record is available from the Library of Congress

ISBN 1-85043-563-4 hardback
ISBN 1-85043-559-6 paperback

Typeset by Columns Design and Production Services Ltd, Reading

Printed and bound in Great Britain by WBC Limited,
Bridgend, Mid Glamorgan

For Rasha

CONTENTS

FOREWORD

In a talk which he gave at a conference on Lebanon in 1989, Walid Khalidi described himself as 'one for whom the twin agonies of Palestine and Lebanon constitute in equal measure the greater part of what T. S. Eliot calls "the damage of a lifetime"'.[1] Born and brought up in Jerusalem, having close family ties with Lebanon and having spent many years there before going to Harvard, his life's work has been the attempt to explain, to himself and to those who would listen, the nature and history of these 'twin agonies'. The essays collected in this book represent one part of that attempt, and make a major contribution to our understanding of the problem of Palestine and Israel by bringing into clearer focus one of the main elements of the problem, the Palestinian Arabs.

In a sense, all the essays are affirmations of a basic fact: the Palestinians exist, and have always existed. Those whom we call 'Palestinian Arabs' are

> not merely the descendants of the Muslim Arab conquerors of the seventh century, but the cumulative stock that included all the races that had entered and settled in Palestine since the dawn of history. They 'preceded' both Jew and Muslim Arab, in addition to 'incorporating' them. (p. 22).

It is necessary, he believes, to insist on this, because it has been so often denied in modern times. The point from which his thought begins, and that from which the 'agony' of Palestine arises, is the war of 1948, which led to the physical dispossession of the greater part of this indigenous population of Palestine, and also to their disappearance from the mind and conscience of much of the world, so that for the next decades it was possible to treat them as if they did not exist.

'There are no Palestinians', declared a prime minister of Israel, Golda Meir. She did not mean by this that they did not exist as individual human beings, but rather that the indigenous inhabitants of Palestine did not form a distinctive entity: they were simply part of a larger entity, Arab or Syrian, and, although they might have left the land where they had lived, they could be absorbed without trace into the surrounding Arab countries.

This was the assumption which underlay the attitude not only of Israel but of the powers called upon to deal with the consequences of the war of 1948: the 'Arab refugees' would sooner or later be absorbed into the societies of the surrounding countries, and 'the Palestinian component of the Arab–Israeli conflict will somehow disappear from the Middle Eastern scene' (p. 82). It was a belief to which the policies of the Arab states gave some support during the age of Nasserist, pan-Arab nationalism. The essential question appeared to be that of relations between Israel and its Arab neighbours; if that was resolved, the 'problem of Palestine' would disappear.

All that Walid Khalidi writes on the subject begins with the assertion that there is a Palestinian entity, given its present shape by the long and continuing experience of the appropriation of its land by others, and that in all attempts to resolve the 'Arab–Israeli problem' without them, the Palestinians will come back as ghosts; they will haunt the chanceries of the world until their existence is recognized, and it is only when it is recognized that the conflict will come to an end.

Of the essays in this book, the longest, Chapter 1 'The Origins and Development of the Palestine Problem 1897–1948', describes the half century of increasing anxiety and conflict which ended in the dispossession of the greater part of the Palestinians. It is history as the vanquished saw it, but many of its conclusions would now be accepted by the new generation of Israeli revisionist historians. This chapter shows how the Palestinian entity was turned into a ghost; others trace the opposite process by which that ghost has come back to life as a nation. At first, the shock of dispossession and the need for countless families and individuals to re-establish their lives on a new basis, prevented any effective assertion of their corporate existence, but the basis of it was still there: the 'umbilical cord' which bound them to each other, as victims of a shared experience, and to the land which some had been compelled to leave, and where the rest lived, after another war in 1967, under a regime hostile to them.

Like all dispossessed peoples, the Palestinians were forced to live by their abilities. They turned themselves into one of the

best-educated peoples in the Middle East, with the highest
literacy rate in the Arab world and more university students than
Israel has. They created their own national institutions: the PLO
and the Palestine National Council and – underlying them and
giving them strength – a network of national associations:
'separate unions for students, women, workers, teachers,
engineers, doctors and pharmacists, writers and journalists,
artists, farmers and lawyers' (p. 8).

It might have seemed likely that the war of 1967, in which what
was left of Palestine was taken under Israeli rule, would once
more scatter the emerging nation, but what happened was
different: 'a barrier of fear has been broken,' Walid Khalidi
suggests, as a result of 'a sense of immunity acquired
incrementally over two decades against the worst the occupation
could do' (p. 133). The occupation has also changed the balance
between Palestinians of the diaspora and those living under
Israeli rule: the centre of gravity has moved from Beirut and
Tunis to Jerusalem, the West Bank and Gaza. Partly because of
this, there has been a gradual change in the political programme
of the PLO and its Arab supporters, from maximalism towards a
viable solution of the problem which could be achieved by
negotiation, with the help of interested parties in the outside
world.

Some of the essays trace this development, from the summit
meeting of the Arab League in Fez in 1982, which put forward 'a
remarkably forthcoming, collectively articulated peace plan'
(p. 135), to the historic meeting of the Palestinian National
Council (PNC) in Algiers in 1988, when the 'two-state solution'
was fully endorsed; and, one might add, beyond that to the peace
negotiations which began in Madrid at the end of 1991.

In this process the work of Walid Khalidi has played an
important part, both in its effect upon the Palestinian movement
and its impact upon opinion in the United States and elsewhere.
His essay, 'Thinking the Unthinkable', is, in some ways, the most
important in the book. For perhaps the first time, the form which
a Palestinian state might take was considered carefully and
realistically, in the broader context of the other political entities
which would be affected by its creation, and Israel in particular.
There are harsh words in some of the essays about the leaders of
the Zionist movement and the state of Israel, but there is nothing

here of Mrs Meir's attitude in reverse. Israel exists: Walid
Khalidi has a sensitive awareness of the European tragedy which
led to its creation, even if he believes that it was unjust for the
world to try to resolve the problem at the expense of the
Palestinians alone. He knows that a Palestinian state can only
come into existence by negotiation and agreement with its
stronger neighbour. His proposals are based on an attempt to
define the 'core values' of the two main protagonists, that which
they can never surrender:

> A vital core demand is involved on each side, and is non-
> negotiable. This is the continued communal and national survival
> of each protagonist. An outcome that concedes this to one side but
> denies it to the other will not work. (p. 158)

Albert Hourani

Note

1   L. Fawaz, ed., *State and Society in Lebanon*, Tufts University and the
    Centre for Lebanese Studies, Oxford, 1991, p. 29.

PALESTINE
REBORN

INTRODUCTION

The Palestine Problem, Past and Future*

I

This chapter will look in three directions: the past, the present and the future.

History, of course, is written by the victorious. And every protagonist in history has wanted to hug the moral high ground. But *Veritas* is an elusive quarry, and it looks different to the maharajah on the elephant than to the footman walking behind. Freedom for the pike is death for the minnow. To the sheep led to slaughter, animal rights is humbug.

I do not look back to incriminate or delegitimize. How things are perceived on the other side of the hill not only helps in understanding actions and reactions, fears and transgressions, but also in the assessment of the parameters of an honourable solution.

II

The crux and the kernel of the Arab–Israeli conflict is the Palestine problem. The Arab–Israeli interstate conflict is derivative from the non-resolution of the Palestine problem. The crux and kernel of the Palestine problem is the struggle between two national movements: on the one hand, the Zionist movement (and, since 1948, its embodiment, Israel) and on the other, the

* Address at the seminar on the Arab world, Harvard Alumni College and the Center for Middle Eastern Studies, Harvard University, 24 March 1991.

Palestinian national movement (and, since 1964, its embodiment, the PLO). The crux and kernel of this struggle has been, and continues to this day to be, the issue of the control or sharing of the land of Palestine.

The earliest stirrings of Zionism as a modern political movement occurred in Russia in the 1880s. But the movement began in earnest in 1897 when the Hungarian Jewish leader Theodor Herzl convened the first Zionist Congress in Basel, Switzerland. Thirty-one Zionist Congresses have been held since then, the latest in Jerusalem in 1987. The first Zionist Congress was attended by 196 delegates, mostly from Eastern Europe. Only four of the 196 were Jews from Palestine. The first Zionist Congress established the World Zionist Organization (WZO), which functions to this day. For the last four decades, one-third of its delegates have come from the American Jewish community.

Zionism was a reaction to the twin challenges to Jewish identity of assimilation by the Christian European environment and persecution by the Christian European environment. In the all-pervasive nationalist climate of nineteenth-century Europe, it was also a positive assertion of Jewish national identity. Its *modus operandi* of massive emigration overseas, land acquisition overseas, and its colonization programme were all in keeping with the policies of the European colonial powers of the time. The first Zionist Congress adopted the Basel Programme, whose aim was to 'establish a home for the Jews in Palestine'. This 'home' – euphemism for a state – was to be established through massive immigration, land acquisition and colonization.

The problem Zionism faced in Palestine was that Palestine was an inhabited country. At the time of the Basel Programme in 1897, the local Jewish community constituted less than 7 per cent of the total population of the land. The rest of the population, 93 per cent, was Palestinian Arab. The Palestinian Arabs were all Arabs in language, culture and collective historical memory. Eighty-eight per cent of the Palestinian Arabs were Muslim, ten per cent were Christian.

The Muslim Arabs had conquered Palestine from Byzantium, the predecessor of the Ottomans, in AD 637, with the help of disaffected Christian Arabs. This was some 400 years before the Norman conquest of Britain, 100 years before the birth of Charlemagne, and 1000 years before the *Mayflower* touched the shores of this continent. The Palestinians of today claim descent, not only from their forebears who defeated Byzantium, but also from the people who inhabited Palestine under Byzantium. These in their turn were descendants, ethnic layer upon ethnic layer and generation after generation, of all previous inhabitants of the land, including the ancient Hebrews and their precursors. In other words, in Palestinian eyes, the Palestinian birthright to their country, Palestine, was as pristine as the birthright of any people to their own country.

To the West, the Zionist argument from Divine Law is eminently plausible, but to the Palestinians, if Jehovah meant to give present-day Palestine to the Jews, then Allah did not. To the West the Zionist argument from Natural Law, based on Jewish need, is eminently plausible, but if Natural Law said the Jews had a greater need for Palestine than the Palestinians themselves, then Palestinians have serious problems with this proposition. Palestinians did not and do not deny the historical and spiritual connection between the Jews and Palestine. What they could not and cannot endorse is that after a lapse of 2000 years, contemporary Jews anywhere have an overriding political right in Palestine which negates, supersedes and annuls the political rights of the Palestinians in their own homeland.

From the early 1880s, and certainly after the Basel Programme, the Palestinians saw in the Zionists a potential dispossessor, displacer and replacer. They saw in the Basel Programme an implicit delegitimization of Palestinian rights, and answered delegitimization with counter delegitimization – an attitude which they maintained until the early 1970s.

The dilemma facing the Zionist founding fathers was monumental. How does one establish a national home in a country that is already the national home of another politically alert people, particularly at a time when the Zionist movement had no military power? The strategy adopted after 1897 was to search, over the heads of the Palestinian population, for a powerful sponsor who would afford the Zionist venture the political and military protection it needed during its formative phase. The premises of this strategy were that:

1 The Basel Programme was to be implemented in spite of the presence and opposition of the Palestinian population;

2 Palestinian consent was not a necessary prerequisite; and
3 In the last analysis, force could be exerted through the
   powerful sponsor.

Thus the genesis of the Palestine problem does not date back to
1948 when the Palestinians and Arabs rejected the establishment
of Israel. Nor does it date back to the rise of the Third Reich,
though this accelerated the rate of Jewish immigration into
Palestine. Nor does it date back to the rise of the PLO in the mid
1960s. It historically dates back to the Basel Programme of 1897.

Palestinians have been on the strategic defensive ever since,
though they have often been on the tactical offensive. From the
Palestinian perspective, the historical record shows that it is the
Zionist movement which challenged the demographic, cultural,
social and political status quo that prevailed in Palestine at the
turn of the century, with all the consequences that flowed and are
still flowing from that challenge to the present day.

Zionist colonization has taken place in two major phases: the
first, from 1918 to 1948; and, after a hiatus of nearly twenty
years, the second phase which began in 1967 and which is still
ongoing today. Zionist colonization actually precedes 1918 and
had its beginnings in the early 1880s, but the Zionist programme
became viable only with the collapse of the Ottoman Empire and
its post-World War I sponsorship by Britain, the paramount
imperial power of the day.

It was under British protection and by the force of British arms
that during the first phase, 1918–48, the demographic, economic,
military and organizational infrastructure of the future Jewish
state was laid – at the expense of the indigenous Palestinian
population and in the teeth of their resistance. It was during this
first phase that the balance of power between the indigenous
Palestinian population and the Jewish immigrant population
slowly but relentlessly shifted in favour of the latter.

At the end of this first phase the Jews were still in the minority
– only one-third of the population – in spite of massive
immigration, and they owned no more than 7 per cent of the
land. But the Jews had an inherent qualitative superiority over
the indigenous Palestinian population. They were a Western,
industrialized, socialistic, centrally controlled, highly mobilizable
urban community led by an efficient, dedicated managerial élite,
supremely confident in its capacity to change the natural order of

things. This leadership had access to the talents and resources of the WZO and to its political clout in the metropolitan centres of the West.

Facing the Jewish community was a decentralized, pre-industrial, predominantly rural society led by a traditional, relaxed, patrician urban élite supremely but naïvely confident in the irreversibility of the natural order of things. This leadership had no institutional links to the neighbouring Arab capitals, which themselves were struggling under various forms of Western tutelage. By the end of this first phase, Britain had in effect become a buffer between the two communities. But Britain had also become superfluous to Zionist purposes. The Zionist leadership now brought tremendous pressure to bear on Britain psychologically, diplomatically and militarily. Unable to hit back in the wake of the Holocaust with the same force it had employed against the Palestinians, its sense of its imperial mission having been drained by the war, Britain referred the matter to the UN as a prelude to its own shabby withdrawal from the country.

An extraordinarily fleeting convergence of interest between Washington and Moscow produced a UN resolution in November 1947 to partition the country into a Jewish and an Arab state against unanimous Palestinian and Arab opposition. To the contemporaneous Palestinian and Arab leadership, partition was no compromise. The resolution did not say to the two principal protagonists: Each side will keep what it has or the bulk of it with reciprocal exchanges. It said to the Zionists: You will increase what you have 800 per cent (from 7 per cent to 55 per cent of the country). It said to the Palestinians: You yield 45 per cent of what you have and let one-third of your population live as a permanent minority under alien rule. In a word, if to the Zionist partition was more than half a loaf, to the Palestinians it was less than half a baby.

With the British smartly departing the country, the Zionists were determined to implement partition by force and the Palestinians equally determined to resist. There followed two wars: a civil war, largely between the Jewish community and the Palestinian community before the end of the British Mandate on 15 May 1948; and a regular war after 15 May between Israel (established on that date) and units of the regular Arab armies. In the civil war, the Palestinian community was pulverized and routed. It was during the civil war that the Palestinian Exodus and Diaspora began to take place. The Arab armies intervened ineffectively and too late and in reaction to the rout of the Palestinians.

The upshot of the two wars was the conquest by Israel of 75 per cent of the country, the creation of 750,000 Palestinian refugees (60 per cent of the population), the fall of ten major Palestinian towns or mixed townships with all their assets, the occupation and total destruction of 416 Palestinian villages, and the seizure of all their lands.

The Nabka, or 'Catastrophe', as the wars of 1948 have been dubbed by the Arabs, sent shock waves throughout the region, adding the Arab–Israeli interstate dimension to the conflict upon which a cold war dimension was presently superimposed when the now radicalized Arab countries turned to Moscow to balance Western support of Israel.

The twenty-year hiatus after the first phase of Zionist colonization culminated in the June 1967 war. During this period, no progress was made in addressing Palestinian grievances and suffering because of international indifference, Arab disarray, the cold war, Israel's solipsistic refusal to accept any responsibility for the fate of the Palestinians and the Arab countries' inability to face the new realities.

During the June war, Israel succeeded in conquering Sinai and the Golan, thus deepening the interstate conflict with the Arab countries. But it also succeeded in conquering the rump of Palestinian territory not incorporated in Israel in 1948: East Jerusalem, the West Bank, and the Gaza Strip, thus taking over 100 per cent of Palestine.

Their humiliating defeat combined with the loss of their territories caused the Arab countries to harden their posture on negotiations with or recognition of Israel. Using this as a pretext, Israel launched the second major phase of colonization of Palestinian territory, as though the only moral to be derived from all that had gone before was Palestinian 'need' for more colonization. This second phase, starting with 1967 and still ongoing to this day, is a repeat performance of the process that had caused the Palestinian Problem (and its derivative, the Arab–Israel conflict) in the first place – except that in this second phase (unlike the first when Britain was a buffer of sorts) Israel is in total control and the Palestinians are hostages to all the administrative, legalistic and military measures that Israel sees fit to take.

In the Palestinian Occupied Territories (East Jerusalem, the West Bank, the Gaza Strip), there had been before 1948 some seven Jewish settlements, and Jewish land ownership constituted at most 1 per cent of the total area. The pre-1948 Jewish population of these territories was at the utmost 5000 including East Jerusalem. After twenty-three years of colonization since 1967:

- East Jerusalem has been formally annexed to Israel with expanded municipal boundaries at the expense of the West Bank;
- 140,000 Israelis now live in East Jerusalem;
- 150 Israeli settlements have been established with the West Bank and the Gaza Strip, with a total population of 100,000 Jews outside East Jerusalem;
- 55 per cent of the lands of the West Bank and 42 per cent of those of the Gaza Strip have been alienated from Palestinian ownership;
- Palestinian building is barred on 68 per cent of the West Bank; and
- all the water resources of the Occupied Territories are under Israeli control – the bulk being diverted to the needs of Israel or of Israeli settlers in the Occupied Territories.

Looming over all this is the dark shadow of a million Soviet Jews expected in the next two to three years to press on the finite water and land resources of Israel and the Occupied Territories. As early as 1983 the Israeli Ministry of Agriculture and the Settlement Department of the World Zionist Organization prepared a master plan for the year 2010, envisaging the expenditure of $2.6 billion for settlement of 800,000 Jews in the West Bank alone. Whence the wherewithal for all this? Grants from the US government to Israel for the period 1952–89 totalled $53 billion. Direct grants from the US to the Palestinians of the Occupied Territories have averaged at $7.4 million per annum.

It is this that partly explains the causes of the latest Palestinian uprising – the intifada – since 1987, and Palestinian reactions to the Gulf crisis.

III

Notwithstanding, the PLO leadership committed a major error in not distancing itself from Saddam Hussein. It should have repeatedly, forcefully and publicly condemned his rape of Kuwait. That it did not is a measure of its utter disillusionment with the US, particularly after the suspension by Washington of its dialogue with the PLO. But this is no explanation, much less a justification.

However, contrary to the general impression in the West, the PLO is a predominantly civilian organization. Its backbone is the professional unions, some of which date back to the early 1920s. There are separate unions for students, women, workers, teachers, engineers, doctors and pharmacists, writers and journalists, artists, farmers and lawyers. Their total membership is in the hundred thousands. The unions are represented in the Palestinian parliament, the Palestinian National Council (PNC) – which has a membership of 600, about one-third of which is allocated to the Occupied Territories but are not allowed by Israel to attend. The mainstream guerrilla groups in the PNC constitute only 13.4 per cent of this body. The largest political organization in the PLO is Fatah, led by Arafat.

The PLO was founded by the Arab states in 1964 towards the end of the hiatus period between the two major phases of Zionist colonization. Its charter was drawn up by a Palestinian lawyer who argued legalistically that since Zionism delegitimized the Palestinians, then the charter considered Zionism and Israel delegitimized and the UN partition resolution null and void. The charter, in the new circumstances, was maximalist and unrealistic and aimed at the total liberation of Palestine.

Indeed, the very creation of the PLO reflected the Palestinian shift in orientation from a pan-Arab to a more particularistic self-image. This shift in itself was an indication of loss of faith in the ability of the Arab countries to help the Palestinian cause. The mood represented by this shift was more militantly represented by the concurrent rise in the mid 1960s of the Palestinian guerrilla movement led by Arafat, which soon captured the leadership of the PLO.

The guerrilla movement amended the PLO charter to specifically include armed struggle as the only means of total liberation.

The guerrilla movement argued that Palestine was not on the agenda of the international community or of that of any of the Arab countries and that there was no alternative to auto-emancipation for placing it on the agenda. It argued that the Palestinians had to take matters into their own hands and through guerrilla operations force the Arab countries kicking and screaming into a military confrontation with Israel.

Palestinian guerrilla operations in the years 1965–7 had little military impact on Israel, but were catalytic in creating the atmosphere that led to the 1967 war. The guerrilla strategy drew its inspiration from the success of the Algerian revolution against French occupation, as well as from the war in Vietnam. But its strategy was intrinsically flawed. It did not recognize the extent of the irrelevance of both the Algerian and Vietnamese analogies. At the heart of the guerrilla strategy was the concept of a putative Arab Hanoi. But there was no such Hanoi because of Israel's massive retaliation policy against the Arab countries 'hosting' the PLO. The Palestinian attempt to secure an Arab Hanoi, or to operate on the assumption that the Arab host country in question was one, ineluctably led to conflict with the Arab country whether it was Jordan, Lebanon or Syria.

The PLO under the leadership of Arafat began from early 1970 to undergo a slow, agonizing but cumulative learning process in the face of these realities. This process is distinctly discernible in the resolutions taken by the successive PNCs of which there have been twenty since the first in 1964. These resolutions show an evolutionary process in the reformulation of the objectives of the PLO away from total liberation and in their reformulation of the means for attaining these objectives away from exclusive reliance on the armed struggle.

The process is slow but steady, patterned and linear. It is all the more remarkable because of the obstacles it had to overcome or bypass: the monumental psychological hindrance to yielding on deeply ingrained historical convictions, the absence of Israeli reciprocity, the fierce opposition of Palestinian ideological rejectionists, the indifference and debunking by the US of the Palestinian groping towards moderation, and the hostility of Arab radical regimes anxious to maintain in their hands the so-called Palestine 'card'.

On the issue of objectives, total liberation in the PNC

resolutions was replaced in succession by concepts of 'a unitary democratic non-discriminatory secular state' including Palestinians and the Jews of Israel; the liberation of 'any part of Palestine as an interim stage'; the setting up of 'a Palestinian authority on the liberated part'; the creation of an 'entity on the liberated part' still as an interim stage; the creation of 'a Palestinian state within the 1967 frontiers' as a *point finale*; and, finally, at the Algiers PNC in November 1988, the formal explicit mention of a 'two-state solution' as a *point finale* based on the legitimacy, ironically, for both the Palestinian and Jewish states, of the UN partition plan of 1947.

Similarly, on the issue of the means there is a movement away from exclusive reliance on 'armed struggle' to armed struggle as an 'aid to diplomacy' to diplomacy with no mention of the armed struggle, as at the Algiers 1988 PNC. The shift is unmistakably 180 degrees.

IV

None of this made any impression on successive Israeli governments. Indeed, the Israeli governments seemed only to escalate the colonization of the Occupied Territories the more moderate the PLO became.

Shamir's policy, as I see it, has three pillars: first, a conviction that the US lacks the will or ability to pressure Israel effectively, whatever Washington's verbal stance might be; second, an adamant refusal to yield an inch of territory; and third, an adamant denial of Palestinian peoplehood. Shamir seems to believe he has taken the measure of Washington. After he had led Secretary Baker up the garden path over his own elections plan for almost a year during 1989, an infuriated Baker announced the suspension of talks with Shamir. He also angrily announced his telephone number, thinking he was throwing down the gauntlet to Shamir. What Baker seemed to overlook was that this was music to Shamir's ears. Shamir virtually willed Baker to go into a sulk.

Let there be no mistake: when Shamir says 'not one inch of territory', he is being as sincere as a devout Muslim attesting that Muhammed is the Prophet of God. This tenet is absolutely central for Shamir and the Israeli Likud Party which Shamir leads. It is cast in concrete. It is moored in the bedrock of Vladimir Jabotinsky's Zionist revisionism, of which Shamir sees himself as the last apostle.

Ideology, not religion and much less security, is the fountainhead of the Likud's thinking. Shamir's triumphalism is not only over Palestinians and Arabs, but equally over Labour Zionism, with which Zionist revisionism has contended for the leadership of Zion since the 1920s.

To be sure, Theodor Herzl founded Zionism, Chaim Weizman secured the Balfour Declaration, David Ben-Gurion established Israel within 75 per cent of Palestine, and Menachim Begin militarily neutralized Egypt. But in this self-image it is Shamir who will join the Zionist pantheon as the architect of Greater Israel.

Shamir's argument that he cannot deal with the PLO, because the PLO is terrorist at least attests to his sense of humour. His rejection of the PLO springs from his territorial tenet. The PLO represents a peoplehood. This people live in the Occupied Territories and in the Palestinian Diaspora. Talking to the PLO is accepting the existence of this peoplehood both inside and outside the Occupied Territories. It is getting into contact with the national and historical rights of the Palestinian people. It is opening the Pandora's box of territorial solutions.

Shamir's elections proposal of 1989 for the Palestinians of the Occupied Territories involved functions of limited autonomy in a territorial vacuum. Being confined to the residents of the Occupied Territories, they enshrine Israeli repudiation of all responsibility for the Palestinians of the Diaspora and formal denial of Palestinian peoplehood.

Already after the Gulf War, Washington seems to be moving along another garden path landscaped by Shamir: direct bilateral interstate negotiations between Israel and the Arab countries on normalization of relations. This ignores that the interstate conflict is derivative from the non-resolution of the Palestinian problem, and that Anwar Sadats do not grow on the trees of the Levant.

Operationally, this concept of Shamir's is designed not only to outflank the Palestinian issue, but to extend the 'not one inch' doctrine to the Golan Heights. When a minister in Shamir's cabinet recently implied in Washington that the Golan was negotiable, Shamir explained, 'What the minister meant to say was that if there are negotiations with Israel, they [the Syrians] will meet and can say to us, "We want the Golan", and we will say, "We won't give them to you". That's negotiations.'[1]

No. Shamir is no candidate for the Harvard Roger Fisher Chair in Yes-able Propositions.

The most precious commodity Shamir is after is time. He seeks this commodity with the avidity the Spanish conquistadors sought gold in the New World. He is not asking for much time: just three or four years – enough to bring in 1 million Soviet Jews. Hence his alternative garden paths – the elections plan and bilateral negotiations. He hopes in this way to assign the Palestinian problem to the dustbin of history.

What he is uncaringly sowing, as we approach the end of the millennium, are the seeds of an Armageddon fought by fundamentalists on both sides.

V

Will not a Palestinian state in the Occupied Territories such as the present generation of Palestinians are now willing to accept – will it not pose an unacceptable security threat to Israel?

I believe a Palestinian state can be devised which is totally compatible with Israel's security. The rock on which this state will be built is its weakness, not its strength. Its defence will not be in its hands, since no defence establishment it can build could possibly match Israel's crushing military preponderance. The defence of this Palestinian state will therefore be based solely on international guarantees. In a word, it would be a voluntarily demilitarized state in its own self-interest and contractually so, except for the requirements of internal security.

The demilitarized regime could be monitored by international observers, and by regular and unannounced on-site inspections. The state could commit itself à la Austria not to enter into any military alliance or arrangement with any Arab or non-Arab country. It will have no defence installations on its borders with Israel. A multinational force could be stationed in it for ten-year renewable periods: to act as trip-wire along the Jordan to deter any hostile move from the East, to police the border with Israel against infiltration into Israel, to act as a strategic reserve to help the Palestinian state against radical Palestinian elements, and to move against any Palestinian radical takeover of the state.

The treaty between the Palestinian state and Israel could be endorsed by the Arab League and guaranteed by the super powers. Violation of the treaty could be subject to sanctions and international military collective action if necessary.

The demilitarized regime could be politically reinforced by some federal/confederal arrangement with the moderate monarchical regime in Amman, whose maintenance is an essential component of the plan. The demilitarized regime could be economically reinforced by economic treaties and arrangements with Israel which could empirically be developed towards a full economic union between Israel and the Palestinian/Jordanian federation/confederation.

VI

The Gulf War has negative and positive implications with regard to the resolution of the Palestinian problem and the Arab–Israeli conflict. But its technical implications underline the irrelevance of the retention of the Occupied Territories for Israel's security. The negative implications for the general resolution of the conflict include: the rift between the Arab coalition partners and both the PLO and Amman, the deepening reciprocal hatred between Israelis and Palestinians, the increased US aversion to the PLO, and American tensions with Amman. Above all, they include this pinnacle of military dominance of the Middle East that Israel has now attained in the wake of the bombing of Iraq back to Ottoman times, and the carnage of the Iraqi military without the firing of a single Israeli bullet. If the conduct of Israel at moments of triumph in the past is an indicator, the chances that this Mother of all Moments of Triumph will generate a greater Israeli disposition to *noblesse oblige* would seem to be slim.

The positive implications of the Gulf War for the resolution of the Palestinian Problem and Arab–Israeli conflict include: the removal of the inter-Arab outbidding pressures from Iraq, the *rapprochement* between Syria and both Egypt and the US, the destruction of the Saladin syndrome among the Arab masses, the increased international awareness of the volatility of the Middle East and of the interconnectedness of its conflicts, the focusing of attention on the need for compliance with UN resolutions, the enhanced awareness of the limits to how *double* double standards can continue to be, and the personal commitment of the President of the US before Congress and the whole world to a just and comprehensive settlement. More problematic, though still potentially positive, are the erosion of Moscow's regional influence, the creation of a precedent for regional cooperation between Moscow and Washington, and the invigoration of the UN and of the concept of collective action.

The technical implications of the Gulf War underline the irrelevance of the retention of the Occupied Territories to Israeli security. The implications include: the destruction of all hope of strategic parity between the Arab states and Israel, the failure of Israeli deterrence – the cornerstone of Israeli military strategy – in spite of the retention of the Occupied Territories, the vulnerability of Israel to missile attack and worse, again in spite of the retention of these Territories, the dependence of early-warning systems on satellites and AWACs rather than territory, the paramountcy of the mastery of the skies (which Israel enjoys) against ground forces, however vast, on the desert battlefields of the Middle East, and the commitment of the US to the direct military defence of Israel.

VII

Great powers impinge on weaker peoples not only by their action but also by their inaction: by acts of omission no less than by acts of commission. Great powers are almost by definition oblivious of their massive, often traumatic, impact on weaker peoples. By definition also, weaker peoples cannot intrude on the attention span of great powers except sporadically. Conversely, weaker peoples obsessively focus their total attention on the great powers' acts of commission and omission.

It is possible in the circumstances for weaker peoples to be at the receiving end of cumulatively catastrophic policies emanating from the great powers without these powers being even aware of the phenomenon. Thus, the view from the Palestinian footman behind the American maharajah's elephant is that successive American administrations have been waging a relentless, gratuitous and undeclared war against the Palestinian people. From this perspective, in short, the US is not only a decisive part of the solution but also of the problem.

The catalogue of imbalances and asymmetries in US policies towards Israel and the Palestinians is truly Himalayan.

The only guiding principle in the Middle East and elsewhere worthy of this great republic is contained in a seven-letter word: *justice*. An ounce of justice is more powerful than megatons of ordnance. There is no absolute justice this side of the grave. But there is pragmatic justice. Pragmatic justice takes cognizance of the genesis and evolution of conflicts, the balance of suffering on both sides in addition to hard contemporary realities. There can be no peace in the Middle East if the Vale of Israel resounds with laughter while the Vale of Palestine resounds with mourning. There can be no peace on the basis of an aristocracy of pain in the Middle East or elsewhere.

Building is more difficult than destroying. But now that President Bush has shown his furrowed imperial brow, let us catch a glimpse of the kinder, gentler profile. Having slain the dragon, let St George take to the plough. There is a tree that is waiting to be planted in Jerusalem: the sturdy oak of peace. This is a fitting task for America. It does no violence to the precept in its Declaration of Independence that 'people seek historically that separate but equal status among the powers of the earth to which the laws of nature and nature's God entitle them'. It could even atone for the dead of the Gulf War.

Notes

1   *Boston Globe*, 19 March 1991.

CHAPTER 1

The Origins and Development of The Palestine Problem

1897–1948*

I

On 1 July 1970, President Nixon of the United States outlined US policy on Palestine. His only reference to the essential merits of the Palestine question was a declaration that the Arabs wanted to drive the Israelis into the sea. It is doubtful whether this declaration indicates the real opinion of the American President or the quality of information available to him in Washington. Less doubtful is that he considered it politically opportune to make it. That he should have done so reflects a peculiar and continuing state of mind on the part of the Western public vis-à-vis the realities of the Palestine problem, which has been both the cause and effect of such cynically inaccurate statements on it as the one made by President Nixon.

Of course the essence of the Palestine problem is something quite different. Nor is there any mystery about it. The Palestine tragedy, for that is what it is, did not unfold in some obscure era of history, in an inaccessible frontier area of the world. It has been enacted in the twentieth century, within the life-span and under the observation of thousands of Western politicians, diplomats, administrators and soldiers, in a country, Palestine, well within reach of modern means of communication. Nor was it the spontaneous outcome of fortuitous circumstances and uncon-

---

* Submitted to the Second International Symposium on Palestine, Kuwait, 13–17 February 1971. An earlier version of this essay appeared in Walid Khalidi, ed., *From Haven to Conquest*, Institute for Palestine Studies, Beirut, 1970.

trollable forces. It was initiated by deliberate acts of will. The major decisions which brought it about were taken in two Western capitals – London and Washington – by constitutional leaders, including the predecessors of President Nixon himself. These decisions were taken in the teeth of the existing realities in Palestine, and against both the agonized appeals of the Palestine Arabs and the warnings and counsels of Western expert observers. As for the Zionists, they acted from the beginning according to a twofold strategy of propaganda and implementation. This strategy was multifaceted and carefully orchestrated and was dominated by a single ultimate political goal: the establishment of a Jewish state. The Zionists were the initiators. But they were also, as they still are, the protégés of their Anglo-American sponsors and the emanations of their power, resources and will.

The Palestine tragedy – of which the current Middle East crisis is but the latest chapter – has, unlike most great upheavals in history, a specific starting point: the year 1897. In this year an international European Jewish political movement, the World Zionist Organization, meeting in its constituent congress at Basel, Switzerland, resolved in a euphemistically phrased programme to work towards the establishment of a Jewish state on Palestinian Arab soil. At the time of the Basel Congress 95 per cent of the population of Palestine was Arab and 99 per cent of its land was Arab-owned. In excluding these realities from their ken, the Jewish leaders assembled at Basel were behaving in a spirit characteristic of their age and continent. This spirit was faultlessly captured in the recent remark of the American-bred Israeli Prime Minister Mrs Golda Meir: 'There was no such thing as a Palestinian people. . . . It was not as though there was a Palestinian people considering itself as a Palestinian people and we came and threw them out and took their country away from them. They did not exist.' Mrs Meir's remark, which was in reference to the population of Palestine early in this century, should not, however, be taken literally. Her denial was qualitative. Properly construed, it underlines the capacity of European colonizers in the heyday of imperialism morally to outflank the issue of the rights of the indigenous populations, in the name of the White Man's Burden, or *Lebensraum*, or whatever. The Zionist refinement of the day was, however, in justifying their ambitions by means of the brilliantly absurd slogans of Divine Promise and Biblical Fulfilment. All the poignant crises that have rent Palestine and the Middle East since then – the great Palestine Rebellion against the British in 1936–9, the Palestine War and Exodus of the Palestine Arabs of 1948, the Israeli invasion of Egypt in 1956, and the Arab–Israeli War since 1967 – flow directly or indirectly from the Basel Congress of 1897. Behind the seemingly labyrinthine complexities of the so-called Arab–Israeli conflict and the baffling maze of claims and counter-claims, there lies a continuous and continuing dual process. On the one hand, Zionist determination to implement, consolidate and expand the Basel 'vision', irrespective of the Arab character and patrimony in Palestine and its hinterland; on the other, a corresponding development of Arab resistance to Zionist encroachment and self-fulfilment at Arab expense. This is the essence of the Palestine tragedy. All else is derivative. This process is continuing at the time of writing: overtly, in the brutal Israeli repressions coyly designated 'environmental punishment' by Moshe Dayan, and best exemplified in the bulldozing of Arab villages and residential quarters in the occupied territories, followed by the setting up of so-called socialist cooperatives for Jewish immigrants on their confiscated and blasted sites; more insidiously, in the cumulative impact of a spectrum of psychological, economic and legislative pressures designed to destroy Arab will and self-respect and subtly suggest that salvation lies in departure.

But if this is the case, how is it that the context of the Palestine problem can be presented in such topsy-turvy terms as was done, for example, by President Nixon? And, further, how can Western public opinion find such presentation persuasive, or palatable at all? This was the point raised in the first paragraph of this chapter. The answer on one level lies in political exigencies. But if these do indeed affect politicians to the extent implied, one is still left wondering why they should equally affect mass opinion in the open and democratic societies of the Western world, themselves typically sceptical of official versions. The customary rejoinder has been that Zionist obfuscation is as thorough as Zionist propaganda is effective. But even this answer is not quite satisfactory. For what one seems to be dealing with here is not mere gullibility in the face of expert public relations. Rather there would seem to characterize the Western public's attitude to the Palestine conflict a certain aversion to the task of identifying the roles of the protagonists and an almost grateful acceptance of the topsy-turvy versions put about. It would seem as if there was an almost conscious turning away from the merits of the case and a positive flight towards the image of the conflict presented by the Zionist propagandist and endorsed by the Western Gentile politician. Without for the moment going into why this should be so, the foregoing analysis could, if true, perhaps explain the spontaneous anti-Arab verdict of the West on matters pertaining to the Palestine problem. It would explain why the Arab (Palestinian and other) is invariably seen as the initiator, whether or not he is reacting, the offender whether or not he is offended against, the impinger whether or not he is impinged upon, the aggressor whether or not the debris of his national and communal life (thanks to the Zionism of Jew and Gentile) lies around for all to see, with the body's eye if not with that of the mind.

These are not, however, the morose broodings of the self-pitying or the obsessed. This Western purblindness is itself a hallmark of the Palestine problem. The Palestinians are not the first and will probably not be the last people to be dispossessed and banished; but so far they are, perhaps, in the unique position where not only is their catastrophe ruled out of the Western court as being irrelevant to their reactions against its perpetrators, but where these very reactions are held to incriminate them. For the Zionists the issue has also an eminently practical aspect. It is this selfsame Western purblindness that has been the indispensable environment for the actualization of the Zionist venture. Its impact is direct and functional. It is preparatory and retroactive: it both paves the way and sets the seal of moral approbation on each new sophistication in the Zionist–Israeli piecemeal progression. As to why the Western mind should be so accommodating, a probable explanation lies in what might be described as the Bible Syndrome. The epicentre is the great dialogue between Christianity and Judaism. This has left in its wake throughout ancient, medieval, and more recent times, and with reason, a mounting burden of guilt on the Western Christian conscience. So brittle has this conscience become vis-à-vis Judaism that in self-defence and excruciating self-doubt it rejects, when we come to the Palestine problem, any train of thought, however warrantable, that might lead to placing the Zionists-as-Jews in the dock. This abdication of judgement is rendered easier by the hiatus in the historical memory of the West as to what happened in the Holy Land in the two thousand years preceding the Balfour Declaration. All this is undergone relatively painlessly – particularly when Western Christian fundamentalism adds its tonic of self-righteousness – because the Arab, like his fellow Afro–Asians, is hardly a three-dimensional phenomenon in popular Western consciousness. But if this explains, it does not justify. To put Zionism in the dock does no violence to any precept of decency; nor of logic, for Jewish past sufferings, however monumental, do not, a priori, preclude the infliction by Jews-as-Zionists of sufferings on others; nor of compassion, for true compassion is universal. Moreover while it may be true that, in problems that have assumed the proportions of the Palestine tragedy, solutions can only be edged towards, it is nevertheless true that a solution divorced from the context of its problem is a solution built on quicksand.

II

The process by which Zionism has sought to wrest control of Palestine and its surroundings from the Arabs passed through two main phases. The first ended in 1948. In this year the Zionists crushed Palestinian resistance, and created both the Palestinian Arab Diaspora and the State of Israel, the latter in the greater part of Palestine. The second phase is still with us. It has been characterized respectively by the consolidation of the territorial conquests of 1948 through the systematic expropriation of Arab homes and farms and the pouring into them of the Jewish Diaspora, the steady and successful probing into adjoining Arab territory beyond the Armistice lines in the years 1949–56, the abortive military bid for the vast Egyptian territory of Sinai in 1956–7, and the trebling of Israeli-occupied territory by the three-pronged invasion of Egypt, Syria and Jordan in 1967.

This chapter covers the first phase only, concentrating specifically on the Palestine problem from the early days of Zionism until the end of the British Mandate in 1948.

III

Underpinning the entire Zionist venture in Palestine is the myth of the Divine Promise. Stripped down to its barest essentials this myth may be presented as the two sides of a coin. The obverse carries the overriding Right of Return deriving from Divine Promise. The reverse carries implicitly, or even explicitly, the dismissal of the millennia-old 'Arab' presence in Palestine. From the viewpoint of Zionism this myth had, as it still has, a key role. It beclouds the strategy of dispossession (as is illustrated by Western acquiescence in the Israeli *Anschluss* of Jerusalem after 1967). It aims at confusing its Arab victims. But above all it taps the vast reservoirs of mass emotion, not only among Jewish, but also of Western Christian audiences. Its currency among Christian audiences (due to the Bible Syndrome) confers a further bonus. It facilitates the task of sponsorship by Western politicians, since these, whatever the real motives for their support, can don the appearance of high-mindedness or, at worst, forgivable 'Old Testament' sentimentality before their own publics in their pro-Zionist or pro-Israeli policies.

Historically, the great watershed in the transformation of this myth to an actual and ominous mode of action threatening the existence of the Palestine Arabs did not take place until 1917. It was only in this year, twenty years after the formal establishment of Zionism as a political movement (the Basel Congress of 1897) that a great power, Britain, through the notorious Balfour Declaration, incorporated Zionism as an integral part of its post-war imperial strategy for the Middle East. Although Zionist infiltration into Palestine had preceded the Balfour Declaration and even the Basel Congress of 1897, the Jewish community in Palestine (the majority of whom were non-Zionist) formed in 1919 only 9.7 per cent of the population and owned 2.04 per cent of the land. The Balfour Declaration revolutionized Zionist prospects overnight, firmly placing the Zionist seeds within the imperial womb of the paramount power in the Middle East.

But to go back to the myth. Professor Alfred Guillaume[1] has decisively dismissed the Zionist claim to a Divine Promise from the point of view of modern Biblical criticism. Indeed, the fundamentally secular and colonial character of Zionism is immediately recognizable from the Basel Programme, from the early Zionist attitudes revealed by the researches of Mrs Leonhard,[2] the utterances of Weizmann in 1919,[3] the *Realpolitik* of official Zionist neutrality during World War I[4] and the territorial ambitions of the Zionist delegation to the Peace Conference in 1919. The antithesis between Zionism and the liberal conception of Judaism was noted at the time by Edwin Montagu[5] and has been examined more recently in the works of Rabbi Elmer Berger.[6]

As for the reverse side of the coin, the fact that 'the Palestinians were there' and had always been there has been made clear by Ilene Beatty.[7] The point is related to the premiss of the Right of Return. The Palestinian Arabs in the twentieth century were not merely the descendants of the Muslim Arab conquerors of the seventh century, but the cumulative stock that included all the races that had entered and settled in Palestine since the dawn of history. They 'preceded' both Jew and Muslim Arab, in addition to 'incorporating' them. They were the true Palestinians. Unlike the Jews, they had never 'left', to 'return'. They had been Arab in culture since the early centuries of the Christian era, but Jewish and pagan before that since primordial times. Their attachment to Palestine has found many witnesses. Burhan ad-Din al Fazari,[8] for instance, showed long ago the depth and poignancy of Muslim Arab love for Jerusalem. Clearly there is no Jewish monopoly of attachment to this golden city. But the distinctiveness of Islam's involvement with it is that it reflects not only its own reverence but that of Judaism and Christianity as well. The intensity of this fascination is evident in the richness of Islamic mystical lore on Jerusalem, by which, according to Miguel Asin,[9] even Christian literature was inspired. Nor was Islam willing to be banished from the city, as Saladin's reconquest of the city from the Crusaders – with a display of crowning mercy that was itself an act of homage to Jerusalem – was to show.[10]

That this was no passing mood is seen from the firm reply a thousand years later, made in 1899 to Zionist approaches by the Arab Mayor of Jerusalem: 'The Jews would be better to go somewhere else',[11] and in the impressive rejection of the Zionist programme in the petitions of the inhabitants of Palestine, Syria and Lebanon received by the American commissioners King and Crane, sent to the area by President Wilson in 1919.

Behind the ostensible biblical sentimentality, there stood two decisive motives for Western sponsorship of Zionism: strategic evaluations and the pressure of Jewish immigration on Britain and the United States. Herbert Sidebotham,[12] himself an ardent Anglo-Zionist, and an architect of the Balfour Declaration, explained, in 1917, the need of Britain for a European population settling in the classical colonial fashion in a buffer region between Sinai and the Arab East for the protection of the Suez Canal and the imperial communications to India. Less known, perhaps, is the immigration issue as a determining factor in Western pro-Zionism.[13] The turbulence of life for the Jews of Tsarist Russia and Eastern Europe, the pressure of the rising middle classes against them, as well as the relative liberalism of Western European countries and the new opportunities offered by the Northern American continent, produced, in the last decades of the nineteenth century, successive tidal waves of Western-bound Jewish migration across the face of Europe towards Britain and the United States; but not, be it noted, more than a trickle to the Land of Promise in Palestine. By the turn of the century, the pressure of Jewish immigration from the Slavonic countries against Britain reached crisis proportions. There were riots in the streets of London and growing demands for restrictive immigration legislation. A Royal Commission was formed, before which Herzl propounded his Zionist thesis as a specific solution to this problem. An Aliens Bill was drafted and became the subject of prolonged debate in the House of Commons in the years 1904–6 during the premiership of no other person than Arthur James Balfour himself. Defending the Bill in 1905 Prime Minister Balfour had unburdened himself as follows:

A state of things could be easily imagined in which it would not be to the advantage of the civilisation of this country that there should be an immense body of persons who, however patriotic, able and industrious, however much they threw themselves into national life, still, by their own action, remained a people apart, and not merely held a religion differing from the vast majority of their fellow-countrymen, but only inter-married among themselves.

Earlier, in 1903, in advising the British Government on the immigration question, Herzl had said: 'If you allow me to say so,

Mr. Chamberlain [J. Chamberlain, the British Colonial Secretary],
I should prefer for England's glory that you do not make such a
Bill. Drain them elsewhere, but don't make an Aliens Bill.'
Palestine, of course, was not under British control at the time,
and at the subsequent Seventh Zionist Congress Balfour was
roundly accused, after the passage of the Act, of 'open anti-
Semitism against the whole Jewish people'.[14]

Substantially the same immigration problem faced the
Wilson Administration in the US. The crux of the matter for
American restrictionists was that racial purity, ethnic balance,
and homogeneity were essential for the preservation of both
nationalism and democracy in the US. The source of the threat to
these values may, perhaps, be inferred from the annual National
Origins quota system eventually adopted by the US. According
to this system 81 per cent of the total annual quota was allotted
to Western Europe, 16 per cent to Southern and Eastern Europe
and 2.7 per cent to non-Europeans. Now the bulk of the Jewish
concentrations was not in Western Europe. Excluding Russia
(from which mass emigration was unfeasible after the Russian
Revolution), the great Jewish population concentrations were in
Eastern Europe, particularly in Poland (3,050,000), Romania
(900,000) and Hungary (500,000). But the annual American
quotas for these three countries were 6,524; 377; and 869
respectively: i.e., a total of 7,770.[15] This total annual quota was
not, of course, at the exclusive disposal of the Jewish communities in these three countries but was available to their entire
populations. But even if it had been, it was hardly designed to
'drain', in Herzl's word, their Jewish communities into the US.
This is the unmentioned and, presumably, unmentionable rock
upon which the Anglo-Zionist and American-Zionist entente was
established in the twenties and thirties of this century, long *before*
the rise of Hitler.

That this Jewish immigration issue was very much on the mind
of the Wilson administration and a determining factor in its
Palestine policy was made clear during the famous interview
between Balfour and Brandeis in 1919. Louis Brandeis, at the
time, was the leading Zionist Jew in the US and the first of a long
line of Presidential advisers on Palestine. The notes on the
interview were meticulously taken by Felix Frankfurter, who
succeeded Brandeis as adviser on Palestine:

Brandeis narrated his own approach to Zionism, that he came to it
wholly as an American, for his whole life had been free from
Jewish contacts or traditions. As an American, he was confronted
with the disposition of the vast number of Jews, particularly
Russian Jews, that were pouring into the United States, year by
year. It was then that by chance a pamphlet on Zionism came his
way and led him to the study of the Jewish problem and to the
conviction that Zionism was the answer. The very same men, with
the same qualities that are now enlisted in revolutionary
movements, would find (and in the United States do find)
constructive channels for expression and make positive contributions to civilisation. Mr. Balfour interrupted to express his
agreement, adding: 'Of course, these are the reasons that make
you and me such ardent Zionists.'[16]

Neither of the two Western powers had any illusions about what
they were doing by endorsing Zionism. However glib his public
utterances concerning the safeguarding of Palestinian Arab
political rights,[17] Balfour knew better. He made some particularly revealing comments in his secret memorandum to the
British Cabinet on the paragraph in the Covenant of the League
of Nations which enshrined the Wilsonian principle of self-
determination. It will be recalled that the Arabs had naïvely
fought for this principle on the side of the Western allies against
their co-religionists, the Ottoman Turks. The paragraph in
question reads: 'The wishes of these communities [i.e., the
independent nations] must be a principal consideration on the
selection of a mandatory'. Balfour comments:

> Let us assume that two of the 'independent nations' for which
> mandatories have to be provided are Syria and Palestine. Take
> Syria first. Do we mean, in the case of Syria, to consult principally
> the wishes of the inhabitants? We mean nothing of the kind. . . .
> Are we going 'chiefly to consider the wishes of the inhabitants' in
> deciding which of these [mandatories] is to be selected? We are
> going to do nothing of the kind. . . . So that whatever the
> inhabitants may wish, it is France they will certainly have. They
> may freely choose; but it is Hobson's choice after all. . . . The
> contradiction between the letter of the Covenant and the policy of
> the Allies is even more flagrant in the case of the 'independent
> nation of Palestine'. . . . For in Palestine we do not propose even
> to go through the form of consulting the wishes of the present
> inhabitants of the country . . .[18]

In this same man-to-man talk with Brandeis, Balfour further
explains that he 'has great difficulty in seeing how the President
[Wilson] can possibly reconcile his adherence to Zionism with
any doctrine of self-determination and he asked the Justice
[Brandeis] how he thinks the President will do it'. Brandeis's
reply is that Balfour himself had 'already indicated the solution'.
The reference by Brandeis is to an earlier remark in the
conversation made by Balfour. Balfour had said that, following
the decision by Wilson to send a Commission of Inquiry to the
Middle East, he (Balfour) had sent a memorandum to the British
Prime Minister which he believed had also gone to Wilson in
which he had asked that Palestine be 'excluded from the terms of
reference because the Powers had committed themselves to the
Zionist programme, which inevitably excluded numerical self-
determination'. Balfour had further explained in his memorandum that in Palestine, 'We are dealing not with the wishes of an
existing community but are consciously seeking to reconstitute a
new community and definitely building for a Jewish numerical
majority in the future.' This was the 'solution' that Brandeis had
referred to; whereupon Balfour commented that he 'supposed
that would be the President's line'. Of course, whether or not
that was the American President's line is a debatable point. On
the other hand it is difficult to dismiss the authority of Brandeis
and Balfour that it was. But whether or not it was the President's
line as explicitly as it was Brandeis's and Balfour's, his
endorsement of the Balfour Declaration certainly made it his
implicit position.

One can easily imagine George Orwell doffing his hat to this
rationalization by Balfour and Brandeis. 'Numerical self-determination' was to be 'excluded'. Did the faintest wrinkle cross the
presidential or academic brow of the propounder of the principle
of self-determination? What is the opposite of 'numerical self-
determination'? 'Self-determination'? Or 'non-numerical self-
determination'? In fairness to President Wilson, he did seem,
according to Frank Manuel,[19] to drag his feet before his
endorsement of the Balfour Declaration; perhaps because he was
pondering over this puzzle, perhaps (less charitably) because he
was too busy conducting the war. But the precise moment and
manner in which the US uttered its verdict against the Palestine
Arabs might perhaps be recalled for the record. On 13 October

1917, exactly eighteen days before the Balfour Declaration was issued, President Wilson, fishing a paper out of his jacket (how long had he been carrying it around on his person and why?) wrote to his aide, Colonel House: 'I find in my pocket the memorandum you gave me about the Zionist movement. I am afraid I did not say to you that I concurred in the formula suggested from the other side. I do, and would be obliged if you would let them know it.' President Wilson's attitude to the Balfour Declaration has been treated at some length partly because a sub-theme in the Zionist mythology is that the Declaration enshrines the principle of self-determination, and partly because the ambivalence surrounding the presidential line at the time might help subsequent occupants of the White House to focus more rigorously on the essence of the Palestine problem.

Political scientists are increasingly concentrating on the decision-making process as a key to the understanding of international politics. The process leading to the Balfour Declaration is revealing in several other respects. Manuel's work brings out clearly the dynamics of the inter-governmental pressures between London and Washington in relation to the Declaration. The picture that emerges is that of one decision-making centre (London) being of two minds with regard to a decision (support of Zionism).[20] The official pro-decision pressure group in this centre uses the intermediary of a non-official pressure group (Weizmann and his Zionist circle) which is the potential beneficiary of the decision, to solicit the help of the counterpart of this pressure group (Brandeis and his Zionist circle) in the decision-making centre of another allied country (Washington). The object of this solicitation is to bring pressure through the counterpart group on the foreign decision-making centre in favour of the contemplated decision, so that this foreign centre would throw its weight behind the official pro-decision faction in the first centre and so tip the scales against its own official opposition. In other words London, acting for reasons of her own, uses 'British' Zionists to recruit American Zionists to pressure Washington to pressure herself in favour of Zionism. This interpretation indicates that, contrary to popular conception, the Zionists did not themselves set the pace, at the time, in either London or Washington. Nor was Washington the pace-setter as yet. This was indubitably, in the editor's opinion,

London. What this interpretation also indicates is the metropolitan status of the Zionist pressure groups in both London and
Washington – a status which was to grow parallel to the growth of
the Zionist venture in the field (Palestine), until it became a
pace-setter in its own right, first in London, then in Washington
and, finally, in both simultaneously and cumulatively. This
metropolitan status of the World Zionist Movement has not been
unique for a 'white' lobby acting on behalf of settlers overseas;
the French Algerian, British Rhodesian and Portuguese Angolan
lobbies have had a similar metropolitan status. But the unique
advantage enjoyed by the World Zionist Organization was that it
was an internationally organized movement based on the
scattered Jewish communities of the world, and commanded
incomparably vaster resources[21] and more diversified political
leverage than any enjoyed by the others, in addition to the halo
of morality, however meretricious, that it alone sported as well.

IV

No sooner had Britain (with the help of the Arabs) defeated the
Ottoman Turks in 1918, than she began to implement her Zionist
policy in contravention of international law, in the newly
occupied territory of Palestine. It was not until 1922 that Britain's
juridical position was 'regularized' under the aegis of the League
of Nations. She now became the Mandatory over Palestine with a
mandate from the League to administer the country, ostensibly in
accordance with the Covenant. The whole Mandate structure
after World War I was, of course, little more than a framework
for the division of colonial spoils between the victorious Western
allies;[22] while the choice of Britain as Mandatory over Palestine
had not only *not* been solicited by the Arabs, but had been
categorically rejected by them. Britain's position in Palestine,
therefore, was based on force of arms and continued to be so
until the end of her catastrophic regime in 1948.

Nothing, perhaps, illustrates more clearly the *colon* status of
the Zionists than the wording of the Mandate instrument itself.
The preamble of this document incorporates the Balfour
Declaration, while the bulk of its twenty-eight articles are
devoted to the modalities of its implementation. The four-letter

word 'Arab' occurs not once throughout the text, with the presumably unavoidable exception of the mention of 'Arabic' in Article 22, where it is thenceforth declared to be one of three official languages, alongside Hebrew and English. The operative article is Article 2, which states: 'The Mandatory shall be responsible for placing the country under such political, administrative and economic conditions, as will secure the establishment of the Jewish national home as laid down in the preamble, and the development of self-governing institutions.' As in the Balfour Declaration, there were several reasons why the euphemism 'Jewish national home' was used instead of a 'Jewish state'. The Zionist movement represented only a tiny minority of the Jewish people, and there was deep concern among the Jews of the world as to the repercussions that such a concept might have on their standing in their respective countries of origin. The Zionists could not ignore this, since their success depended on winning Jewish support. Obfuscation had obvious tactical advantages also with regard to the Arabs. But perhaps the most important consideration was that it was much too premature to declare the ultimate aim, the objective conditions for which had still to be created. Article 2, just quoted, reflects the dilemma of its authors: on the one hand, specific authority is given to create these conditions, on the other, a bow, however sardonic, is made in the direction of the grandiloquent Wilsonian principles. We have seen what the line was with regard to the antithesis between the Zionist programme and the principle of self-determination noted by Balfour and Brandeis. When it came to the implementation of the Zionist programme the reasoning behind this line was actually reversed. For implicit in Article 2 is that the Zionist goal is *reconcilable* with 'the development of self-governing institutions'.

This fiction of reconcilability between the Zionist goal and Arab aspirations for self-government became in fact the 'moral' linchpin of British administration in Palestine. It was only in 1937, some fifteen years later, that a British Royal Commission was to fall upon the Archimedean discovery – this time, that the two objectives of Article 2 were not, in fact, reconcilable.

Meanwhile, the key operational mode of Anglo-Zionist action was Jewish 'immigration', since '*numerical* self-determination' was to become operative in Palestine only *after* the Jews had become the majority. Blessing for this role assigned to 'immigration' was forthcoming from Winston Churchill, who, as Colonial Secretary, laid down in an authoritative gloss on the Mandate in 1922, that for Palestine the sole criterion for Jewish immigration was to be the 'economic absorptive capacity' of the country. The phrase has the resilience of Churchillian prose, and, by excluding political, psychological and social criteria by which all human societies (e.g., those of Britain and the US) regulate even non-politically motivated immigration to their territories, Churchill's ruling was a magnificent example of charity at some distance from home. His empathy with the Zionist *colon* is in intriguing contrast to the incomprehension, displayed throughout his life, of the hopes and aspirations of hundreds of millions of human beings living to the south of certain latitudes. Given this definition and role of Jewish migration to Palestine, it is obvious that 'invasion' is the only word that accurately describes the process.

This, then, was the environment in which the Zionist myth began its translation to reality. In fairness, however, it must be mentioned that many British voices were raised at the time in protest and foreboding. The flavour of these early days is reflected in the forthright speeches of Lords Grey and Buckmaster in the House of Lords as well as in the writings of colonial officials like W. F. Stirling and C. R. Ashbee. As for the new Zionist design, we are indebted to the elucidations of Arlosoroff, written in 1932.[23] Arlosoroff fixed his gaze, as Director of the Political Department in the Jewish Agency, on the one factor that mattered to him, if Zionism was to succeed: the relation of forces between the Zionist *colon* and the indigenous inhabitant. He saw the need for a steady manipulation of this relation until Zionist supremacy was assured. This he characteristically called the point of 'equilibrium', a description which is not without contemporary echoes today in American declarations about maintaining the balance of power between the Arabs and Israel. He projected an escalatory ladder of power leading to the desired end, categorizing the rungs already mounted and the mechanics of further progress. He was realistic enough to see a corresponding and inevitable increase in Palestinian resistance by which he was already impressed; as well as in tension between the Zionist *colon* and the British Metropolis. He was aware that these latter developments ran counter to the Anglo-Zionist strategy of achieving Jewish domination through 'immigration'. But he had an answer. In the last analysis there would have to be 'a transition period during which the Jewish minority would exercise organised revolutionary rule' – in other words a Rhodesian-style Unilateral Declaration of Independence must be brought off, if need be. Arlosoroff's strategic blue-print was Herzlian in inspiration, but the founder's legacy was enriched by a remarkable adaptation of Leninist doctrine with a Clausewitzian *deus ex machina* in reserve. Arlosoroff's intellectual brilliance was matched only by his prophetic accuracy.

Several writers have shed light on the more operational aspects of Zionist strategy. Sir John Hope Simpson[24] analysed in 1930 the constitutions of the two principal colonizing institutions of the World Zionist Organization: the Keren Kayemeth, Jewish National Fund (founded in 1901), and the Keren Hayesod Palestine Foundation Fund (founded in 1920). He noted that both these were based 'on the principle of the persistent and deliberate boycott of Arab labour . . .' a situation which he described as 'not only contrary to the provisions . . . of the Mandate but . . . in addition a constant and increasing source of danger to the country'. He concluded: 'It is impossible to view with equanimity the extension of an enclave in Palestine from which all Arabs are excluded . . .' A study by Granott[25] has placed this expanding enclave in the perspective of total Zionist strategy. 'Thus the various objectives – national policy, security, and strategy – were linked through land acquisition with the settlement objective, all being welded together in a united, systematic, purposeful and farseeing policy . . .'. Granott also brings out a somewhat neglected aspect of the strategy. Land was acquired and even 'settlement' thereon carried out 'not from the viewpoint of agricultural development'. This was the policy of acquiring land 'reserves'. According to Granott: 'At the time the intent was not their immediate utilization but just maintenance even though they lay fallow, while title was preserved against all encroachment . . .'

The figures of population and land ratios for the period reveal the full impact of all this on the Arab community in Palestine.[26] Thus the Arab percentage of the population dropped from 91.3 per cent in 1919, to 83.2 per cent in 1925, to 82.2 per cent in 1930, to 71.4 per cent in 1935, to 69 per cent in 1939; while Jewish land ownership rose from 2.04 per cent in 1919, to 3.8 per cent in 1925, to 4.5 per cent in 1930, to 5.3 per cent in 1935, to 5.7 per cent in 1939. These figures on Jewish land ownership are of particular interest in view of the ubiquitous Zionist propaganda theme that it was Zionist enterprise that made Palestine soil productive, and its rider, that on the Mediterranean shores of Palestine trees grew only in kibbutzim. The Zionist proposition is proved false by the fractional size of Jewish land ownership up to the eve of the establishment of the state of Israel. And it is belied by the actual statistics on cultivation and agricultural production. The truth of the matter is that Jewish land settlement was qualitative; not only in the sense described above by Sir John Hope Simpson and Granott but, literally, in that it occurred in the richest and most fertile parts of Palestine e.g., the littoral plain between Jaffa and Haifa, the inland plain between Haifa and Tiberias and the Upper Jordan Valley.

Under the Mandate there was no constitutional redress for the Arabs. In spite of the fiction of reconcilability between the two sections of Article 2 of the Mandate, British policy in practice, and for obvious reasons, was never to accept the principle of 'one man one vote' in Palestine, and no self-governing institutions were ever developed for the country at large. To be sure, the Arabs could air their grievances before the Permanent Mandates Commission of the League of Nations, but the terms of reference of this Commission precluded the questioning of the provisions of the Mandate. The circle was Kafkaesque in its completeness. Arab resistance, therefore, escalated from delegations, petitions, demonstrations and strikes, to riots and violent clashes with the British security forces and the Zionist colonists. Invariably the British responded with the time-honoured and time-winning device of a commission of enquiry. Just as invariably these commissions reached the conclusion that the root cause was Arab fear of creeping Zionist encroachment and ultimate Zionist purposes. Arab reactions to the Zionist attempts on the Wailing (Western) Wall in 1929 were particularly violent and bloody. It was in the aftermath of these disturbances that Sir John Hope Simpson had reported. The British Colonial Secretary at the time was the liberal Sidney Webb (Lord Passfield). He could not ignore the evidence from the field and his was the first sincere British official attempt since 1917 to look into Arab grievances. History tells us what he got for his pains. Clearly the metropolitan status of the Zionists had been vastly consolidated since the Balfour Declaration. Links forged with Anglo–Jewish constituencies and pressure groups enabled the Zionist leadership to bring direct pressure from within the nerve centre in London and upon it. Weizmann goes into a sulk or two, opposition leaders are contacted, a letter published in *The Times*, a quiet horse-trading of pressure for votes in a timely British by-election; and the result? Sidney Webb is cut down to size, and the British Government swallows whole its White Paper endorsing the views of its royal commissioners and responsible minister. The moral of all this is that, at least in normal times, pressure from a non-*colon* community (the Arabs in Palestine) is peripheral and therefore taken in the imperial stride as a nuisance to be suppressed in the interests of law and order. But pressure from the autonomous metropolitan base of an overseas *colon* community is part of the balance of power system at the decision-making centre – a different story altogether. The Webb-Weizmann encounter was the prototype of many subsequent showdowns in more than one Western capital between the Arabs (Palestinian and other) on the one hand, and Zionists and later Israelis, on the other.

With the suppression of Webb, the Mandate machine could again grind forward. A new High Commissioner, General Sir Arthur Wauchope, whose political credentials seem to have included command of a Black Watch brigade on the Western Front, was despatched to Palestine with instructions that the Jewish national home policy should go into high gear. In the next few years Jewish 'immigration' reached what can only be described as invasion proportions: 9553 (1932), 30,327 (1933), 42,359 (1934), 61,854 (1935) total of 144,093 in four years. Concurrently, for example, Jewish immigration into the US was: 2775 (1932), 2372 (1933), 4134 (1934), 4837 (1935), a total of 14,118 in the same period. In despair, the Arabs clutched at an offer for the establishment of a legislative council made by the Colonial Office in a fit of even-handedness in 1935. The formula for the Council could by no stretch of the imagination be said to be based on the principle of 'one man one vote' for the Arabs. But even this proposal was defeated in the British House of

Commons on the grounds of unfairness to the Zionist *colon*. The Arabs of Palestine now braced themselves up for national revolt.

The great Palestinian Arab Rebellion, probably the boldest native challenge to Britain in her colonial empire in the first half of the twentieth century, fell into two main phases: from April 1936 to July 1937 and from late 1937 to the autumn of 1939. The first phase ended with the arrival of yet another commission of enquiry headed by Lord Peel. The second phase started as soon as Peel's recommendations were published. It was Peel who made the discovery that the two objectives of Article 2 of the Mandate were not reconcilable. Another of his discoveries was that the 'economic absorptive capacity' criterion for immigration ignored fundamental political and psychological criteria. His solution? The partition of Palestine. He not only recommended the principle but promptly interpreted it in an impressionistic map appended to his report. The author still recalls the breathless incredulity, with which he, as a boy, first saw the proposed map. Ever since 1917 the Arabs had been saying that the 'Jewish national home' was merely a euphemism for a Jewish state, only to be referred by London to the 'safeguard' clause in Article 2 of the Mandate about 'self-governing institutions'. The Arabs, of course, were horrified at the very principle of partition, which they saw as the vivisection of their country. But they were equally horrified at its interpretation which gave the Jews 40 per cent of Palestine at a time when their land ownership did not exceed 5.6 per cent. The envisaged Jewish state included hundreds of Arab villages and the solid Arab bloc of Galilee north of Nazareth. But the cruellest provision of all was that there should be, if necessary, 'a forcible transfer of Arabs' from Arab lands allotted to the Jewish state. This was indeed a nightmare come true.

Peel's partition proposals served only to fan the flames of Arab rebellion. The British replied with massive repressive measures, including environmental punishments, frequent executions, and the terrorization and murder of Arab villagers by special British-trained Jewish squads (in which Moshe Dayan was recruited) in 1938. A conservative estimate of Arab casualties during 1936–9 would be about 5000 killed and 15,000 wounded, out of a population of one million Arabs.[27] Translated into British and American figures (populations 40 million and 200 million respectively) this would amount to 200,000 British and 1 million Americans killed and 600,000 British and 3 million Americans wounded. These figures do not include the numbers of Arabs detained which reached 5600 in 1939 alone, or, 224,000 and 1,120,000 in comparative British and American figures respectively. Accompanying this massive repression there were three other developments. First, the systematic disarming of the Arab population of Palestine, a process which continued well beyond the end of the rebellion in 1939.[28] Second, the large-scale arming of the Jewish population, through direct British aid, as attested to by Ben-Gurion, and indirectly (by Britain looking the other way), as can be inferred from Ben-Gurion also.[29] And, finally, the breaking-up of Arab political organization.[30]

The British were taken aback by the violence of Arab reaction to the partition plan. This did not affect their military measures, as we have seen. But it did contribute to the shelving of the plan. A technical commission, sent to study the feasibility of partition in 1938, reported sceptically after considering both Peel's plan and two variants. Reid,[31] a member of this commission, was more forthright than his colleagues in criticizing partition on the grounds of absence of consent, of equity, of security and of solvency as well as on those of the dismemberment of the country. Writing in 1938 he concluded:

> In stating that partition is impracticable I am in accord with nearly 100% of non-Arab and non-Jewish persons in Palestine in direct contact with the problem, who by experience and impartiality are best qualified to judge. . . . I am not a lonely recusant flying in the face of the facts or of the evidence . . .

The Arab struggle against partition also evoked the sympathy of Mahatma Gandhi[32] who wrote in 1938: 'Surely it would be a crime against humanity to reduce the proud Arabs so that Palestine can be restored to the Jews partly or wholly as their National Home'. And again, 'according to the accepted canons of right and wrong, nothing can be said against the Arab resistance in the face of overwhelming odds.' But although the partition plan was shelved, the confrontation between the British and the Palestine Arabs in the years 1936–9 had a decisive impact on the future of the country. Until the mid thirties the British shield had

had a deterrent effect on the Arabs. But the burgeoning Zionist entity behind the British outworks gradually eroded this effect and left the Arabs no alternative but to launch a frontal attack on the British themselves. The shield turned into a battering-ram with which the Arabs, in Gandhi's words, were 'reduced'. The British now proceeded to conquer the country from its Arab inhabitants in 1936–9 as they had conquered it from its Ottoman rulers in 1917–18. This was partly the inexorable logic of a powerful military machine set in motion. It was also a function of the efficacy of the metropolitan Zionist lobby so clearly demonstrated in 1931 and, more recently, in the quashing of the Legislative Council proposals in 1935. But Peel's conception of a Jewish state in 1937 had also the same strategic and geo-political parentage as the ideas put forward by Sidebotham in 1917. The persistence of these ideas in the mid thirties was illustrated by Main[33] writing only two years before Peel's partition proposals; and was perhaps best brought out in the chummily bantering tone adopted by Weizmann in his discussion of partition in 1937[34] with Ormsby-Gore, the British Colonial Secretary, and the deferential alacrity with which every remark of the Zionist leader was conceded. Another consideration, already noted in the background of the Balfour Declaration, was the question of Jewish immigration into Western countries, including the British dominions. This question, of course, re-emerged with the rise of the Third Reich and the building up of pressures against Jewish communities in Eastern Europe, particularly in Poland. But, whatever the British motivation, the Anglo–Arab confrontation in 1936–9 had a devastating impact on the power position of the Arabs in the country and constituted in effect a giant stride towards the 'equilibrium' sought by Arlosoroff.

The Zionist attitude to partition had been ambivalent. The official leadership (Weizmann and Ben-Gurion) representing the actual centres of power inside Palestine were jubilant. This was the first time that the 'Jewish national home' was being officially and publicly equated with a 'Jewish state'. The idea of Jewish sovereignty was being propounded by a great power who was itself the Mandatory. This was a telling argument to be wielded against the hesitant as well as the anti-Zionist Jews. It, incidentally, illustrates an interesting aspect of the dynamics of Zionism. These are based on a triangular relationship between the Zionist leadership, the Gentile great-power sponsors, and the Jewish masses inside and outside Palestine. The more the sponsors endorse or, better still, initiate pro-Zionist policies, the greater the leverage of the Zionist leadership on the Jewish masses. This was true in 1917 and 1937 as it was to be true later, and as it is still true today. Peel gave both respectability and ostensible practicability to the idea of a Jewish state. He made it morally respectable by successfully anchoring his recommendation of partition to a fallacy; under the guise of giving half a loaf to each protagonist he blurred the simple fact that the loaf already belonged in its entirety to one of them. This was in strict consonance with the Balfour Declaration, but Peel went further by supplying the idea of Jewish sovereignty with the ostensible practicability it desperately needed in the face of mounting Palestinian resistance. His plan presented a direct operational formula for the implementation of Zionist demands in which emphasis shifted from 'immigration' (Churchill's formula) to territory; a shift, moreover, that was supremely adjustable to the piecemeal land strategy of the Zionists. It was therefore in its territorial aspects that Peel's plan constituted such a windfall. Sixty years of Zionist 'pioneering' since the 1880s had succeeded in acquiring no more than 5.6 per cent of the territory of Palestine. Now, with a stroke of Peel's pen, 40 per cent of the land fell into the Zionist lap, with a bonus – that its Arab inhabitants could be expelled from it if necessary. This last recommendation showed the lengths to which Peel was prepared to go in ignoring the evidence of his senses – reflecting, no doubt, current British attitudes on the rights of natives versus those of white settlers in colonial overseas territories.

The ambivalence of the Zionist reaction to partition derived partly from Peel's generosity and partly from Britain's evident determination to shatter Palestinian Arab power. A new gargantuan appetite was stimulated. Hence the tension between Weizmann and Ben-Gurion on the one hand, and Jabotinsky, the leader of the numerically small Zionist opposition on the other. At bottom there was no fundamental difference between the three; or, for that matter, between them and Herzl. There is a direct line of thought linking Herzl's idea of working the poor population across the frontiers *'unbemerkt'* (unobserved) and Weizmann's remarks to Ormsby-Gore concerning the 'transfer'

of the Arab population in accordance with Peel's recommendations.[35] The differences with Jabotinsky were not on the ultimate
aim. To Weizmann and Ben-Gurion, there was time enough to
acquire the rest of Palestine, a possibility that would indeed be
facilitated by acceptance of Peel's frontiers.[36] To Jabotinsky,
unwilling to let the opportunity slip by for outbidding his two
political rivals, acceptance of Peel's Heartland was a betrayal of
the vision of Greater Israel on both sides of the Jordan – a vision
made more feasible with Peel's frontiers in the bag. In the event
it was American Jewry, whose financial backing was essential,
which hesitated on the brink of statehood. As an American
Jewish wag put it: 'Non-Zionists were alarmed that Jews had
prayed 2000 years for a Palestinian Restoration and now *it had to
happen to them.*'[37] The Gentile sponsor was too far ahead of the
Jewish masses. Nevertheless, the permanent breakthrough quality
of Peel's recommendations lay in their very articulation. This
made the wildest expectations of the official Zionist leadership
seem matter of fact. It served to translate them, on levels both
theoretical (concept of sovereignty) and cartographic (territorial),
into a new acquired right, a new irreducible minimum, a new
starting line. This in turn paved the way for the even more
ambitious partition proposals of 1947 and to horizons of conquest
far beyond.

The work of Jon and David Kimche[38] has shed light on the
delicate question of the Zionist policy of selective immigration in
the late thirties. Kimche and Kimche have produced irrefutable
evidence from Zionist archives to show that this selective policy
was persisted in, in the five years *after* the rise of Hitler and
almost up to the outbreak of World War II. Ironically, it was to
bring the Zionist authorities into headlong clash with Eichmann,
the Nazi official in charge of Jewish 'emigration' from Germany.
Whereas Eichmann's emphasis was on numbers, that of the
Zionists was on 'quality'. In other words, Zionist policy was not
as preoccupied with the rescue of European Jewry as with the
selection of suitable 'pioneering' material among the physically fit
and doctrinally amenable Jewish youth of Central Europe. An
even more poignant aspect has been described by Robert
Briscoe.[39] The Rabbinical leaders of Poland in 1939 were
adamantly hostile to mass Jewish emigration *to Palestine*, on the
grounds that 'all forms of Zionism are to us "traif" [unclean].' If,

in their obsession with *Realpolitik*, the Zionists had slowed down the process of Jewish emigration from Europe[40] in the crucial years 1933–8, and had failed to communicate with the Jewish leadership in Poland, which included the bulk of European Jewry outside Russia, it was this same obsession that inhibited them from making direct appeals, in time, to the conscience of vast Western countries with almost unlimited 'economic absorptive capacities'. This last point was brought out brutally in the moving, if abject, testimony of the leading American Zionist, Stephen Wise, before the United States Joint Congressional Hearings on Immigration, in 1939.[41] The inference is unavoidable that an accusing finger should be pointed as much in the direction of Western immigration legislation, as in that of official Zionist leadership. And the accusation is monumental. It is that the Herzlian advice to Chamberlain to 'drain' Jewish immigration away from the West[42] seems to have been seriously taken up by the British and American governments. Reference has already been made to the Brandeis–Balfour talks of 1919, where the deflection of Jewish immigration from the US was explicitly declared to be a foundation of American pro-Zionism. Subsequent restrictive Western immigration legislation, both American and British, indicates that a tacit understanding seems to have been reached between the West and the Zionists under which the Zionists would not embarrass the West with criticism of Western immigration policies, provided that the West lent support to Zionist plans for Jewish immigration to Palestine. Upon this tacit bargain the entire Zionist immigration policy towards Palestine seems to have been based in the period 1917–39. But whatever the Zionist achievement in Palestine, this surely is dwarfed when compared with humanitarian results that could have been obtained from a less politically orientated approach enabling the maintenance of more options for emigration before the embattled pre-World War II Jewish communities of Europe. It is intrinsic to this proposition that Western immigration policies in the twenties and thirties were functionally related to Zionist immigration policy and the Western-Zionist entente on the subject since 1917. And that callous as the Western response was at, for example, the Evian Conference in 1938, this was the bitter harvest sown during the preceding decades by the Zionist leaders themselves in their collusion with the two leading Western capitals, Washington

and London. Nor will it do to argue that, even if the Polish
Rabbinate were willing, there was no possibility of mass
emigration to Palestine at the time. This merely begs the
questions eternally posed to the Zionist leaders both dead and
alive: 'Why Palestine?' 'Why *only* Palestine?'

The British retreat from partition was not in itself a cause of
concern to the Zionists, partly because of the ambivalence of the
Zionist attitude to the proposal and partly because the proposal
had been made at all. There could be no denying, however, that
this retreat was related to the impact made on Britain by the
desperateness and steadfastness of Palestinian Arab resistance to
the dismemberment of their country, as well as to the rapidly
deteriorating world situation. To the extent that British abandon-
ment of partition, however temporary, was in acknowledgement
of these factors, it reflected the potential of strain that existed in
Anglo–Zionist relations. This was inevitable, since, irrespective
of the origins and course of the Anglo–Zionist relationship,
growing Zionist autonomy was bound to produce, eventually, the
usual tensions between any two political entities. Far from
negating the metropolitan *colon* nature of the Anglo–Zionist
relationship, the development of such tension is only too
characteristic of it (e.g., Algeria, and Rhodesia). In the
Palestinian context this strain has been noted in the Webb crisis
of 1931 and to a lesser extent in the abortive Legislative Council
proposals of 1935. It underlines the fact, which is not without its
contemporary relevance today, in 1970, that the terms of
reference of the metropolis are bound to be larger than those of
the *colon*, if only because of the regional and global responsibilities and susceptibilities of the metropolis, particularly when
it is a great power and more so in times of threatening
international crisis. This fact was becoming increasingly evident
in British policy in Palestine as the clouds of World War II began
to gather. It explains Britain's next move – the calling of a round
table conference in London, in 1939, to which delegates from the
neighbouring Arab countries, as well as Palestinian Arab and
Zionist representatives, were invited. The moving spirit behind
the conference was Malcolm Macdonald, the new Colonial
Secretary. Macdonald's stand on Palestine was embodied in a
White Paper issued at the inconclusive end of the conference.
The White Paper of 1939 said, in effect, that the blank cheque

given to Zionism in 1917 had been honoured for some twenty-two years, but that neither equity nor expediency demanded an indefinite extension into the future of its time limit. It was, therefore, time to start attending to Britain's other obligation of developing self-governing institutions. To this end there would be progress, after a transitional period of ten years, towards the independence of the country. The statement contained many loopholes, on account of which the Palestinian Arab delegates, in contrast to the delegates of the Arab countries, found themselves unable to accept it. The Zionists saw it as the most serious challenge to their maximalist ambitions since Webb. Macdonald was promptly dubbed an 'appeaser', the dirty word of the late thirties – a fantastic designation, considering that Britain had just finished the systematic destruction of all organized Palestinian Arab political and military power. In the event, Macdonald was 'banished' from the United Kingdom as soon as Churchill, an arch-Zionist, assumed the premiership. It was only after Britain had absorbed the facts of life created by World War II that he was called upon to regulate relations with the crumbling empire. But by then it was too late for Palestine.

V

Undoubtedly the most important development during the period 1939–47 was the transfer by the Zionists of their main metropolitan base from London to Washington. The White Paper of 1939 had been a danger signal that saturation point in London's susceptibility to Zionist influence was being approached. This was certainly the view of the overseas Zionist establishment in Palestine represented by Ben-Gurion. But it was not shared by Weizmann, the metropolitan Zionist leader operating from London. This difference in the evaluation of London's future role between the two Zionist leaders has usually been interpreted as reflecting the moderation of the one and the extremism of the other. There is no evidence for the moderation of Weizmann. His reliance on London stemmed from the fact that as metropolitan leader his constituency *was* in London, whereas Ben-Gurion's was in the field, in Palestine. What we have here is not only estrangement between the Zionists as a whole and their Gentile metropolis discussed earlier, but an estrangement also between the British Zionist metropolitan establishment and its overseas extension, partly as a result of this more general estrangement with London, and partly on account of the growing confidence of the overseas Zionist *colons* led by Ben-Gurion. Overlying this there was the restlessness of these overseas *colons* at the remote control from London even though this was exercised by Weizmann. In other words there was also developing a struggle for the leadership of the entire Zionist movement between Ben-Gurion and Weizmann, with the former taking the offensive. Ben-Gurion's American orientation from 1939 onwards was therefore as much a reflection of his evaluation of future British policy as of his desire to establish a new power base without Weizmann's patronage. Conversely Weizmann's British orientation was as much a reflection of his style of operation, based as it was on *tête-à-têtes* with key British politicians, whom he had been indefatigably charming for the previous quarter of a century, as of his fear of losing the threads of Zionist control to Palestinian or American Zionist leaders. In the event, Zionism suffered little from these differences. While Weizmann continued to work on Britain, Ben-Gurion stormed the US.

The success of Ben-Gurion in his American venture is a striking illustration of the unique advantage possessed by the World Zionist Organization as a *colon* system in having more than one metropolitan base and in its ability to exploit this fact to the full in response to pressures both external and internal. It also provides insights into the strategy of Zionism.

By 1939 the Anglo–Zionist entente had by no means come to an end; Churchill, the British war premier, was an unqualifiedly dedicated Zionist.[43] Such was Zionist influence with the British Labour Party during the war that the Party's National Executive in 1944, inspired by Peel and almost certainly prodded by its mentor, Harold Laski, advocated: 'Let the Arabs be encouraged to move out [of Palestine] as the Jews move in.' Nevertheless the message conveyed by the White Paper of 1939 could not be ignored. Its most disturbing feature for the Zionists was that it was an index of the extent to which the leverage formerly enjoyed by British Jewry on Britain's Palestine policy had been eroded. As a result of growing tensions between London and Tel Aviv, British Zionists, in the words of Kermit Roosevelt,[44] 'would seem to have been aware – as indeed, British citizens should be – to some extent, at least, of *British* as well as Zionist interests . . .' Ben-Gurion[45] has described his deliberations in 1939 with the Zionist leaders Golomb and Shertok on precisely this issue. The account by Ben-Gurion shows the role assigned to the metropolitan base in Zionist strategy and the desperate search for an alternative to the British one. All nationalist movements in overseas territories have tried to marshal public support for their cause in the metropolitan country. But no nationalist movement has, in degree or kind, needed or depended on a metropolitan base as, according to Ben-Gurion, the Zionists did. While to a nationalist movement public support in the metropolitan country is at best auxiliary, the entire strategy hammered out by the three Zionist leaders in 1939 seemed to hinge on the activation of American Jewry to replace the reduced influence of the Jews of Britain. This exclusive organizational link with similar ethnic groups in the metropolitan country also differentiates the Zionist *colon* system from nationalist movements whose links with favourably disposed groups in the metropolitan country are diffuse and ungoverned by considerations of ethnic solidarity. Moreover, whereas with other nationalist movements the relations with the favourably disposed metropolitan groups are usually of an ad hoc nature and contingent upon the existence of a state of confrontation between the metropolis and its overseas territory, the links forged between the Zionist *colons* and their metropolitan base and vice versa primarily reflect this ethnic common denominator between them. Other aspects of Ben-Gurion's deliberations in 1939 are also of interest. The 'plan' to harness the US was decided upon by him and his two colleagues consciously and deliberately. The decision was taken on Palestinian, not on American, soil. None of the three architects of the plan (Ben-Gurion, Shertok, Golomb) were American citizens or even residents of the US. The main asset that they possessed in the US was their ethnic link with American Jewry. The principal feature of their plan was that American Jewry should be activated by the Zionist *colon* leadership in Palestine. The purpose of this activation was to use American Jewry to bring pressure to bear on the American Legislature and Administration so that the latter, in its turn, would pressure London into toeing the Zionist line. It will be recalled that in 1917 London had itself encouraged the British and American

Zionists to use their leverage in Washington to persuade herself
(London) to adopt the Balfour Declaration. But what was
happening now was radically different. The initiative came not
from London, not from the British Zionists, not even from the
American Zionists but from the Zionist *colons* in Palestine.
Listen to the appraisal of Shertok in 1939 as quoted by Ben-
Gurion:

> There are millions of active and well-organised Jews in America,
> and their position in life enables them to be most dynamic and
> influential. They live in the nerve-centres of the country, and hold
> important positions in politics, trade, journalism, the theatre and
> the radio. They could influence public opinion, but their strength
> is not felt since it is not harnessed and directed at the right target.

That it took the planners only about five years to revolutionize
the American scene indicates its extraordinary permeability in
the face of the Zionist *colon* system. Of course, London had
shown a similar susceptibility to Zionist pressure in the twenties
and thirties – but with two principal differences. London's Zionist
policy was based on a conscious evaluation of British national
interests in the Middle East, however misguided it may have
been. And the main pressure on London came from the British
metropolitan Zionist base. But the most remarkable aspect of
Ben-Gurion's performance in the US is that it had an external
origin in the Zionist establishment in Palestine and was carried
through to success against the advice and policies of the
specialized agencies in the US Administration, i.e., the State
Department and the Pentagon.

Ben-Gurion's task was not easy. American Jewry seemed
indifferent. In the words of Golomb in 1939: 'Dire tragedies have
befallen the Jews of Europe. Did this arouse American Jewry to
increase their material support? No, it did not. Quite the
opposite . . . ' At the same time the Zionist Organization of
America was 'disunited and incapable of action. It has no faith in
its own ability to gain the support of the American Jewish
masses, and to conduct any worthwhile activity'. A specific index
of this state of affairs is the level of contributions by American
Jewry to the two leading Zionist colonizing institutions, the
Keren Hayesod and the Keren Kayemeth. In the four years
1939–42 these contributions showed little increase: $3,500,000
(1939), $3,700,000 (1940), $3,500,000 (1941), $4,200,000 (1942).

How to galvanize American Zionists, and through them American Jewry, into action was Ben-Gurion's problem. And the means he chose to do this was to define Zionist objectives in maximalist terms and to persuade and cajole American Zionist leaders to endorse them openly. Hence the so-called Biltmore Programme adopted by 600 American Jews in New York on 11 May 1942 in the presence of both Ben-Gurion and Weizmann. It is clear from Ben-Gurion's memoirs that he considered the Biltmore Programme a principal achievement of his career which he probably viewed in the perspective of Zionist history as 'cancelling out' Weizmann's role in achieving the Balfour Declaration. And it is intriguing that Weizmann in *his* memoirs makes no reference to the Programme at all, confirming the proposition that Ben-Gurion's drive towards this Programme was at least partly a function of the struggle for leadership between the two men. The operative paragraph in the Programme is the final one:

> The Conference urges that the gates of Palestine be opened; that the Jewish Agency be vested with control of immigration into Palestine and with necessary authority for upbuilding the country, including the development of its unoccupied and uncultivated lands; and that Palestine be established as a Jewish Commonwealth integrated in the structure of the new democratic world.

Behind the controlled language the intention is crystal clear: to take over the whole country. Not a '*national home* in Palestine' (the Balfour Declaration), not a Jewish state *in* Palestine (the Peel partition formula), but 'Palestine . . . as a Jewish Commonwealth'. The use of the word 'Commonwealth' still betrays the Zionist predilection for happy euphemisms but there is no doubt about what it means, viz. undisputed control of immigration and land acquisition. When it is remembered what the roles of Jewish 'immigration' and land 'development' were, and when it is recalled that in the year 1942 Jewish land ownership in Palestine stood only at 5.9 per cent of the total area of the country and the Jewish community at only 31.2 per cent of the total population it is clear that what Ben-Gurion had really succeeded in doing was to secure the support of American Zionists for Arlosoroff's proposal for 'a transition period during which the Jewish minority would exercise organized revolutionary rule'[46] – in short a

Rhodesian-style Zionist Unilateral Declaration of Independence in the whole of Palestine. It will be noted that the Biltmore Programme wields Wilson's name for the benefit of the American public. The reader is best left to his own devices to scrutinize these credentials.

With the Biltmore Programme the American Zionist metropolitan base came into its own. It was no longer to be only the milch cow but the centre of political gravity setting the framework and the pace for decisions on Palestine taken in Washington, and, through Washington, in London. A repeat performance now took place on the American scene of the whole gamut of tactics and pressures exercised earlier during the twenties and thirties on the British Government. But the opportunities offered by the American theatre of operations were more conducive to Zionist success than the British, partly because of the peculiarities of the American political system, partly because of the vastly more significant potential power of the American Jewish community, and not least of all on account of the diverse repertory of Zionist skills in the strategy of political leverage acquired in the long rehearsals with Britain. But the announcement of the Biltmore Programme was only the first step. The supreme objective was that of harnessing the White House itself, to as much of this Programme as was feasible at any point of time. The developments of the Palestine problem since 1942 to this very day of writing, in 1970, have been influenced by the graduated progress of Zionism in attaining this objective, more than by any other single factor.

The green light from the White House did not flicker until the accident of Roosevelt's death in 1945 brought Harry Truman to the presidency of the US. President Roosevelt's standing with American Jewry was very high indeed, partly because of his relatively liberal domestic policies and partly because of his leadership of the Western World against Nazism. From about the mid thirties onwards the vast majority of American Jews voted in his favour in presidential elections. On Palestinian matters he was sympathetic to Zionism, and he had intervened on its behalf with London during 1938–9. His support for Zionism was, however, measured. This was perhaps due to the strength of his personal position with American Jews, which made it difficult for the Zionists to mobilize them against him. But it was also due to the context in which he seemed to view the whole issue of Jewish migration from Europe. As early as 1938 he had called for an international conference, which had met at Evian to discuss the problem. To be sure, his instructions to the American delegates to the conference were that additional Jewish immigrants would be accepted in the US but only within the annual quotas. This was hardly designed to bring dramatic relief to the problem, as has already been noted. On the contrary the American emphasis on the immutability of the existing quotas influenced the other delegates to the conference to tighten rather than liberalize their offers of help. What is, however, important about the Evian Conference is its international character. And it is this international context, in which Roosevelt saw the Jewish migration problem, that is relevant to his attitude to Palestine. The gist of this attitude was that Palestine by itself (or presumably the US?) could not provide the necessary relief for the problem of Jewish migration from Europe and this was an international responsibility in which all countries should share. Roosevelt became increasingly preoccupied with this problem after war broke out. He foresaw that the Jewish refugee problem would become a major issue at the end of the war. He also foresaw that there would be increasing pressures on Palestine (and the US?) which the country could not meet. His new plan was to secure by private diplomacy specific commitments from individual countries to admit an agreed number of Jewish immigrants at the end of the war. His envoy on this mission, Morris Ernst, has related how the bitter Zionist opposition to it ensured the failure of the mission.[47] Whether Roosevelt was primarily worried about the post-war flooding of the US or Palestine by European Jewish refugees is, of course, a moot point. But he was certainly aware of the limitations of Palestine, a country of 10,000 square miles, as compared, for example, with the US (3,600,000 square miles), Canada (3,850,000 square miles) or Australia (2,960,000 square miles). This awareness is perhaps exemplified in his serious discussion of the possibility of a 'supplemental' Jewish National Home, in addition to the one in Palestine, to be located, mercifully, not in the Middle East. In addition to this scepticism that Roosevelt seemed to show with regard to the 'absorptive capacity' of Palestine, his interest in the Middle East grew with the American military and political involvement in the area during the war and the development of oil and strategic interests in Saudi Arabia. Meanwhile the pressures generated by the Biltmore Programme began to permeate the American political system through the Zionist lobby. An index of the progress made by the Biltmore Programme in mobilizing American Jewry is again the level of contributions to the Keren Kayemeth and Keren Hayesod. These are $4,200,000 (1942), $6,100,000 (1943), then $10,300,000 (1944), and $14,800,000 (1945). In February 1945, on his way back from the Yalta Conference, President Roosevelt met King Ibn Saud, to hear from him the Arab position on Palestine. William Eddy, who acted as interpreter at the meeting, has described the impression made on Roosevelt by the Arab monarch.[48] In a letter dated 5 April 1945, which President Roosevelt sent Ibn Saud, the predecessor of President Nixon then stated, according to Eddy, that '(1) He personally, as President, would never do anything which might prove hostile to the Arabs; and (2) the U.S. Government would make no change in its basic policy in Palestine, without full and prior consultation with both Jews and Arabs.' One week later, F. D. R. was dead, and Harry Truman President of the US.

Hardly had the new president eased himself into his chair at, presumably, the Oval Office, than he fired his first missive on behalf of Zionism in the direction of London. The letter was addressed to Churchill, the British Prime Minister who had been nagging Weizmann about the lukewarmness of Roosevelt on Zionism. The letter was dated 24 July 1945. But by 26 July the results of the British election had brought the Labour Party, headed by Attlee, to power. The first paragraph of the letter that Attlee read stated:

> There is great interest in America in the Palestine problem. The drastic restrictions imposed on Jewish immigration by the British White Paper of May 1939 continue to provoke passionate protest from Americans most interested in Palestine and the Jewish problem. They fervently urge the lifting of these restrictions which deny to Jews who have been so cruelly uprooted by ruthless Nazi persecutions entrance into the land which represents for so many of these their only hope of survival.

The focus on the immigration issue was not fortuitous. It was directly and explicitly aimed at the White Paper of 1939. The abrogation of the White Paper was the immediate Zionist objective. This was after all largely why the transfer of the metropolitan base to Washington had taken place.

With the White Paper out of the way progress could continue towards the Biltmore Programme objective of Zionist political domination of the whole of Palestine. And given the world climate of opinion aroused on behalf of Europe's Jews by Nazi barbarism, what better Zionist line could there be than to present the abrogation of the White Paper as the one available solution on humanitarian grounds? This line had already been adumbrated in the Biltmore Programme itself which had stated: 'The policy of the White Paper is cruel and indefensible in its denial of sanctuary to Jews fleeing from Nazi persecution.' Now no less a person than the President of the US was endorsing it. The lifting of the White Paper restrictions are equated by him with the 'only hope of survival' available to the refugees. This is inexplicable in terms of logic and indeed of equity. The war had ended and Nazism had been crushed. The wretched inmates were removed from their horrible surroundings into various relief centres. These were under the surveillance of Allied troops (including the American army and units of the Palestinian Jewish Brigade). They were organized by international teams including American Zionist and Palestinian Jewish organizations. Tragically, the number of Jews was small, about 300,000 in all, representing the pitiful remnants of the Holocaust. Seared to the soul, these were unquestionably entitled to refuse 'repatriation' to the scenes of their destruction in Central and Eastern Europe. Their plight was an indelible scar on the conscience of Western Christendom, crying for immediate and permanent remedy by the collective efforts of mankind. Nor would that have been beyond the human ingenuity and incomparable resources of the victorious powers. Even the Palestine Arabs were morally called upon in the circumstances to make their contribution, however modest, and irrespective of the background of Zionist machinations and ambitions in Palestine. But to exploit the plight of the European Jewish refugees for the political purpose of tearing the White Paper of 1939, itself the end result of two agonized decades of Palestinian Arab struggle for national and communal survival, is to open to question the motivation of the White House. For an inkling of the extent of America's cynicism in her ostensibly humanitarian concern with the Jewish refugees the reader is referred to Robert Divine,[49] the American authority on his country's immigration legislation, who describes the hostile attitudes of the Congress and various American pressure groups in the years 1945–7 on the question of admission of these very remnants of Hitler's gas chambers into the United States itself. There is nothing basically new in Divine's revelations. They are in consonance with earlier American attitudes already described. What they do emphasize, however, is the persistence of these attitudes even in the circumstances created by World War II. As for President Truman, he had hardly chosen the road that winds uphill all the way. Not for him to lead the world by setting the example 'at American expense'; nor the need to honour the commitments of his predecessor to Ibn Saud, nor the collective approach advocated by President Roosevelt, but the Churchillian 'magnanimity' of 1922, far away from home.[50] The temptation, clearly, was too great for the Vice-President turned President. The terrible pressures on men in his predicament at the White House to vindicate themselves in their own right at the next elections (due in 1948) is now commonplace knowledge since Harvard ex-Kitchen Cabinet members have taken to reminiscing about their experiences at the pinnacle of American power. In his letter to the British Prime Minister in July 1945 Truman, with sure awareness of the exigencies of political survival, scored several bulls-eyes. He allayed the fears of Congressional leaders and the American public that the US would 'alone' bear the brunt of this invasion by 300,000 miserable human beings; he relieved the leaders of American Jewry from the embarrassing task of seriously demanding access to the US for thousands of their European co-religionists; he won the hearts of the Zionist leadership. And he did all this in the name of the most cherished values of his civilization, to the loud applause of his public. On the debit side he brought himself into possible conflict with London. But with Lend Lease abruptly terminated at the close of the war, Britain was down on her knees. He also propelled the Arab world on its journey of alienation from the West, but then, as he explained in October 1945 to his assembled American diplomats from the Arab countries: 'I am sorry, gentlemen, but I have to answer to hundreds of thousands who are anxious for the success of Zionism; I do not have hundreds of thousands of Arabs among my constituents.' One is at least grateful for the candour, which pinpoints one of the most unbalancing influences on developments in the Middle East since the 1940s – the role of the domestic factor in American decision-making on Palestine. This factor is never absent in any process of foreign policy-making, whatever the country, and its influence can be to the good or towards imbalance. It is the latter if domestic considerations operate in defiance of the merits of the case and at the expense of the regional realities of the issue in question. Truman's posture falls squarely into the latter category. And to bring about just such a state of affairs was the basic intent of the strategy of Ben-Gurion and his two principal colleagues in 1939. This strategy had been tantamount to throwing a bait at the White House, which Roosevelt had dodged but which Truman firmly bit on. What was the anatomy of this bait? Two correlations to be made simultaneously by the incumbent American President: (1) between idealism and Zionism, and (2) between pro-Zionism and presidential longevity. In taking the bait Truman became a presidential prototype (compare in particular the policies of Presidents Johnson and Nixon on Palestine) by starting an ineluctable process. For as already noted there is a triangular flow between the Gentile great power sponsor, the Zionist metropolitan establishment and the metropolitan Jewish community. The more the Gentile sponsor's partiality for Zionism, the greater the self-confidence of the metropolitan Zionist establishment. The greater the self-confidence of this establishment, the greater its leverage against the metropolitan Jewish community. The more the metropolitan Jewish community is mobilized, the greater its leverage against the Gentile sponsor. The greater the leverage against the sponsor, the greater the latter's partiality. Ben-Gurion's achievement was in seeing early enough the limitations on the operation of this cycle in Britain and its feasibility in the US. An immediate indication of American Jewry's response to presidential partiality was the sudden unprecedented leap in the American revenue of the Keren Kayemeth and Keren Hayesod from $14,700,000 in 1945 to $26,800,000 in 1946.

President Truman's letter to the British Prime Minister of 24 July 1945 was only a shot across the bows. It was followed by

a series of escalating moves against Britain steadily nudging it in
the direction desired by the Zionists. It will be recalled that the
British Labour Party, now in power, was staunchly pro-Zionist.
Bevin, the new Foreign Secretary, had a long working relationship with British Zionists that stretched back at least to 1931,
when his intervention on their behalf had been decisive in
neutralizing Webb. But Britain had by now some twenty-seven
years of first-hand experience of Zionism, and unlike the US she
also had a Middle Eastern policy of sorts. She needed some time
to regain her breath after the war and was thinking out her next
moves in the Arab World in the new conditions that now
obtained. Aware of her own tergiversations on Palestine since
1917, and having no illusions about the sensitivity of the issue in
the Middle East, she was, in short, taking her time. But it was
precisely this that the Zionist leaders and their American Zionist
allies could not stomach. There were many reasons for Zionist
haste. The Zionist leaders were aware that immediate post-war
international environments are generally characterized by fluidity
and are therefore most propitious for territorial surgery. World
public opinion, shocked to the core by the Holocaust, was at the
peak of its potential sympathy for Zionism, whatever it
understood Zionism to be. President Truman and American
Jewry were all keyed up and their momentum needed to be
exploited before it flagged. Arab public opinion was being stung
by the partisanship of the US and in 1945 the Arab League had
been established and had committed itself to the preservation of
the Arab character of Palestine. But the most important
consideration was of a different order altogether. The Zionists
had claimed the leadership of 'World Jewry' since 1897. After
almost half a century of this leadership, the Jewish people
suffered the greatest catastrophe in its history since that at the
hand of the Assyrians. There is a definite correlation between
this catastrophe and the axioms of Zionist doctrine in the inter-
war period, which demanded the exclusive orientation of Jewish
immigration towards Palestine and, as a corollary, Zionist silence
towards immigration restrictions imposed upon Jews by the
West.[51] In retrospect (and any verdict on policies can only be
made in retrospect) the chief Zionist miscalculation lay, as
noted, in emphasizing the political formula for the solution of the
Jewish problem at the expense of the humanitarian one. This was

becoming increasingly clear as the news of the extent of Nazi bestiality against the Jews began to percolate to the outside world. The timing of the Biltmore Programme reflects signs of early Zionist self-consciousness on this score. Hence, when the full extent of the Nazi horrors became known by the end of the war, the desperate need for the Zionist leadership to *vindicate* themselves and their old political formula. Hence their otherwise irrelevant and untypical equation of this formula with the far too belated 'rescue' of the Jewish Displaced Persons. Hence the significance of Truman's acceptance of this line. And hence the extraordinary efforts made to project this image of the work of Zionist organizations for illegal immigration to Palestine in the immediate post-war period.[52]

Pressure through the White House represented the major thrust of the Zionist offensive against London. It also formed what the Americans would call the 'backdrop' for the other arm of the giant pincer operation. This subsidiary arm was two-pronged. One operation was the lavishly financed and carefully orchestrated organization of the illegal immigration of specially trained Jewish Displaced Persons 'trying to reach' their 'only hope for survival' in Palestine. This, while ramming home the new image of the Zionist leadership, maximized the embarrassment of the British Mandatory. The second was the equally carefully orchestrated campaign of violence against the Mandatory[53] based on the powerful Zionist military establishment in Palestine.[54] The coordination between the three levels of action, the 'diplomatic' (the White House), the 'histrionic' (illegal immigration), and the 'military' (the controlled violence in Palestine) was, of course, central, attesting to the transcontinental scope and resources of the World Zionist Organization. But although action was on three levels, the fulcrum was in Washington's relations with London, not in the histrionic or the military 'confrontation' with the British in Palestine. The sure awareness by both the Zionists and the British of where the fulcrum was, gave the former immense leeway against the latter and made the subsidiary histrionic and military operations devastatingly effective. And it is precisely the extent of this leeway which confirms the intrinsically *colon* character of the Zionist establishment in its two wings, metropolitan and overseas. For never in the history of truly nationalist struggle, either before or since the Anglo–Zionist 'confrontation' in the years 1945–7, have any 'rebels' enjoyed the immunity that the Zionists did. Never have the 'security forces' faced with such immobilism the onslaughts of the violators of 'law and order'. Never has the ratio of casualties between the former and latter been so fantastically in favour of the latter. Never have the rebels emerged in their economic, political and military infrastructures literally unscathed from their confrontation with an imperial power as the Zionists did. Never was so much won at such little cost. To be sure, Britain was war weary and at her wits' end as to what to do, but she had 100,000 crack troops in Palestine (one for every six Jews in the country). And if Britain's immobilism, in contrast to her handling of the Palestine Arab Rebellion (1936–9), and indeed to Israel's conduct in her occupied territories since 1967, points to any significant truth, it is to the apparent fact that some people are more 'equal' than others and especially more so if shaded by a White House umbrella.

Just how strong the White House pressures were has been related by Francis Williams,[55] who records the account of London's dealings with Washington in the years 1945–6 as he heard it from Attlee the British Prime Minister. But a word of caution is due at this stage. It will not do to get too maudlin at Britain's plight, for importunate as Truman was, he was not without his uses as an alibi. Meanwhile American revenue to the Keren Kayemeth and Keren Hayesod doubled again from $26,800,000 in 1946 to $59,000,000 in 1947. The American Zionist lobby tightened the screws and these were applied to key American Jewish congressional members. Most notable of all was the impact of Zionist pressure on American Cabinet decision-making as recorded in the diaries of William Forrestal, the American Defense Secretary of the time. The entry describing a Cabinet lunch on 4 September 1947 begins:

> At the end of the lunch Hannegan [Postmaster General] brought up the question of the President's making a statement of policy on Palestine, particularly with reference to the entrance of a hundred and fifty thousand Jews into Palestine. He said he didn't want to press for a decision one way or the other but simply wanted to point out that such a statement would have a very great influence and great effect on the raising of funds for the Democratic National Committee . . .[56]

But the issue of immigration had long served its purpose. By August 1946 the Zionist leadership was spelling out its territorial conditions. To show how cooperative they were they would not insist on the Biltmore Programme. They would settle for three quarters of a loaf, i.e., the Peel frontiers plus the Negev. Truman promptly endorsed the new Zionist strategy.

The Biltmore Programme, it will be recalled, envisaged Zionist control of the whole of Palestine. What the Zionists seem to have had in mind, as already noted, was a Rhodesian-style Unilateral Declaration of Independence (UDI) to take place immediately after the war. Zionist thinking and planning in this direction was far advanced. As an official publication explained in 1943, one year after the Biltmore Programme: 'The Zionist authorities now feel that the Mandate has outlived its usefulness. . . . *Now*[57] the time has come for us to demand what we have been working for during the last twenty years.'[58] The same publication quotes Ben-Gurion as saying:

> The main readjustment . . . is a new regime – political, legal, and administrative – especially designed for the maximum development of the resources of the country and the absorption of the maximum number of immigrants in the shortest possible time. . . . Only a Jewish administration can be equal to that task – an administration *completely identified with the needs and aims of the Jewish settlers*.[59]

The emphasis is on political control. This has an overall priority over immigration. Indeed political control is seen as the *sine qua non* for massive immigration and settlement. Through political control the numerical Arab majority can be subverted 'in the shortest possible time.' Through political control again the juridical status quo with regard to the Arab ownership of the bulk of the land can be negated by legalistic strategems of direct and indirect dispossession at which the Israelis have proved themselves to be second to none since 1948. This actual emphasis on political control contrasts with the public emphasis on immigration subsequently propagated through President Truman. At the same time the language used by Ben-Gurion, viz. 'an administration completely identified with the needs and aims of . . . the Jewish settlers' is an excellent example of *colon* disregard for the 'needs and aims' of the indigenous majority. But what it does reflect most of all is the Zionist assessment that the relation of forces inside the country had at last shifted in their favour, irrespective of Palestinian Arab numerical superiority. This assessment stemmed partly from the fact that Palestinian Arab military strength had been shattered by the British during 1936–9, and partly from the immense development in the Zionist military establishment during World War II. This development took place on several levels. A total of 27,028 Palestinian Jews were recruited by the British Army (1016 in the Royal Navy, 2652 in the RAF and 23,270 in the Army). Towards the end of the war Churchill authorized the formation of a Palestinian Jewish Brigade Group which was 5258 strong. The significance of this Brigade Group was not lost on the Zionists. In the words of Ben-Gurion, this was 'an independent unit with auxiliary forces (artillery, armour, etc.) so that it can operate as a small division'. Subsequently this formation became the model combat unit of the Israel army, just as the British-trained Jewish Palestinian officers and NCOs became its backbone. Expertise was also forthcoming from other sources. The British estimate, for example, that a total of 3600 Jewish deserters from the Polish forces (many of them with their weapons) joined the Palestinian Jewish community during the war. But the most far-reaching development was in the vast expansion of the Jewish military industry. Jewish Palestinian industries were already producing mortars, together with their bombs, as early as 1939. During 1942–4 they supplied orders to the British military totalling £33 millions. These included 3,634,000 anti-tank mines, tank engines, small naval craft, parachutes, etc. It was on this military establishment that the Zionists based their assessment of the feasibility of a UDI in the whole country. And indeed a General Military Plan known as Plan Aleph (Plan A) was drawn up in February 1945, precisely to implement this UDI strategy. Its premiss was that the general situation in the Arab world was such that resistance to the UDI would come from the Palestinian Arabs only. Plan Aleph was designed to crush their resistance to a Zionist take-over.

Within a few weeks of the end of World War II the Zionists must have realized that a UDI on the scale planned was not immediately feasible. Hence the concentration of their fire on the

White Paper of 1939. By early 1946 and thanks to Truman this had been torn to shreds by a joint Anglo–American Committee. Ironically, this Committee recommended, *inter alia*, the immediate admission of 100,000 Jewish immigrants into the country, but also pointed to the undesirability of the existence of illegal armies. The reference was to the Zionist military establishment described already, the disbandment of which the British made a condition for the admission of the 100,000 Jews. But the disbandment of the Zionist military establishment would have deprived the Zionists of the military means to implement their UDI when the opportunity presented itself. At the same time a joint Anglo–American team of experts studied various political formulae for the solution of the problem and reached unanimity on a plan for Arab–Jewish provincial autonomy. Fearing that the American experts would win Truman's approval for this plan, the Zionists immediately changed their strategy. They would drop their insistence on a UDI in the whole country and accept a UDI in the greater part of the country. This new objective was suitably formulated in the phrase 'a Jewish State in a viable area of Palestine'. What they meant by a 'viable area' was the Peel frontiers plus the Negev. This proposal was promptly endorsed by Truman who, in August 1946, submitted it, in his turn, to the British, thus blowing sky-high the provincial autonomy plan of the Anglo-American team of experts.

Meanwhile the Arab League had shown growing concern. In December 1945 it had instituted a counter boycott of Zionist goods in belated retaliation for the discriminatory practices against the Arabs of both the Keren Hayesod and Keren Kayemeth. In May 1946, at the first Arab Summit meeting at Inshass in Egypt, the Arab heads of state pledged themselves to preserve the 'Arab status' of Palestine. In June, at Bludan in Syria, the Arab League reaffirmed the Inshass pledge. In September the Arab delegates to a conference called by the British in London put forward their plan for Palestine. They envisaged a unitary Palestinian state, the citizenship of which would be Palestinian. Qualification for this citizenship would be ten years' residence in the country. Jews with Palestinian citizenship would have full civil rights equally with all others. Special safeguards would be provided to protect Jewish religious and cultural rights. These safeguards would be alterable only with

the consent of the majority of the Jewish members of the
Legislature. Jewish representation in the Executive and Legislative branches would be proportionate to their numbers on the
principle of 'one man one vote'. Legislation on immigration and
land transfers would require the consent of the majority of the
Arab members of the Legislature. There were, incidentally, no
provisions for throwing the Jews into the sea.[60] Perhaps the most
important feature of the Arab proposals was the provision that
citizenship would be Palestinian *not* Arab. On 4 October 1946
the President of the US publicly announced his support for the
Zionist UDI proposals of the previous August, killing this
imaginative and positive Arab initiative in the bud.

President Truman's October endorsement of the latest Zionist
map for Palestine was the most important event in Zionist history
since the Balfour Declaration in 1917. It was directly responsible
for starting the chain of events that led to the catastrophic climax
of the British Mandate – the destruction of the Palestinian Arab
community in the 1948 War and the rise of Israel. At the time
when Truman made his October statement, Palestine was divided
into sixteen sub-districts, in only one of which (Jaffa sub-district,
containing the all-Jewish city of Tel Aviv) the Jews constituted
the majority, though even in this sub-district they owned only 39
per cent of the land, as opposed to 49 per cent owned by the
Arabs. The Truman-sponsored Zionist map envisaged the total
incorporation into the proposed Jewish State of *nine* of these sub-
districts. These were the sub-districts of Beisan (Arab population
70 per cent), Tiberias (A. pop. 67 per cent), Safad (A. pop. 87
per cent), Acre (A. pop. 96 per cent), Haifa (A. pop. 53 per
cent), Nazareth (A. pop. 84 per cent), Jaffa[61] (A. pop. 29 per
cent), Gaza (A. pop. 98 per cent), Beersheba (A. pop. 99 per
cent). In addition, the Jewish state was to incorporate the bulk of
two other sub-districts viz. that of Tulkarm (A. pop. 83 per cent)
and Ramleh (A. pop. 78 per cent) as well as portions of a *third*
sub-district, that of Hebron (A. pop. 96 per cent). The Arab
rump state would include wholly only *three* out of the sixteen sub-
districts, as well as the remainder of Ramleh, Hebron, Tulkarm,
and Jerusalem[62] (A. pop. 62 per cent) sub-districts. The three sub-
districts were those of Jenin (A. pop. 100 per cent), Nablus (A.
pop. 100 per cent) and Ramallah (A. pop. 100 per cent). In terms
of territory the Truman-sponsored Zionist map would give 75 per

cent of the total area of Palestine to the Jews at a time when their land ownership constituted 7.0 per cent of this area – an increase of more than 1000 per cent at Arab expense. The number of Jewish settlements to come under Arab rule was *ten* with a total of some 2000 inhabitants or a quarter of 1 per cent of the total Jewish population of the country. The number of Arab towns and villages to come under Jewish rule would be about 450, with a total of about 700,000 inhabitants, or 58 per cent of the total Arab population of the country. The Arabs would lose *all* their richest lands including *all* their citrus groves, which latter produced their most lucrative export crop. They would lose *all* control of the vital head-waters of the River Jordan, and all contact with the sea except for a tiny corridor leading to the largest Arab city of Jaffa, which from a bustling prosperous city would become a waif dependent on Jewish mercy.

The endorsement by Truman of these Zionist territorial ambitions was as devastating in its implications for the Arabs as it was shameless in its timing. The day which Truman had chosen on which to make his public announcement, 4 October, was Yom Kippur – a Jewish holiday. The choice of this day carried the flagrant hint of a special presidential offering to his Jewish constitutents on the occasion. The additional nuance of awaited reciprocity from these same constituents was implicit in the fact that the far-reaching scope of the announcement was specifically designed to pre-empt a political rival. This rival was Dewey, chief prospective Republican candidate in the forthcoming presidential elections in 1948, who on Yom Kippur was reported to be about to relieve himself of a sweeping pro-Zionist pronouncement in his campaign for the governorship of New York. President Truman's own Yom Kippur statement was a crowning triumph for the strategy conceived by Ben-Gurion and his two colleagues seven years before in 1939.[63] Commenting on Truman's statement, James Reston said:

> The President went against his advisers on foreign policy and chose to follow the promptings of those who were primarily interested in retaining Democratic majorities in Congress. The general conclusion is that if the Palestine question is approached from the viewpoint of American politics it is not likely to be solved and America's prestige and authority in the world are likely to be impaired.[64]

These words are as true and relevant today as they were twenty four years ago.

Truman's Yom Kippur statement had a decisive effect on the Zionists and British alike. To the Zionists, the green light from the White House was now a powerful beam lighting the road ahead. To the British the signal was equally clear. They were to lay their hands off the Hagana, the Zionist underground army, whose disbandment they had demanded, and to acquiesce to Zionist demands. American leverage against the British was particularly effective in the financial circumstances in which post-war Britain found herself. Already in August 1946 the balance of an American loan negotiated to replace Lend Lease had been frozen. It was to remain frozen until British compliance on Palestine was forthcoming.[65] Such were the privileges of the Zionist *colon* system in its 'confrontation' with the British. The White House attitude also had a more subtle effect on the British. It gave them the opportunity to follow in the footsteps of Pontius Pilate and wash their hands of the whole affair. On February 18 1947, in an uncharacteristically self-effacing confession, His Majesty's Government declared that they had 'no power under the terms of the Mandate to award [sic] the country either to the Arabs or to the Jews or even to partition it between them'. They had therefore reached the conclusion that 'the only course now open to us is to submit the problem to the judgement of the UN.' It has been suggested that the British believed that the UN would fail to reach agreement and that the problem would be returned to them. The new circumstances then obtaining would vastly strengthen their hands against all the other protagonists, particularly the US. There is evidence that the British did consider the possibility of such an outcome. But this could hardly have been the main motivation for the reference of the problem to the UN. With the White House virtual veto on military action against the Zionists, the British had indeed reached a dead-end. Meanwhile the Zionist military establishment was expanded still further. In May 1947 a new General Military Plan was drawn up to replace Plan Aleph. This new plan, Plan Bet (Plan B) was designed to take into account the increasing concern felt by the Arab countries and the new situation created by Britain's reference of the problem to the UN. In short, its purpose was to ensure the implementation of the UDI plan endorsed by Truman on Yom Kippur 1946, even if the Palestinian Arabs received help from the neighbouring Arab countries.

VI

The British Mandate over Palestine reached its terrible climax in the war of 1948. In response to Britain's request, the General Assembly met in special session in April 1947, only to send yet another commission of inquiry, the United Nations Special Committee on Palestine (UNSCOP). The committee was composed of representatives of eleven member states: two were Asian (India and Iran), two British white dominions (Canada and Australia), three Latin American (Uruguay, Guatemala and Peru), three Western and Central European (the Netherlands, Sweden and Czechoslovakia), one communist (Yugoslavia). Of the eleven states represented on the committee one was Moslem; the rest, with the exception of India, were Christian. Iran and India were potentially sympathetic to the Arabs, while Sweden was at least potentially neutral. The others were, alike, potentially pro-Zionist. But uppermost in the minds of all must have been the knowledge that the US had already committed itself to a particular 'solution' of the problem. And in the last analysis the committee was not a juridical tribunal. In the event, and after a brisk tour of the Middle East, the majority of the committee recommended a territorial solution substantially along the lines of the Yom Kippur statement by President Truman. The main difference from the Yom Kippur frontiers was the subtraction from the proposed Jewish state of the sub-districts of Acre, Nazareth and Gaza (Arab population, respectively, 96 per cent, 84 per cent, 98 per cent).

The principal feature of the UNSCOP plan, like that of Yom Kippur was, of course, the incorporation of the Negev in the Jewish State. This has usually been justified on the grounds that since the Negev was a desert, it was only appropriate that it should be 'given' to the Zionists who were adept at making deserts bloom. So much nonsense has been written about the subject that a digression will be made here to look more closely at it. The Negev is generally the area of Palestine south of a line drawn East–West through Gaza. This is a vast region totalling 12,577,000 dunums, almost half the total area of the country. Rainfall is poor, averaging 220 millimetres as compared to 550–611 on the coast between Tel Aviv and Acre. For centuries the area had been inhabited by bedouin tribes. In 1947 these were seven in number: the Tarabin, Azazmeh, Tiyaha, Jebarat, Saidiyin, Hanajra, and Luhaiwat, themselves sub-divided into about eighty clans. Although the bedouins are usually on the move, their movement is confined within a certain area which is jealously guarded against encroachment from others. These tribal areas contain focal centres of tribal life such as holy shrines, ancestral tombs, sites commemorating tribal memories, etc. In addition, as in the case of the Negev bedouins, these tribes were half-sedentary, deriving a considerable part of their livelihood from dry-farming. Indeed they grew most of the barley and much of the wheat produced in the country. Thus attachment to the tribal area was strengthened by the traditional and prescriptive rights acquired in the lands put under cultivation. The area actually cultivated by the bedouins was vast. As early as 1935 this amounted to 2,109,234 dunums.[66] By 1946 the number of bedouins in the Negev was 100,000. Now the year 1935 has just been given because it precedes by five years the *first* Jewish settlement in the Negev. By October 1946 the number of Jewish settlements in the Negev was only *four*. These were the settlements of Beit Eshel, Gevulot, Beer Yitzhak, and Revivim. Their total population was 475, and their landholdings amounted to 21,000 dunums only. Plainly, and despite all the talk, the Jews simply did not make the desert bloom, nor were they indeed very interested in doing so. And if there *was* any blooming in the desert, this was the work of the wretchedly poor bedouins. Perhaps more to the point is that the area put by the bedouins under cultivation in the Negev was *three* times the *total* area cultivated by the *entire* Jewish community in Palestine, after more than sixty years of loudly trumpeted 'pioneering'.[67] It remains to note that in the *two weeks* immediately following the 4 October 1946 Yom Kippur statement by President Truman which endorsed the incorporation of the Negev into the proposed Jewish state, *thirteen* new 'agricultural' settlements were established in the Negev. The occupants of these settlements were members of the Hanegev Battalion of the Palmach Brigade, the shock-troopers of the Hagana. Nevertheless (or should one say 'consequently'?) UNSCOP saw fit to 'give' the Negev to the Jewish state.

Politics is the art of misnomers. The General Assembly was now seized of the Zionist plan in the form of a recommendation by the 'majority' of UNSCOP. The name of the plan was the old one of partition. But whereas in 1937 partition had been recommended by the royal commission of an imperial power it was now the ostensibly disinterested verdict of an impartial international body. This endowed the concept with the attributes of objectivity and even-handedness – in short, of a compromise solution. But a compromise by definition is an arrangement acceptable, however grudgingly, to the protagonists. The 'partition' of Palestine proposed by UNSCOP was no such thing. It was Zionist in inspiration, Zionist in principle, Zionist in substance, and Zionist in most details. The very idea of partition was abhorrent to the Arabs of Palestine and it was against it that they had fought their bitter, desperate and costly fight in the years 1937–9. Also, 'compromise' implies mutual concession. What were the Zionists conceding? You can only really concede what you possess. What possessions in Palestine were the Zionists conceding? None at all. Again, a compromise implies that you concede what in the last estimate is expendable in order to preserve the substance of your position. We all know what the 'concessions' demanded of the Arabs were in the UNSCOP plan, and what the residual Arab state in the country was to be after the concessions were made. Concessions of such a kind and scale are demonstrably alien to the very idea of compromise. It is surely utterly alien to this idea that one party should so revolutionize its position vis-à-vis the other, and at the latter's expense, that the relative positions between the two would be actually reversed. It surely goes against the grain of human nature to expect the party that would suffer this reversal to enter into the transaction just because some third party, itself affiliated to the potential aggrandizer, chose to befog the issue by calling this transaction a 'compromise'. One might say all this is very well except that it ignores the power factor. True enough, but if we are talking about power, then we should say so and not pretend that we are talking about compromise – except that UNSCOP and subsequently the UN General Assembly did talk about this process of dictation and blackmail as though it were indeed a genuine compromise transaction. It may be relevant in this context to quote Peel himself. In the final paragraphs of his report in 1937, Peel addressed the Palestine Arabs as follows: 'Considering what the possibility of finding a refuge in Palestine means to many thousands of suffering Jews, is the loss occasioned by partition, *great as it would be*,[68] more than Arab generosity can bear?' and later: 'If the Arabs at *some sacrifice*[69] could help to solve that problem they would earn the gratitude not of the Jews alone but of all the Western World'. We are not concerned with the hypocrisy of such an appeal from a country whose own record on the admission of Jewish immigrants even contemporaneously with these very words as they were being written by Peel bears little examination. Nor with the absurdity of an appeal by one people to another that they should, out of generosity, yield their homeland to a third party. What is relevant is that the author of the partition plan knew what partition was about long before the term had been neutralized to suit the purposes of its beneficiaries and sponsors. And the Peel frontiers, flagrant as they were, were still less so than those of UNSCOP.

On 29 November 1947, the UN General Assembly resolved by a two-thirds majority to endorse the partition plan of UNSCOP with minor modifications. In this way partition was elevated to the status of 'the will of the international community'. The mechanics of bulldozing employed by the White House during this session of the General Assembly are described by many observers. Eban,[70] the South African-born Jewish Agency delegate, has described how President Truman's direct personal intervention in response to Zionist demands, but against American expert advice, ensured that the Negev was finally incorporated in the proposed Jewish state. Sir Muhammad Zafrulla Khan,[71] the Pakistani delegate, has disclosed the procedural manipulation (including the notorious postponement of the General Assembly vote on Thanksgiving Day) which was resorted to by the UN Secretariat under American pressure in order to channel proceedings in the direction of partition. Kermit Roosevelt[72] has also given an account of an extraordinary web of intrigue and strong-arm tactics that operated from White House circles against the smaller UN members who were lukewarm on partition. The diaries of Secretary of Defence Forrestal[73] reveal graphically what happens to an American cabinet member who tries to hold this ground against the fully mobilized Zionist forces of the United States.

Three other specific aspects of the UN deliberations on partition are worthy of attention. The first aspect pertains to the legality of the partition resolution. The Arab delegates at the General Assembly requested, *inter alia*, that before further action by the UN a resolution should be adopted to consult the International Court of Justice. The draft resolution asked:

> Whether the UN or any of its member States is competent to enforce or recommend the enforcement of any proposal concerning the constitution and future government of Palestine, in particular, any plan of partition which is contrary to the wishes, or adopted without the consent of the inhabitants of Palestine.

The voting of the General Assembly meeting as an Ad Hoc Committee on this draft resolution was 21 votes to 20. Only 21 of the 57 members of the General Assembly considered that the UN had the necessary competence. And yet the subsequent partition resolution was given overnight the sanctity and imperativeness of holy scripture – such are the ways of Democracy.

Secondly, the UNSCOP proposals had included a set of unanimous recommendations, one of which specifically pertained to the Jewish Displaced Persons. This unanimous recommendation urged that the UN General Assembly:

> undertake immediately the initiation and execution of an *international arrangement*[74] whereby the problem of the distressed European Jews . . . will be dealt with as a matter of extreme urgency for the alleviation of their plight and of the Palestine Problem.

In its unanimous comment on this unanimous recommendation UNSCOP pointed out that the distressed Jews of Europe were 'a legacy of the Second War' and as such 'a recognised international responsibility'. It further stated that:

> It cannot be doubted that any action which would ease the plight of the distressed Jews in Europe would thereby lessen the pressure of the Palestinian immigration problem and consequently create a better climate in which to carry out a final solution of the question of Palestine.

In the spirit of this unanimous recommendation and comment of UNSCOP's, the Arab delegates proposed a draft resolution, which would recommend, *inter alia*:

> that those Jewish refugees and displaced persons who 'cannot be repatriated should be absorbed in the territories of members of the United Nations in proportion to their area, economic resources, *per capita* income, population, and other relevant factors.

The result of the voting on this draft resolution in the General Assembly as an Ad Hoc Committee should by now occasion little surprise. It was 16 votes to 16 with 25 abstentions. In other words it was not carried. The closeness of this vote shows, however, how near to the marrow of Western pro-Zionism the Arab delegates had come: Jewish immigration to Palestine, even if it means flooding the Arabs out – by all means; but a modest contribution by each Western country to reflect the ostensibly humanitarian concern for Jewish refugees – nothing doing. Such are the ways of Charity.

Thirdly, the role of the USSR. As early as the special session of the General Assembly called in April 1947 to discuss Britain's reference of the problem to the UN, the USSR had indicated its interest in 'partition'. Earlier, the Soviet authorities had encouraged the movement of illegal Jewish immigration to Palestine from Soviet-occupied East European countries. During the discussions by the General Assembly of the recommendation of UNSCOP, the USSR emerged as a staunch supporter of the idea of a Jewish state. The Soviet Bloc controlled four votes in the Assembly (those of the Byelorussian SSR, the Ukrainian SSR, Poland, and the USSR),[75] and all these were firmly cast in support of a Jewish state. But the influence of the Soviet attitude on the UN Palestine deliberations far exceeded its voting strength, since it allayed fears that a pro-Jewish state attitude by the United States might exacerbate the cold war. What was the motivation for Soviet pro-Zionism? The question is of obvious relevance today. Now, if we are to believe W. Z. Laqueur,[76] the possibility cannot be excluded that Soviet endorsement of a Jewish state 'was recommended by some Foreign Ministry adviser and approved by Stalin in a fit of absentmindedness'. The explanation is less of a tribute to Laqueur's Kremlinology than to his public relations zeal vis-à-vis Western audiences on behalf of Zionism. There was nothing absent-minded about Soviet support of the Jewish state. The voting record of the Soviet Bloc during the crucial debate in the General Assembly leading to the partition decision on 29 November 1947 was determinedly pro-Zionist. It was to remain consistently so in the subsequent debates of all the UN bodies throughout the various stages of the Palestine War of 1948. Indeed, when, under State Department influence, and as a result of the increasing chaos in Palestine early in 1948, the US Government showed signs of wanting to reappraise its pro-partition policy, it was the USSR which insisted on its pound of flesh. Soon after the partition resolution, Soviet broadcasts to the Middle East, as well as the Soviet press, launched a campaign of abuse and psychological warfare against the Palestine Arabs and the Arab countries for opposing the establishment of a Jewish state. This campaign was sustained until the end of the fighting in 1949 and beyond. The fiercest attack on the UN mediator Count Folke Bernadotte came from the USSR, for suggesting modifications in the partition plan in partial redress of its excesses. Nor was Soviet policy confined to political support and propaganda. The largest single consignments to Palestine of specially trained illegal Jewish immigrants were released from Soviet-controlled Black Sea ports during 1947–8. But the most important Soviet contribution to the establishment of the Jewish state came in the form of a massive supply of heavy arms, tanks, and planes through Czechoslovakia, after the Communist take-over in that country in March 1948. Arnold Krammer has given the details of this Soviet-sponsored arms deal to the Jewish state,[77] and it is as well to remember that this deal preceded the subsequent deal to Egypt by seven years. It was this Soviet arms deal to the Zionists in 1948 that tipped the military scales against the Arab countries, facilitating the fall of Palestine and the rise of Israel.

Everything about Soviet Palestine policy during 1947–8 indicates that it was the result of cold calculation and long-term planning. The immediate objective of USSR policy was to exploit Anglo–American differences on Palestine in order to oust Britain from the country. With the British expelled from Palestine, British influence throughout the area would be undermined. On the long-term view, and knowing the intense Arab opposition to

Zionism, the USSR hoped that the creation of a Jewish State would produce a fluid situation in the Middle East which was bound to present it with more than one avenue of exploitation. Given its freedom from public pressure at home, its policy could shift from support of one side to the other. Such a shift would enable it to compensate for its earlier misdemeanour in supporting Zionism while polarizing Arab opinion, itself cumulatively alienable from the West by the latter's unrestrained Zionist partisanship. The Russian *entrée* into the Middle East was therefore the direct result of the banal motivation of White House policy on Palestine. Nor is the predicament relieved by reacting to the Russian moves with yet more Western pro-Zionism. This would serve, as it has already done, to accentuate the polarization and make the circle more vicious and unbreakable. If there is a moral to all this, it is the need for Western perception of the 'causal flow', i.e., an identification of just what is cause and what effect.

In blunt terms the need is for the occupant, any occupant, of the White House, to look rigorously into his pro-Zionist motivation, no matter how easy it is to sell his posture to his public in terms of preventing 'the Jews from being thrown into the sea', or of 'countering Soviet penetration', and no matter how glittering the immediate rewards.

After the partition resolution by the UN General Assembly on 29 November 1947 the scene shifted to Palestine. The intentions of the British were a key factor. What were they? The British line was that they could not support a solution that was not acceptable to both parties. They would not oppose partition but they would not help implement it. They would give up the Mandate by 15 May 1948, but until then they would be the sole sovereign power in the country. After 15 May the UN would be free to supervise the transitional interregnum leading to the establishment of the successor regimes based on partition. This seemed to be good enough for the White House, for on 10 December 1947, the balance of the American loan frozen since August 1946 was released.

What did the British attitude signify to the Zionists and the Palestine Arabs? To both, the most important feature of the rapidly developing situation was the *combination* of the partition resolution and the British withdrawal, to take place within a period of six months. Since the UN had not provided for an international force to implement its resolution, the British decision to withdraw was an invitation to both sides to fight it out. Given the balance of power inside Palestine,[78] which was crushingly in favour of the Zionists – a fact of which all parties were well aware – the British withdrawal was an open invitation for a Zionist military take-over of the country. But there was one imponderable which worried the Zionists – the possibility that help to the Palestine Arabs would come from the Arab countries. As we have seen, the Zionist General Military Plan of May 1947 (Plan Bet) had taken this into account.[79] Nevertheless it was difficult to foresee precisely what the scale of outside Arab help would be, in view of mounting anxiety felt for Palestine by the Arab countries. The problem fell into two parts: external Arab help in the six month period *between* 29 November 1947 and 15 May 1948, i.e., *during* the remaining period of the British Mandate; and Arab help *after* the termination of the British Mandate on 15 May 1948. Obviously what happened in the earlier period *up* to 15 May 1948 would largely determine the situation after it. The British provided an answer to Zionist worries on this score. They would remain the sovereign power until 15 May. This meant that the entry before this day of the regular Arab armies, such as they were, would involve a confrontation with the British. This was enough to rule out this possibility. There remained the possibility of help by external irregular Arab forces. But since these would be militarily of lesser significance, would take time to organize to an appreciably effective level, and would still have to be well below the threshold of a confrontation between the Arab countries that sponsored them and the British, the British 'sovereign' presence in the remaining six month period of the Mandate acted virtually as a shield against external Arab help behind which the Zionist military forces could conduct their business. Another feature of the British withdrawal plan played into Zionist hands, as it was expected to do. The Mandatory regime in Palestine was thirty years old. This had to be dismantled within six months. Obviously this could not be done in the twenty-four hours preceding 15 May 1948. Here the situation, as it evolved, was that the British yielded *de facto* authority in successive areas of the country while retaining *de jure* sovereignty over it as a whole against outside intervention. The general pattern of British withdrawal was away from the areas of Jewish concentration, starting with Tel Aviv and its hinterland, and towards those with Palestinian Arab concentration. Given the total absence of central Palestine Arab political and military control (thanks to British repression) and the existence of powerful, purposeful, multifaceted central institutional Zionist control (thanks partly to British immobilism in the face of Zionist provocation),[80] the pattern of British withdrawal, even when it affected areas of Arab concentration, merely *increased* the fragmentation of the Arab scene while it furthered the cumulative consolidation and extension of Jewish power. It is true that in certain localities individual British officials and soldiers showed favouritism to the Arabs, but these instances were balanced by corresponding individual instances in favour of the Jews, and were totally eclipsed by the overall desire of the British not to clash with the Zionist central forces even under extreme provocation from them or from the so-called dissident military groups, the Irgun and Lehi.

The immediate problem which which the Zionists were faced by the UN partition resolution and British withdrawal plans was largely novel. Until 1947 and since the 1880s Zionist land acquisition was based on purchase. Their land acquisition strategy had, of course, always been determined by politico-military considerations and there were numerous instances of thuggery and terrorization of Arab tenants and neighbours during the take-over of particular sites. The 'Operation Negev', as it was called, involving the establishment of thirteen new settlements after President Truman's Yom Kippur statement,[81] was not the only such operation clearly military in nature which had been carried out before 1948. But all these instances of settlement followed in the wake of legal or at least legalistic transactions involving the change of ownership of the site to be settled from the original owners to the new ones. Almost seventy years of this activity since the 1880s had netted a mere 7 per cent of Palestine by 1947. Now the partition resolution had 'given' the Zionists about 55 per cent of the country. What this signified was that the Zionists were asked literally to move into these additional areas of Palestine involving an almost 800 per cent increase of the territory that they actually held at the time. They were to move in gratuitously as occupiers and rulers, not as the legal owners of purchased real estate. But these additional areas were not empty. The frontiers of the proposed Jewish state included hundreds of Arab villages and scores of Arab towns and suburbs. To the Arab inhabitants of these towns and villages life under Jewish rule did not only mean life under foreign rule. It meant that, given Zionist ideology, their personal and communal property rights would be negated in the interest of the Jewish settler,[82] their status as a majority would be reduced to that of a minority in their own country, and the whole character of their society and communal life imperatively stamped with the stamp of an alien culture and alien values – not to mention the dismemberment of their country. These inhabitants had no option but to fight Zionist encroachment, UN resolution or no UN resolution. Militarily they were weak, but at least they were thick on the ground. Many of their villages occupied historically strategic sites astride the lines of communication of Jewish settlements. They would count on the help of the rest of the Palestinians who would fight partition for the same reasons as themselves. They could expect help from the neighbouring Arab countries. In short, the Zionists knew that the new phase of Zionist growth inaugurated by the UN partition decision would have to be based on a military take-over. But it was not so much the need for military action that presented them with a novel situation – their thinking along UDI lines had all along been based on the assumption of such action. What was novel in the circumstances was the need for military action within a definitely circumscribed time-table (the six months between 29 November 1947 and 15 May 1948) and on a scale commensurate with the task of occupying at least the area 'given' to them by the UN.

Zionist military planning and organization were superbly fitted to mesh in with British withdrawal plans. The Anglo–American Committee of Inquiry in 1946 had given the following breakdown of the Zionist military organization known as the Hagana. There was (a) a static force of 40,000 settlers and townsfolk; (b) a field army trained in more mobile operations 'based' (sic) on the Jewish Settlement Police with an estimated strength of 16,000; and (c) a full-time force (Palmach) with an estimated peace establishment of 2000 and a war establishment of 6000. What this breakdown blurs is the role of the Jewish Settlement Police

(JSP). This was an official British sponsored force created during the Palestine Arab Rebellion in 1936–8. The British had not seen fit to disband this force, which was under their control, even after failing to secure the disbandment of the illegal Hagana in 1946. The JSP was 15,410 strong in June 1947.[83] It served several purposes. Service in the JSP was known to be a preliminary step towards service in the field army of the Hagana, so that in effect the British continued to train and expand the Hagana's field army through the JSP while officially demanding the disbandment of the Hagana. In addition, as a recognised official force, the JSP had freedom of movement in the country. Since the command of the JSP was ultimately in the hands of the commanders of the Hagana, it was easy to move units of the Hagana's field army in the guise of the JSP. But the point to remember is that the JSP was a force separate in structure from the field army and additional to it. It is this point that is largely blurred by the breakdown given by the Anglo–American Committee. Another force not mentioned by the Anglo–American Committee was the Home Guard.

The breakdown of the main Zionist forces on 29 November 1947,[84] was therefore as follows: (a) the Home Guard (Mishmar Haam); (b) garrison troops (KHIM) referred to by the Anglo–American Committee as a 'static force'; (c) the 'field army' (KHISH); (d) the JSP; and (e) the Palmach. These were not full-time forces in 1946. Also, they were all organized on a territorial basis, i.e., they were tied in small units at company or platoon strength at the places of residence or work of their members. But starting from May 1947, and in accordance with Plan Bet, the Zionist military planners set themselves the task of converting the KHISH and the Palmach to a war footing. This was to be done by (a) disconnecting the units of these forces from their *local* territorial base, (b) regrouping them in larger units at battalion and brigade strength, and (c) assigning the new brigades specific theatres of operation to fit in with the British withdrawal plans and the requirements of the military take-over in the light of the partition decision. Meanwhile the JSP operated as an excellent cover for (a) the movement of arms and men, and (b) their protection *en route* to their new areas of operation. As the plan got into stride the Palmach, placed increasingly on a war establishment, was assigned the role of a general strategic reserve to spearhead operations in the various brigade areas and for other 'emergency' tasks.

Basing themselves upon this reorganization, the Zionist military planners drew up in late 1947 two new general plans: Plan Gimmel (Plan C) and Plan Dalet (Plan D).[85] These were strictly operational plans. Plan Dalet was the master plan for the military take-over of as much Arab territory as was feasible in the name of the partition resolution. Its overriding objective was the seizure and retention of territory. The minimum area to be seized was, of course, that assigned to the Jewish State. But certain Jewish settlements, e.g., in Upper Western Galilee lay outside the area of the Jewish state and these had to be 'defended'. The Jewish sector of Jerusalem[86] lay in the middle of the proposed Arab state and this was 'undesirable'. Jewish settlements in the plains were 'dominated' by Arab villages on higher ground, and these villages, although in the proposed Arab state, presented a 'security threat' to the Jewish settlements. The area of the Jewish state proposed by the UN partition plan had already been described by Zionist leaders as the 'irreducible *minimum*'. There was no telling what Plan Dalet would yield in terms of territory, since the Arabs were resisting partition and by so doing inviting 'retaliation'. But there was one constraint – the time factor. Plan Dalet should achieve its principal objectives *before* or *by* 15 May 1948. On that day, it will be recalled, the British Mandate would end and a juridical vacuum would be created in Palestine unless it was filled by the military *fait accompli* of the rise of Israel.

Plan Gimmel's role was to buy time for the mobilization of the forces necessary to carry out Plan Dalet. It would seize strategic points vacated by the British, terrorize the Arab population and undermine its will to resist, destroy any Arab concentrations, keep Arab forces off balance, maintain lines of communication *through* Arab territory between Jewish localities. When would Dalet replace Gimmel? This depended on the pattern and pace of the British withdrawal, the mobilization rate of the KHISH and Palmach brigades, but above all on the nature of Palestinian Arab resistance. Indeed Dalet might not be needed at all if the resistance of the Palestine Arabs collapsed under Gimmel. But it did not. Although Palestinian Arab strength had been pitifully inadequate since 1939, the Palestinian Arabs had no doubt why they had to fight, badly led and poorly organized though they were. Also, after endless verbal attitudinizing and dithering by the Arab League, a force of irregulars – the Arab Liberation Army – was trickled into Palestine, and this, absurdly small as it was,[87] boosted morale and stiffened resistance.

Between 29 November 1947 and 15 May 1948 Palestine was plunged into all the horrors of civil war, with Britain, to be sure, retaining its sovereignty over the country. Although strained to breaking point, the Palestine Arabs held their ground throughout the months of December, January, February and March under the blows of Plan Gimmel, supplemented by the barbarities of the Irgun and Lehi. By mid March Palestinian Arab steadfastness was making an impression on the UN. The US State Department, in particular, began to reconsider its position and spoke of the need for a special session of the General Assembly to discuss the possibility of a UN trusteeship over Palestine.

At the news of this reappraisal by the US of its attitude on Palestine, 'a frenzy of rage and disappointment', according to Eban, 'rolled through the Jewish World'.[88] But Weizmann put matters right again in a *tête-à-tête* with President Truman held on 18 March. The President, we are told, 'gave his visitor a specific commitment. He would *work for the establishment and recognition of the Jewish state*,[89] of which the Negev would be a part'. (Many years later, in May 1967, Eban himself was to perform similar miracles at the White House). The way was now clear for Plan Dalet.

Zero-hour for Plan Dalet was 1 April 1948. *Thirteen* operations were carried out within this plan's framework. There were only six weeks to go. Hence the merciless fury of the assaults. The greatest Arab asset was that they were there, on site, in their towns and villages. But this was the historic opportunity to de-Arabize the land of Israel, to negate Arab presence by simply removing it, to solve with a few crushing blows all the problems presented by the fact that, in the UN proposed Jewish state, the Arabs were equal in number to the Jews and owned the bulk of the land. Plan Dalet was conducted on two levels, the military and psychological. On the military level, the main strategy was of massive surprise attack against civilian populations softened by continuous mortar and rocket bombardment. On the psychological level, this was accompanied by intermittent announcements broadcast in Arabic from clandestine Hagana radio stations and from loudspeakers mounted on armoured cars in the target areas. The announcements threatened dire punishment, warned of the spread of epidemics, and named specific escape routes which the inhabitants could take to flee the carnage. Supplementing this dual strategy were carefully calculated acts of histrionic cruelty against small villages, designed to increase the credibility of Israel's might and induce an exodus from the countryside parallel to the exodus from the towns. Close-ups of some of these operations have been provided by Jacques de Reynier[90] in his account of the Deir Yasin massacre on 10 April, by Harry Levin[91] in his description of the destruction of the village of Kolonia on 12 April; and by Jon Kimche[92] in his account of the rape of Jaffa on 27 April.

The Palestinian Arabs broke under the full impact of Plan Dalet. The combination of military and psychological techniques produced a panic of mass proportions. The inhabitants of the coastal towns, Jaffa, Haifa and Acre, cut off from their hinterlands, were, for President Nixon's information, literally thrown into the sea.[93] Hundreds of men, women and children were drowned in the scramble under fire for any vessel or fishing craft to take them to safety. A vast exodus of hundreds of thousands of refugees was driven before the victorious Jewish brigades across the borders. Plan Dalet was supremely successful and the road was open for the restoration of the historical frontiers of Israel in the whole country.

Already by 23 April, and with the fall of Haifa, it was clear that Plan Dalet had achieved its purpose. On that day President Truman sent word to Weizmann in New York via Judge Samuel Rosenman, 'one of President Truman's closest political advisers'. The President had told Rosenman 'I have Dr. Weizmann on my conscience' [sic]. But the substance of the message was: 'If a Jewish State was declared, the President would recognise it immediately'. Incidentally, 23 April was Passover Eve. (Does the American President look at other calendars?).

With the President's renewed support, operation Dalet reached its climax. Eight new operations were mounted between 23 April and 14 May, four of which were outside the area of the proposed Jewish state.

On 14 May a letter was sent to the White House by Eliahu Elath, representative of the Jewish Agency in the United States, as 'representative of the Jewish state' *which had not yet been proclaimed.* The letter, sent in a taxi, requested American recognition of the Jewish State. Before the cab reached the White House news arrived from Palestine that a Jewish state had been proclaimed. At 5.16 Truman authorized the recognition of Israel by the US. (The year 1948 was also a presidential election year.)

The fall of hundreds of Palestinian Arab villages and the towns of Tiberias, Safad, Acre, Haifa and Jaffa, as well as the threat to Arab Jerusalem, compounded by the arrival of hundreds of thousands of Arab refugees in the Arab countries, forced the Arab governments, under tremendous public pressure, to act, however belatedly. Units of some of the Arab regular armies went into Palestine on 15 May. This has been described in Zionist mythology as the invasion of Israel by overwhelming Arab hordes, although the Arab forces were only about 14,000 strong[94] and vastly outnumbered by the Zionists. But Arab intervention was the logical and inevitable response to plans Gimmel and Dalet and the only hope of *stemming* the tide of refugees and averting the complete loss of Palestine in 1948.

VII

On 14 May 1948, the Chief Secretary of the British administration called a press conference in his office in the King David Hotel in Jerusalem. This was the last day of the Mandate. After a statement on the achievements of His Majesty's Government in the country and the unhappy circumstances of the termination of the Mandate, one of the assembled journalists asked: 'And to whom do you intend to give the keys of your office?' The Chief Secretary, blushing, and valiantly forcing a smile, replied: 'I shall put them under the mat'. A fitting epitaph to perhaps the shabbiest régime in British colonial history.

Notes

1   Compare A. Guillaume, *Zionists and the Bible*, in *From Haven to Conquest*, ed. Walid Khalidi (Institute for Palestine Studies, Beirut, 1970), pp. 25–30.

2   Compare L. M. C. van der Hoeven Leonhard, *Shlomo and David, Palestine, 1907*, in *From Haven to Conquest*, pp. 115–24.

3   Compare *Chaim Weizmann in Jaffa and in Paris*, in *From Haven to Conquest*, pp. 189–91.

4   Compare L. Stein, *The Balfour Declaration* (London, 1961), ch. xxxvi.

5   Compare *Edwin Montagu and Zionism 1917*, in *From Haven to Conquest*, pp. 143–51.

6   Compare E. Berger, *The Jewish Dilemma* (New York, 1946), pp. 169–208.

7   Compare Ilene Beatty, *Arab and Jew in the Land of Canaan* (Chicago, 1957), pp. 27–49 and 50–2.

8   Compare Burhan ad-Din al Fazari, *On the Merits of Jerusalem and Palestine*, in *From Haven to Conquest*, pp. 31–3.

9   Compare Miguel Asin, *Islam and the Divine Comedy* (London, 1926), pp. 67–76.

10   Compare Stanley Lane-Poole, *Saladin and the Fall of the Kingdom of Jerusalem* (Beirut, 1964), pp. 224–34.

11   The best account of early Palestinian Arab opposition to Zionism is Neville Mandel's article 'Turks, Arabs and Jewish Immigration into Palestine, 1882–1914.' (St. Antony's Papers, *Middle Eastern Affairs*, ed. A. Hourani, Oxford University Press, 1965).

12   Compare Herbert Sidebotham, *England and Palestine* (London, 1918), Chap. x.

13   Compare Oskar Rabinowicz, *Winston Churchill on Jewish Problems* (New York, 1960), pp. 46–50, 64-72, 78–80, and 164–67.

14   All quotations are from Rabinowicz, *op. cit.*

15   The population and quota figures refer to the year 1933, the eve of Hitler's assumption of power in Germany.

16   Compare *Documents on British Foreign Policy, 1919–1939*, ed. Woodward and Butler, pp. 1276–78.

17   Compare his statement in the House of Lords in 1921: 'I cannot imagine any political interests exercised under greater safeguards than the political interests of the Arabs of Palestine.'

18   Compare Balfour's Memorandum on Syria, Palestine and Mesopotamia in *Documents on British Foreign Policy, 1915–1939*, ed. Woodward and Butler, pp. 340–7.

19   Compare Frank E. Manuel, *The Realities of American–Palestine Relations* (Washington, 1949), pp. 164-70.

20   Compare also *Edwin Montagu and Zionism 1917*, in *From Haven to Conquest*, pp. 143–51.

21   Compare *From Haven to Conquest*, Appendix V, p. 851, for details

of American Jewry's financial contributions to Zionist institutions in Palestine.

22 For the best analysis of the Mandate system, see W. E. Hocking, *The Spirit of World Politics* (New York, 1932).

23 Compare Chaim Arlosoroff, *Reflections on Zionist Policy*, in *Jewish Frontier*, October 1948, pp. 7–11.

24 Compare Sir John Hope Simpson's *Palestine, Report on Immigration, Land Settlement and Development* (HMSO, London, 1930), pp. 52–6.

25 Compare A. Granott, *Agrarian Reform and the Record of Israel* (London, 1956), pp. 30–9.

26 Compare Appendices I and II of *From Haven to Conquest*, pp. 841–4 for the relevant statistics.

27 Compare Appendix IV of *From Haven to Conquest*, p. 846 ff for these estimates.

28 Compare Appendix III of *From Haven to Conquest*, p. 845.

29 Compare David Ben-Gurion in the *Jewish Observer and Middle East Review*, September 27, 1963, pp. 15–8.

30 Compare Appendix VIII of *From Haven to Conquest*, p. 858.

31 Reid's reservations on the plan appear in the Palestine Partition Commission *Report, 1938* (London, HMSO, 1938), pp. 263–81.

32 Compare M. K. Gandhi, *My Non-Violence* (Ahmedabad, 1960), pp. 70–4.

33 Compare Ernest Main, *Iraq: From Mandate to Independence* (London, 1946), pp. 43–6.

34 Compare the *Jewish Chronicle*, August 13, 1937, pp. 24–5, for a report of the discussion.

35 Compare *Jewish Chronicle*, August 13, 1937, pp. 24–5.

36 Compare Ben-Gurion's remark on Peel's frontiers: 'The Jewish state now being proposed to us is not the Zionist aim. But this will be a decisive step in bringing about the great Zionist aim. In the shortest possible time it will build up the real Jewish strength that will carry us to our historic objectives.' (Michael Bar-Zohar, *The Armed Prophet* (London, 1967), p. 61). Weizmann made a similar remark in reply to a criticism that the Negev should have been demanded for the proposed Jewish State, commenting that 'it would not run away.' (Nevill Barbour, *Nisi Dominus* (London, 1946), p. 185.)

37 Author's italics: Samuel Halperin: *The Political World of American Zionism* (Detroit, 1969), p. 119.

38 Compare Jon and David Kimche, *The Secret Roads* (London, 1954), pp. 15–9 and 28–38.

39 Compare Robert Briscoe with Alden Hatch, *For the Life of Me* (Boston, 1958), pp. 266–70.

40 i.e., to *any part* of the world.
41 Compare Chapter 46 of *From Haven to Conquest*, pp. 451–9, dealing with Rabbi Wise and the immigration of German Jewish children to the US.
42 Compare p. 24 above.
43 Churchill even expressed worry about possible interpretations of the self-determination clause of the Atlantic Charter on the ground that these might obstruct Zionist settlement in Palestine. (See Churchill's letter to Roosevelt of 9 August, 1942, in *The Second World War*, Vol. IV (London, 1948–54), p. 786.)
44 Compare Kermit Roosevelt, *The Partition of Palestine* in *The Middle East Journal*, II, No. 1, pp. 1–13.
45 Compare Ben-Gurion in the *Jewish Observer and Middle East Review*, January 31, 1964, pp. 14–6.
46 Compare p. 30 above.
47 Compare Morris L. Ernst, *So Far So Good* (New York, 1948), pp. 170–7.
48 Compare William A. Eddy, *F. D. R. Meets Ibn Saud*, (New York, 1954), pp. 33–7.
49 Compare Robert A. Divine, *American Immigration Policy, 1924–1952* (New Haven, 1957), pp. 112–28.
50 Compare p. 30 above.
51 Compare p. 38 above.
52 Compare, for example, Jon and David Kimche, *The Secret Roads*, Ch. 13.
53 Compare the British White Paper on violence in Palestine issued in July, 1946.
54 Compare the Anglo–American Committee of Enquiry *Report, 1946* (London, HMSO, 1946), pp. 39–42.
55 Compare Francis Williams, *A Prime Minister Remembers* (London, 1961), pp. 181–201.
56 Compare *The Forrestal Diaries* (New York, 1951), pp. 306, 309–10.
57 Present writer's italics.
58 The *'Jewish State' Idea in Zionism*, Zionist Federation of Great Britain & Ireland, 1943, p. 10.
59 The *'Jewish State' Idea in Zionism*, p. 11. Present writer's italics.
60 Compare President Nixon's statement, p. 16 above.
61 Except for the city of Jaffa.
62 The Zionists envisaged some special regime for the city of Jerusalem proper.
63 Compare pp. 43 ff above.
64 *New York Times*, Oct. 7, 1946.
65 Joseph Alsop, *Washington Post*, Dec. 10, 1947.

66 *The Area of Cultivable Land in Palestine*, Jewish Agency for Palestine (Jerusalem, 1936), p. 13.

67 The area under cultivation by the Jews in the whole of Palestine was estimated in 1944 at 716,750 dunums, or about 60 per cent only of their total landholdings. *Survey of Palestine*, Government of Palestine (Jerusalem, 1946) Vol. I, p. 379).

68 Present writer's italics.

69 Present writer's italics.

70 Compare A. Eban, *Tragedy and Triumph*, in *Chaim Weizmann: A Biography by Several Hands*, ed. Weisgal and Carmichael (London, 1962), pp. 301–3.

71 Compare Muhammad Zafrulla Khan, *Palestine in the U.N.O.* (Karachi, 1948), pp. 6–23.

72 Compare Kermit Roosevelt, *The Partition of Palestine*, in *The Middle East Journal*, II, No. 1, pp. 13–6.

73 Compare Millis, *The Forrestal Diaries*, pp. 346–9 and 362–5.

74 Present writer's italics.

75 Yugoslavia, although communist, had shown an independent attitude from that of the USSR. As a member of UNSCOP, Yugoslavia, together with India and Iran, had recommended federation as a solution.

76 W. Z. Laqueur, *The Soviet Union and the Middle East* (New York, 1959), p. 147.

77 Compare Arnold Krammer's article in *The Wiener Library Bulletin*, No. 3, N. S. 12, pp. 19–23.

78 Compare Appendices VIII & IX-A of *From Haven to Conquest*, pp. 858–66.

79 Compare p. 60 above.

80 Compare p. 53 above.

81 Compare p. 59 above.

82 Compare the *Report* of Sir John Hope Simpson, 1930, pp. 52–6.

83 Compare Appendix IX-A of *From Haven to Conquest*, p. 862.

84 Excluding the so-called 'dissident' groups and various British sponsored Jewish police forces other than the JSP.

85 For a Zionist version of this plan see Lorch, *The Edge of the Sword* (New York, 1961), pp. 87–9.

86 Jerusalem and its environs were to become a UN supervised *corpus separatum* according to the UN partition plan.

87 Compare Appendix IX-B of *From Haven to Conquest*, p. 867.

88 Compare Eban's contribution to *Chaim Weizmann*, ed. Weisgal and Carmichael, pp. 303–8.

89 Present writer's italics.

90 Compare Jacques de Reynier, *Deir Yasin*, in *From Haven to*

Conquest, pp. 761–6. The massacre was part of Operation Nach-shon, carried out within the framework of Plan Dalet.

91 Compare Harry Levin, *Jerusalem Embattled* (London, 1960), pp. 64–7. This attack was also part of Operation Nachshon.

92 Compare Jon Kimche, *Seven Fallen Pillars* (London, 1940), pp. 217–8 and 222–4. This attack was part of Operation Chametz, also carried out within the framework of Plan Dalet.

93 Compare Nixon's remarks, p. 16 above.

94 Compare Apendix IX-B to *From Haven to Conquest*, p. 867.

CHAPTER 2

Thinking the Unthinkable: A Sovereign Palestinian State*

I

Every time the Palestinian resistance is clobbered, or appears to be so, there is new hope in some quarters that the Palestinian component of the Arab–Israeli conflict will somehow disappear from the Middle Eastern scene. Such was the case after the showdown in Jordan in 1970–1 and the Syrian intervention in Lebanon in 1976; such is the case today after the Israeli invasion of Lebanon [in mid-March, 1978]. However, the hope will remain elusive because it is based on a fallacy. This is that the salience of the Palestinian component of the Arab–Israeli conflict is necessarily a function of the organizational strength or military prowess of the Palestinians.

II

The Arab states' system is first and foremost a 'pan' system. It postulates the existence of a single Arab nation behind the façade of a multiplicity of sovereign states. In pan-Arab ideology, this nation is actual, not potential. It is a present reality, not a distant goal. The manifest failure even to approximate unity does not negate the empirical reality of the Arab nation. It merely adds normative and prescriptive dimensions to the ideology of pan-Arabism. The Arab nation both *is*, and *should be*, one.

* Essay first published in *Foreign Affairs*, Vol. 56, No. 4, (July 1978) pp. 695–713.

From this perspective, the individual Arab states are deviant and transient entities: their frontiers illusory and permeable; their rulers interim caretakers or obstacles to be removed. Champions of pan-Arabism speak in the name of *vox populi*. Their mandate is from the entire Arab nation. Before such super-legitimacy, the legitimacy of the individual state shrinks into irrelevance. It is these credentials that pan-Arabists of various hues have presented and continue to present, be they a dynasty (the Hashemites), a party (the Arab Nationalist Movement, the Ba'ath, the Popular Front for the Liberation of Palestine), a charismatic leader (Nasser), or an aspirant to his mantle (Qaddafi).

The oneness of the Arab nation has corollaries in the concepts of the dignity of the nation, and the oneness and therefore the inviolability of its territory 'from the [Atlantic] Ocean to the [Arab/Persian] Gulf'. These concepts together constitute the central value system of the Arab states' system. To be sure, they are not uniformly manifested in the five great regions that make up the Arab world – the Fertile Crescent, the Gulf, the Peninsula, the Nile Valley and the Maghreb – nor in the countries of each region. But for historical, religious and cultural reasons they find powerful resonance among the vast majority of Arabs at every level of society throughout these regions. It is this resonance that gives them sanctity as dogmas. And it is this sanctity that gives them their key functional role within the parallelogram of '*raisons*' that make up the resultant stuff of the Arab political process. These are: *raison d'état, raison du status quo, raison de la révolution*, and *raison de la nation*.

Unlike the four natural seasons of the universe, the four '*raisons*' of the Arab political universe operate concurrently – not in two compartments in opposition to one another but diagonally and dialectically. *Raison d'état* no less than *raison de la révolution* can invoke *raison de la nation*, while even *raison du status quo* can invoke both these latter. Only explicit or transparent *raison d'état* is heresy. The other side of the coin is that 'pan-Arab' interventionism, whether offensive or defensive, does not operate only at the level of incumbent élites. It is geared also to counter-élites in the target states. Perpetually Janus-faced, incumbents (whether conservative or radical) look both across the border and at their counter-élites. These latter look across the same border for 'pan-Arab' help against their incumbents. Irrespective of the degree or kind of commitment to them, the concepts of pan-Arabism are functionally the most effective tools of change and legitimization in the hands of the Arab political élite.

III

The Palestine problem encapsulates the concepts of pan-Arabism. It is not difficult to see why. By definition the Palestinian people are an integral part of the Arab Nation. Therefore, by definition the injustice suffered by the Palestinian people was suffered by the Nation. Again, the loss of Palestine is the de-Arabization of Arab territory. It is thus a violation of the principles of the unity and integrity of Arab soil, an affront to the dignity of the Nation.

Until recently these premises have held unchallenged sway, setting Arab perceptions of Zionism and Israel into a seemingly unbreakable mould. Within this mould the Zionist colonization of Palestine appears as a latter-day Crusade. (The conquest of East Jerusalem in 1967 instantly reactivated memories of its fall and reconquest by Saladin.) Simultaneously, Zionist colonization is but an extension of nineteenth-century European encroachment on Asia and Africa. Building on the debris of Western World War I promises to the Arabs, it matured within the womb of imperial Britain. The UN partition resolution of 1947 was the outcome of superpower manipulation, a travesty of the principle of self-determination by a country's (Arab) majority.[1] Western support of Jewish immigration to Palestine was an exercise in charity at the expense of others. The Arabs and Muslims have had little difficulty in rejecting Jewish political title to Palestine on the basis of Divine Right. They have some difficulty in understanding the morality of punishing the Palestinians for the Holocaust.

To the Arabs the loss of Palestine was all the more poignant because it entailed the dismantling of Palestinian communal life and the pauperization of the bulk of its people. It was more threatening than the form of European colonialism experienced by most of them. This had been characterized by the imposition of an alien regime of control and administration. As in the case of French colonization of Algeria, Zionist colonization of Palestine involved the double process of the displacement of the resident population and its replacement through massive alien immigration. It was all the more antithetical to the principles of pan-Arabism because Israel occupied a pivotal part of the Arab world, separating its Asiatic from its African halves. It was all the more feared because of its territorial dynamism and the seemingly inexhaustible reservoir of Western and particularly American support it commanded. To many Arabs, especially the bulk of the younger generation, Israel is the beachhead of American imperialism in the Middle East and its executioner. With independence achieved by all Arab states and the process of decolonization almost completed in the Third World, the unique and anachronistic plight of Palestine became all the more intolerable in Arab eyes.

These were some of the basic Arab perceptions, however outrageous they may sound, of the Palestine problem. Their currency and hold were fundamentally unrelated to the popularity or credibility of the Palestine Liberation Organization (PLO), or indeed to its presence or absence. In the first two decades following Israel's creation (1948–65) there was no PLO, and Arafat was an unknown name. This did not prevent these Arab perceptions from conditioning the conduct of Arab states toward one another and toward Israel. Their dominance over Arab minds during this period and to a lesser extent since then (together with Israeli intransigence) has been the principal factor inhibiting the Arab states from realistically coming to grips with the Arab–Israeli conflict. This inhibition is a tribute to the functional role of the Palestine problem in inter-Arab politics. It is congruent with Arab altruism toward or alienation from the Palestinians or their leaders.

This is not to say that the PLO is irrelevant to a solution of the Palestine problem and therefore the Arab–Israeli conflict. It is precisely the potentially constructive role of the PLO that the West (particularly the United States) is blind to. (Conversely, perhaps because of the Soviet Union's communist character, Moscow shows greater insight into the PLO's transnational catalytic role.) Western strategy is addicted to the assumption of the autonomy of *raison d'état* in the Arab world. In a sense this is an extension of the European colonial incapacity to understand

Afro–Asian nationalism (Churchill, for example, never understood how Gandhi could possess power). To attribute autonomy
to *raison d'état* in the Arab world is to transfer Western concepts
prematurely to it. It is to misconstrue the nature of the phase
through which the Arab states' system is passing. Hence
American (and Israeli) reliance on the 'dominoes in reverse'
sequence: with Sadat hooked, Jordan's Hussein will follow, then
Saudi Arabia's Fahd, then Syria's Assad. Meanwhile, the
Palestinian dust will have been swept or reswept away under
some carpet or other.

To the Arabs, the Arab–Israeli conflict derives from the non-
resolution of the Palestine problem. The cause (the Palestine
problem) has to be seen to have been adequately addressed
before the effect (the Arab–Israeli conflict) can be resolved. Only
the representatives of the Palestinians have it in their power to
transmit the relevant signal to pan-Arab sentiment. This cannot
be done by quislings or Uncle Toms, present or future. It is here
that the PLO, if willing (which it is), can play a crucial role. With
pan-Arab sentiment apprised of the attitude of the PLO, the
Arab incumbents, their political pudenda appropriately covered,
could endorse the settlement. And with that endorsement such a
settlement would have an excellent chance of survival.

A PLO-endorsed Arab–Israeli settlement could have a decisive
effect on the dynamics of the Arab political process and the
future orientation of the entire Arab states' system. Paradoxically
it could lead to the consolidation of *raison d'état*. Such a result
would require an alternative model to the existing one. Its central
premiss could be the concept of the Arab nation in the state of
becoming rather than that of being. From this perspective, Arab
unity is a potential, the multiplicity of Arab states actual. Thus
unity becomes a programmatic goal, not a metaphysical imperative. It would be approached via the existing sovereignties. Its
modality would be interstate cooperation and gradual, cumulative, consensual evolution.

Several developments have tended to make possible such an
orientation. Chief among these are: (1) the collapse of the
United Arab Republic in 1961 and the falling out not only
between the Baath Party and Nasser but also among the various
factions of the Baath itself; (2) the redistribution of power in the
wake of the independence of the North African littoral and the

oil affluence of the smaller or less-developed Arab countries, offsetting the advantages of territorial size, cultural pre-eminence, geo-political position, historical role, and enterpreneurial and other human resources of the more established states; (3) the death of Nasser; (4) the emergence of a technocratic, development-orientated élite; and (5) the possibilities inherent in inter-state cooperation exemplified by the Arab performance in the October 1973 War.

These developments have had a profound, if indirect, influence in generating a mood of greater pragmatism vis-à-vis regional and global relations, including the Arab–Israeli conflict. More directly influencing a pragmatic approach to the Arab–Israeli conflict have been several other developments: (1) the crushing defeat of the 1967 war; (2) the growing awareness of the extent of the US commitment to the security and independence of Israel; (3) a parallel awareness of the limits of Soviet support against Israel; (4) the new self-confidence deriving from oil wealth and the Arab military performance in the 1973 war; (5) the growing Palestinian awareness of what the revolutionary armed struggle can and cannot achieve.

Whether the new model of the Arab states' system will have a chance to prevail over the existing flamboyant and apocalyptic one hinges primarily on whether an honourable overall settlement of the Palestine problem and therefore the Arab–Israeli conflict is possible.

IV

What solution of the Palestine problem would constitute a viable component of such an honourable overall settlement? What follows is not a blue-print but rather an inventory, followed by some reflections. It represents the personal viewpoint of the writer.

The Juridical Status of the Palestine State

The cornerstone is the concept of Palestinian sovereignty. Not half-sovereignty, or quasi-sovereignty or ersatz sovereignty. But a sovereign, independent Palestinian state. Only such a state would win the endorsement of the PLO. Only such a state is likely to

Israeli-occupied Arab territories prior to the Camp David peace
agreement.

effect a psychological breakthrough with the Palestinians under occupation and in the Diaspora. It would lead them out of the political limbo in which they have lingered since 1948. It would end their anonymous ghost-like existence as a non-people. It would terminate their dependence on the mercy, charity or tolerance of other parties, whether Arab, Israeli or international. It would be a point of reference, a national anchorage, a centre of hope and achievement.

Of all peoples, the Jewish people are historically qualified to understand this. Only such a state, through PLO endorsement, would win the support of Arab opinion and the majority of Arab states. These results could not ensue from a Bantustan 'federal' formula under a Hashemite dressing, or the perpetuation of Palestinian minority status under international guardianship. They are less likely to result from an Israeli mosaic of Indian reserves and hen-runs, crisscrossed by mechanized patrols and police dogs and under surveillance by searchlights, watchtowers and armed archaeologists. But there is no reason why the concept of Palestinian sovereignty should not accommodate provisions designed to allay legitimate fears of neighbours on a reasonable and preferably reciprocal basis.

The Frontiers of the Palestinian State

The frontiers of 1967 with minor and reciprocal adjustments are the most realistic under the circumstances. They would include East Jerusalem, the West Bank and the Gaza Strip. Contact between the West Bank and the Gaza Strip could be maintained through guaranteed freedom of access along a specified route or routes. This need not necessarily entail the extra-territorial status of the routes.

Such a solution embodying Palestinian sovereignty is a reversion to the old concept of partition. The difference is that no former partition proposal (Peel in 1937, Woodhead in 1938, and the UN Special Commission and UN General Assembly in 1947) gave the Jewish state anywhere near as much territory as a settlement along the 1967 frontiers would. Given the historical context of the evolution of the Palestine problem, a partition solution (particularly along the 1967 frontiers) does no violence to Zionism. Within the lifetime of most readers the following

words were addressed by Lord Peel to the Palestine Arabs in
1937 in the recapitulation of his report recommending partition:
'Considering what the possibility of finding a refuge in Palestine
means to many thousands of suffering Jews, is the *loss* occasioned
by partition, *great* as it would be, more than Arab *generosity* can
bear?'[2] It should be borne in mind that on the eve of the UN
General Assembly's partition resolution ten years later and six
months before the declaration of the state of Israel, Jewish land
ownership in Palestine did not exceed 6.5 per cent of the total
territory of the country.[3]

The fact that partition is an old formula is no argument against
its validity today. After all, the idea of a Jewish return to
Palestine is of considerable vintage. Nor is it a valid argument
against partition that Palestinian and Arab leaders rejected it at
the time. Given the context and circumstances, it was inevitable
that they should do so. This was known beforehand to all
proponents of partition including its chief beneficiary, the
Zionists. A different generation of Palestinian and Arab leaders
in different circumstances today are prepared to say that they
accept it with all the implications of such acceptance for
Israeli–Palestinian and Israeli–Arab reciprocal recognition and
coexistence.

It if is wondered why it was that throughout the period 1948–67
no one talked of a Palestinian state on the West Bank and the
Gaza Strip, the answer is simple: Palestinian and Arab opinion
was not prepared for it. It aspired to the recovery of the whole of
Palestine or the establishment of a democratic secular state in it.
Acceptance of partition or a state on the West Bank and in the
Gaza Strip was treason. In some Palestinian and Arab quarters, it
still is. Therefore, if partition is accepted today over a much
smaller area of the country than under any previous partition
formula, this is a measure of the evolution in the last decade or
so of Palestinian and Arab pragmatism. It is the development
that has long been awaited by outside observers and Israelis. It
would be tragic if it were not recognized when it occurred. It
would be more tragic if it were recognized and ignored.

The Foreign Relations of the Palestinian State

Given the security concerns of its neighbours and the balance of
power between it and them, it would make sense for the
Palestinian state to declare its non-aligned status vis-à-vis the

superpowers and other powers particularly in the defence and military fields. Some variant of the Austrian model could be applicable in this connection. This could involve agreement between the superpowers, their allies and clients to recognize this non-aligned status. Those Arab states party to the settlement as well as other powers could subscribe to this agreement. The arrangement could be guaranteed by the UN Security Council and the Arab League.

This does not mean that the state need be demilitarized. Nor would it preclude its membership in the United Nations, the Arab League and other international organizations. Nor would it prevent it, again like Austria, from having a foreign policy.

The closest relations of the Palestinian state would naturally be with Arab League members. These relations could cover the political, economic, commercial, cultural and social fields. But its most intimate relations are likely to be with Jordan. Consanguinity, historical ties and common economic interests would all demand this. Jordan would be the nearest Arab neighbour, the gateway to the Arab world and the sea. Naturally, relations with Jordan would have to be on an interstate basis of equality. But this does not preclude a consensual evolution of relations toward greater intimacy.

The Armed Forces of the State

A state bristling with the most sophisticated lethal weapons systems is unrealistic. A demilitarized state would be self-defeating. Without national armed forces the political leadership of the state would become the laughing stock of the Arab world. Their eunuch-like image would be enhanced by the formidable Israeli arsenal next door. So would their own sense of insecurity. This would increase their vulnerability to criticism by opponents of the settlement at home and abroad. For several years large segments of the population would continue to live in 'refugee' camps, posing security problems to the authorities. There would be a need to curb adventurism across the border into Israel. There would be a need to stand in the way of armed excursions by extremist Israeli groups of would-be settlers. The Palestinian state would be likely to become a great centre of tourism and pilgrimage for Diaspora Palestinians, Arabs and Muslims, as well as for Jews and Christians. This could involve the influx of hundreds of thousands annually. Reliance for all this on borrowed security made available by UN forces would be impracticable. It would be unstable politically and psychologically. But this does not preclude the use of such forces in a supplementary role or for specific purposes. They could be stationed, for example, along the borders as well as at airports, harbours, and the points of exit from and entrance to the West Bank–Gaza Strip highway.

Heinous as this may sound, an attempt will be made to visualize hypothetical levels of strength for the national armed forces of the Palestinian state. Table 1 is merely an illustration of how the situation in two scenarios might look on the ground. The Palestinian forces are, for argument's sake, computed on two alternative bases, one-half and one-third of Jordanian strength. They are deployed on a one to two scale in the Gaza Strip and the West Bank respectively. The result is compared system by system to Israeli and Jordanian strengths. Only certain systems have been chosen for purposes of comparison.

TABLE I

	Israel	Jordan	½ Jordan		⅓ Jordan	
			West Bank	Gaza Strip	West Bank	Gaza Strip
Combat Aircraft	574	78	26	13	18	8
Transport Aircraft	117	11	3	2	2	1
Trainer Aircraft	144	29	10	5	7	3
Helicopters	186	18	6	3	4	2
Tanks	3065	520	174	86	115	57
Armoured Fighting Vehicles (AFV)	3600	140	47	23	30	15
Armoured Personnel Carriers (APC)	4000	720	240	120	160	80
Self-propelled Howitzers	560	55	18	9	12	6
Guns/Howitzers	450	126	42	21	28	14

Source: *Military Balance, 1977–78*, London: International Institute for Strategic Studies, 1977.

These totals are merely illustrative. They do not preclude desirable qualitative mixes within each system. The other additional systems available to both Jordan and Israel or only to the latter are listed.[4] Possible comparisons of doctrine, command, training, administration, communications, technical maintenance, industrial infrastructure, etc. are, for brevity's sake, not touched upon.

East Jerusalem

Without East Jerusalem there would be no West Bank. It is the navel, the pivotal link between Nablus to the north and Hebron to the south. Together with its Arab suburbs it is the largest Arab urban concentration on the West Bank. It is the former capital of the *sanjak* (district) of Jerusalem under the Ottomans, as well as of Mandatory Palestine.[5] The highest proportion of the Palestinian professional élite under occupation resides in it. It is the site of the holiest Muslim shrines on Palestinian soil. Muslims first turned to it in prayer before they turned to Mecca. Toward it the Prophet Muhammed journeyed on his mystical nocturnal flight and from it he ascended to within 'two bow-lengths' of the Throne of God. It is the fountainhead and focus of Sufism – the deepest spiritual tradition of Islam. Within its precincts are buried countless generations of Muslim saints and scholars, warriors and leaders. It evokes the proudest Palestinian and Arab historical memories. It contains the oldest religious endowments of the Palestinians, their most prestigious secular institutions – the cumulative and priceless patrimony of a millennium and a quarter of residence. Architecturally it is distinctively Arab. In ownership and property, it is overwhelmingly so. It is the natural capital of Arab Palestine.

To make it so would involve the partition of the city along the 1967 lines. But not necessarily a return to the *status quo ante bellum* in all its details. The Israeli argument for a unified city must not obfuscate the military conquest of East Jerusalem. The argument contains two themes. The first is an implicit justification for Israeli annexation. The second endows this annexation with an ecumenical purpose. Neither is sacrosanct. Continued Israeli occupation precludes an overall settlement. This in itself frustrates any ecumenical purpose. Such a purpose is best served if a Jerusalem settlement symbolizes and consecrates the principles most worthy of association with the uniqueness of the Golden City. These are the principles of non-exclusivity, co-equality, non-dominance, co-sharing, non-coercion, palpable justice, the absence of a victor–vanquished equation, the non-dictation of spiritual hierarchies.

There is no monopoly in history or common sense for any one of the three great monotheistic faiths over the fate or future of Jerusalem. But if only because of the chronological sequence of its occurrence, it is Islam alone of the three faiths that encompasses in its reverent ken the other two. Abraham and Moses, David and Sarah, Jesus and Mary occupy the same pedestal alongside Muhammed in Muslim adoration. A partition solution does not mean the erection of a wall. The frontiers could remain open between the capital of Israel in West Jerusalem and the capital of Arab Palestine in East Jerusalem. Provisions could be agreed to at the interstate level for freedom of movement and residence between the two capitals. Regulation of entrance and exit between the capitals and the two states could also be included. A joint interstate great municipal council could operate and supervise certain essential common services, while residual services would fall under the separate municipalities of each sovereign state. Another grand inter-faith council of senior representatives of Christianity, Judaism and Islam under a UN or rotating chairmanship could oversee the special interests, holy places and institutions of each religion and act as an arbitration and conciliation body for disputes or claims arising with regard to them. An irreversible right of access to the Wailing Wall would be an integral part of the settlement, while a special regime for the Jewish-owned properties adjacent to the Wailing Wall could be created.[6] These arrangements could be overseen by the grand inter-faith council or by a special interstate Israeli–Palestinian body, under the guarantees of the UN Security Council, the Arab League and the Islamic states. It would be supremely fitting if both capitals could be demilitarized in part or wholly except for essential internal security forces.

Only some such solution for Jerusalem is likely to capture the imagination of the world and stamp out for all time the ugly embers of holy wars. Only by some such solution would Jews,

Christians and Muslims translate their veneration of Jerusalem from rhetoric to the idiom of accommodation and love.

The Internal Politics of the Palestinian State

If the PLO is to endorse the settlement, it has to participate in the government of the Palestinian state. The likelihood is that the centrist Fatah, the backbone of the PLO, will be the backbone of any Palestinian government. Those Palestinian elements that do not subscribe to the settlement will of themselves decline to participate in such a government. A Palestinian government built around Fatah will almost certainly be a national coalition. And the Palestinians who have lived under occupation since 1967 will in the nature of things play a major role in any coalition. Given their experiences, they will strengthen the centrist tendencies in Fatah. So will the monumental task of state- and nation-building facing the new government. This will demand the extensive support of the entrepreneurial and professional Palestinian élite in the Diaspora. These centrist tendencies will be further strengthened by economic dependence on international and foreign sources as well as on oil-rich Arab countries. The need for close cooperation with Jordan will promote the same result. There is little reason to believe that Fatah and its coalition partners will want to squander overnight the fruits of decades of terrible struggle and sacrifice by the Palestinians. Considerations of pride will impel them to demonstrate how Palestinian genius can build, those of prudence to avoid playing into the hands of others, those of self-interest to survive and prosper.

One of the first tasks of the new Palestinian government will be to draw up the constitution of the new state, to replace the National Charter.

The Refugees

As many refugees as possible need to be settled in East Jerusalem, on the West Bank and in the Gaza Strip. Cooperation with Jordan is essential for the fullest exploitation of the Jordan Valley.

UN General Assembly Resolution 194 III of 1948, providing the refugees with the choice between compensation and return,

will have to be implemented.[7] It is impossible to know how many
will choose to return to pre-1967 Israel. While Israel may not be
expected to welcome inundation by all those who will want to
return, its acceptance of a mere handful will offer no solution.
Many Diaspora Palestinians in the Arab countries have become
middle class. Most of those in the Gulf countries and the
Peninsula have not been granted and are unlikely to be granted
the nationalities of the host countries. Their acquisition of a
Palestinian nationality, in addition to its psychological impact on
them, will regulate their status in their countries of residence and
make it easier for them to return or commute to the Palestinian
state. The balance of the Diaspora refugees who cannot return to
pre-1967 Israel (because of Israeli objections) or to the
Palestinian state (because of lack of absorptive capacity) will still
have the options of compensation and Palestinian citizenship.

The Israeli Settlements on the West Bank and in the Gaza Strip

Given the need for every inch of territory in East Jerusalem, on
the West Bank and in the Gaza Strip to solve the Palestinian
refugee problem, it would not make sense to maintain the Israeli
settlements established in these territories after 1967.[8] Their
presence would become a ready target for criticism and agitation
by refugees (and their supporters) who had been barred by Israel
in the past from return under Resolution 194 III, or who were
unable to settle in the Palestinian state because of lack of space.
The protection of these settlements and their inhabitants *en route*
to or from them would develop into a major security risk. The
circumstances in which these settlements were established would
be a constant reminder of the hated occupation. The rights and
claims of villagers trespassed upon during their establishment
would continue to plague the Palestinian authorities. Far from
contributing to or symbolizing Israeli–Palestinian harmony or
coexistence, the settlements are likely to exacerbate inter-racial
relations. Palestinians would not stop wondering why, after
having acquired 77 per cent of Palestine, Israelis should want to
settle in yet more Palestinian territory. The continued presence
of the settlements would undermine the authority of the
Palestinian government and the stability of the overall settlement. There would be challenge enough for Palestinians and

Israelis to try out the experiment in 'hostile symbiosis' in Jerusalem. It would be folly to overload the system.

V

Theological arguments have been adduced against the establishment of a Palestinian sovereign state in East Jerusalem, on the West Bank and in the Gaza Strip. The serious arguments are three and will be addressed below:

1 The Absorptive Capacity of the State

The thrust of this argument is that a Palestinian state within virtually the 1967 frontiers (and *a fortiori* within smaller ones) would be too small and too poor in resources to absorb the bulk of the refugees. The refugee problem and therefore the Palestine problem would persist even after the establishment of the Palestinian state. It follows that the establishment of such a state would not be a definitive solution of the Palestine problem.

A few comments are in order.

It is true, of course, that a Palestinian state within (at best) the 1967 frontiers would not itself be able to absorb all the Palestinian refugees. That is why the closer the frontiers are to those of 1967, the greater will be the capacity of the Palestinian state to do so. Israel could also help by meeting its obligations under Resolution 194 III and by withdrawing its settlers from the West Bank and the Gaza Strip.

A Palestinian state along the lines described above is likely to win PLO endorsement. The responsibility for tackling the question of the balance of refugees after the absorption of others by Israel and the Palestinian state will fall upon the shoulders of the PLO and the Arab states party to the overall settlement.

The psychological effect on the refugees of the mere establishment of a Palestinian state should not be ignored. They have been alluded to earlier; no one can predict what advantage the refugees might take of the opportunity to choose compensation and citizenship in the event of the establishment of a Palestinian state. The miraculous impact of Israel on the Jews in the Diaspora may be relevant in this connection.

Without a state there is no hope of PLO endorsement of an overall settlement. Without such endorsement it is difficult to see who would have the will or the power to tackle the refugee problem.

Even if an overall settlement that does not involve a state were feasible (which it is not), it would have no obvious advantages over a state formula with regard to the refugees.

2   The Economic Non-Viability of the State

The short answer to this argument is that the Palestinian state would be joining a populous club whose membership list includes its neighbour to the West. But there could be worse prospects facing fledgling states. The Arab oil countries do not suffer from a dearth of capital. They would have a vested interest in the stability of the state. So presumably would some affluent industrial countries. The United Nations and other international organizations would be deeply involved in technical aid and assistance programmes for the foreseeable future.

A *sine qua non* for economic progress would be some form of common market arrangement with Jordan. But the greatest asset of the state will be high-level Palestinian manpower. Relatively speaking this exceeds that of all Arab states (with the possible exception of Lebanon) and of most Third World countries.[9] It will be attracted by the novel challenge of building a country for its own kith and kin. Specialized new light industries as well as off-season agriculture could depend on this human resource as well as on imported capital, including that of the Palestinian Diaspora.[10] Palestinian entrepreneurs, sick of the humiliations of exile in Arab and other countries, are likely to transfer their main or regional offices to the state. A restored East Jerusalem could become a cultural and artistic showpiece of the Arab and Muslim worlds. Arab heads of state would vie with one another to endow and embellish its monuments and institutions as their ancestors had done in medieval times. Individual Palestinian cities could be 'paired' with prosperous Arab municipalities. East Jerusalem could become the site of ecumenical, Third World and Islamic conferences. The pilgrimage industry would boom. Expenditure on the armed forces would be modest. The climate of the hills of Jerusalem and those of Nablus and Hebron is ideal for the development of a large-scale summer tourist industry for the Arab world. Jericho and the Dead Sea are equally ideal for a winter tourist industry. Remittances from the Palestinian Diaspora would be sent with greater incentive and confidence. The country could even become a retirement haven for Palestinians aspiring to die within earshot of the muezzins of the Aqsa Mosque or the bells of the Holy Sepulchre.

3   The Dangers of a Radical State Militarily Threatening to Israel

The thrust of this argument is that the government of the state would be taken over by radical groups. These would be bent upon the prosecution of revolutionary armed struggle, not only against Israel but also against Jordan. They would offer the Soviets or Soviet clients military bases that would put the slender urban waist of Israel under the constant threat of annihilation.

The likelihood that any radical group would seize, much less maintain, power is negligible for reasons already given. More-over, any Palestinian regime would be subject to several constraints:

First, there would be *the global context of settlement*. An overall settlement to which the Soviet Union is not a party is a non-starter. A settlement involving the application of some variant of the Austrian model demands the specific agreement of the superpowers, their allies, and their clients to respect the non-aligned status of the Palestinian state. The Soviets might well welcome such an arrangement if acceptable to other parties, including the PLO. It would give them a responsible, integral role in the settlement. It would be welcomed by their Palestinian and Arab allies. It would save them from a potentially embarrassing military commitment in a highly vulnerable place (the West Bank) where the balance of local power is crushingly in favour of Israel. Within such a framework, under UN Security Council and Arab League guarantees, the possibility of entangle-ment by the Palestinian state in dangerous military alignments would be precluded.

Next, there would be *the regional context of the settlement*. An overall settlement would have to remove the causes of a specifically Egyptian and Syrian irredentism. It would have to involve full withdrawal to the 1967 frontiers on the Golan and in

Sinai. This need not entail the stationing of Egyptian or Syrian troops on the frontiers. With pan-Arab irredentism defused by a PLO endorsement of the Palestinian state, and Egyptian and Syrian irredentism defused by return to the 1967 frontiers, the stage will have been set for the generation of an Arab consensus in favour of an overall settlement. Within such a framework, a collective Arab guarantee of the settlement could be made and the modalities elaborated for economic assistance to the Palestinian state. Given its non-aligned status, it is difficult to see what expectation would prompt a Palestinian regime to withdraw from such an arrangement.

Third, let us look again at *the military balance between Israel and a Palestinian state.* As we have already seen, even if for argument's sake a Palestinian state acquired armed forces one-half or one-third those of Jordan, the balance of power between it and Israel would be crushingly in favour of the latter. The deterrence Israel would command would be eminently credible. It would be all the more enhanced by a sober assessment of the military implications of the new state's geography. Note specifically the following:

(a) *Discontinuity.* The Gaza Strip and the West Bank are separated from one another by Israeli territory from twenty to thirty-five miles wide. Even with East Jerusalem restored to the Palestinian state, West Jerusalem dominates the main road linking Nablus to the north and Hebron to the south.

(b) *Encirclement.* Both the Gaza Strip and the West Bank are almost completely surrounded by Israel, the former on the north and east, the latter on the north, west, south and southeast.

(c) *Accessibility of Palestinian territory.* If Tel Aviv is fifteen miles from the West Bank, the West Bank is the same distance from Tel Aviv. Accessibility is not only a function of distance. It is a function of terrain, vegetation, communication routes and transport capacities, but above all it is a function of the balance of power. Visual accessibility with the naked eye is a bonus.

The Gaza Strip is five to ten miles wide, thirty miles long. Every square yard is penetrable from the Israeli side by foot within an hour, by vehicle within minutes. It has no warning time against aircraft. It is totally accessible to the naked eye from land and sea.

The West Bank is some eighty-five miles long. Its greatest width is under forty miles, its narrowest at Jerusalem is under twenty miles. No point on the West Bank falls outside a twenty-five-mile radius from the nearest point along the Israeli frontier, and most of it falls within a twenty-mile radius of the frontier. No impenetrable vegetation or inaccessible terrain prevents arrival from the Israeli frontier anywhere on the West Bank, by foot within six hours, by vehicle within one. Warning time against aircraft is to all intents and purposes nil. No dense forests cover any part of it.

(d) *Links to the outside world.* The Gaza Strip has no direct land link to the outside world. If the Israelis dismantled their settlements in the Arish area on the southern frontier of the Gaza Strip, they could be replaced by a UN buffer zone. The single airport in the Strip is a stone's throw from Israel. The only harbour is small and makeshift. The figures for the Palestinian forces that might be deployed in the Strip under the formulae discussed above and their relation to the Israeli forces speak for themselves. The Israeli Navy is also available to monitor the Gaza coastline.[11]

The West bank has no direct access to the sea. It has one airport north of Jerusalem with limited capacity. It is within medium mortar range from the Israeli frontier. It is accessible to the naked eye to aircraft flying within Israeli airspace. The West Bank's land link to the Arab world is through Jordan. Vehicular travel to and from Jordan is along two main routes with two crossing points on the Jordan River. The routes leading to the crossing points from the Jordanian side pass through gorges and open country. As they come out of the open country on the Palestinian side, they start their climb up the mountains of Nablus and Jerusalem. Given Israeli air superiority, the terrain on both sides of the Jordan River is an ideal burial ground for armour.

As a party to the settlement, Jordan would be anxious to monitor the armed forces of the Palestinian state. Its position astride the land routes of access to the state as well as the state's only contact with the sea through Arab territory (Jordanian Aqaba) enables it to exercise effective control on vehicular traffic to the state. This could be reinforced by UN inspection and verification personnel at the two crossing points on the Jordan River, as indeed at the Jerusalem airport. The orifices of the state would thus be sealed.

The West Bank has the configuration of a bulge abutting on Israel, with its base on the Jordan River. The length of this base from north to south is forty-five miles. A road runs along the base parallel to the river from the Israeli frontier near Lake Tiberias. An army crossing the Syrian desert in the direction of the Jordanian routes of access to the Palestinian state would have to cover hundreds of miles before reaching the eastern frontiers of Jordan, themselves hundreds of miles from the Jordan River. An armoured Israeli column travelling southward from the direction of Lake Tiberias could in less than two hours sever all contact between the Palestinian state and the Arab hinterland. Israel could also draw on its five paratroop brigades and 186 helicopters (not to mention its 574 combat aircraft) to take possession in time of the two crossing points on the Jordan River.

In *conclusion*, therefore, any PLO leadership would take the helm in a Palestinian state with few illusions about the efficacy of revolutionary armed struggle in any direct confrontation with Israel. They would be acutely aware of its costs. They would have little incentive on national or corporate grounds to incur it.

To one observer, the real security question posed by the Palestinian state is: For how long would the Israeli brigadier generals be able to keep their hands off such a delectable sitting duck?

Notes

1   On December 31, 1946, less than a year before the UN partition resolution, the total population of Palestine was estimated at 1,972,559, of whom 1,364,332 were Arabs and 608,225 Jews. (UN Doc. A/AC 14/32, November 11, 1947, paras. 56 ff.).

2   *Palestine Royal Commission: Summary of Report*, Official Communiqué No. 9/37, June 1937, p. 31. The emphasis is the writer's.

3   At the time of the UN partition resolution in November 1947, Palestine was administratively divided into 16 districts. Distribution

Thinking the Unthinkable

of population and land ownership in these districts between Arabs and Jews is shown in the maps accompanying UN Doc. A/AC 14/32, November 11, 1947. These maps indicate (a) that the Arabs were in the majority in 15 of the 16 districts, and (b) owned the bulk of private land in all 16 districts. The UN partition resolution gave the Jews about 55 per cent of Palestine.

4　The additional systems both Israel and Jordan have are mortars, anti-tank guided weapons, missile guns, recoilless rifles, and Redeye surface-to-air missiles. Additional systems that Israel has are surface-to-surface missiles (Ze'ev/Wolf, Lance, Gabriel), rocket launchers, and Hawk surface-to-air missiles. Israeli defence expenditure for 1977–78 is $4.27 billion; Jordanian expenditure for 1977 was $200.6 million. *Military Balance, 1977–78,* London: International Institute for Strategic Studies, 1977, pp. 36–37.

5　The *sanjak* of Jerusalem covered some 60 per cent of what later became mandatory Palestine. From a line drawn east–west from the sea to the Jordan River some ten miles north of Jerusalem, it extended down to the borders of Sinai and the Gulf of Aqaba. The *sanjak* was directly attached to Istanbul instead of to any provincial capital. Palestinian deputies for Jerusalem and other cities in the *sanjak* sat in the Ottoman Parliament of which a Jerusalemite became Deputy Speaker. (Other Palestinians from the *sanjak* became senior diplomats, army officers, provincial governors, and civil servants in the Ottoman Empire.)

6　Jewish property within the municipal boundaries of pre-1967 East Jerusalem did not exceed five per cent of the area of the city. Most of the Jewish quarter inside the Old City was Arab-owned – the pre-1948 Jewish residents being largely tenants of Arab landlords. In Western Jerusalem whole quarters were Arab owned, e.g., Talbiyeh, Katamon, Musrara, Upper Baka, Lower Baka, El Turi, the 'Greek' Colony, the 'German' Colony.

7　The resolution has been repeatedly affirmed by the United Nations and supported by the United States. One of the last direct American references to it was made by Harold Saunders (then Deputy Assistant Secretary of State for Near Eastern and South Asian Affairs) on November 12, 1975. *Department of State Bulletin,* November 1975, No. 8.

8　See Ann Lesch, 'Israeli Settlements in the Occupied Territories,' *Journal for Palestine Studies,* Autumn 1977.

9　See Nabeel Shaath, 'Palestinian High Level Manpower,' *Journal for Palestine Studies,* Winter 1972.

10　A Palestinian refugee from Jaffa, Talal Abu Ghazaleh, who made good in the Diaspora, was recently reported to have donated $10 million to his alma mater, the American University of Beirut, in Lebanon. *New York Times*, May 2, 1978.

11   This includes one submarine (two under construction). 18 naval vessels with surface-to-surface missiles, 40 patrol boats, and 12 landing craft. *Military Balance, 1977–78, op. cit.*

CHAPTER 3

Regio-Politics: Towards a US Policy on the Palestine Problem*

I

Unlike the Carter Administration (with the Brookings Report), the new Administration has not come into office with any known general policy framework of its own for the settlement of the Palestine problem and the Arab–Israeli conflict. In addition to the priority accorded by President Reagan to the domestic economy, the fact that the Israeli elections were to be held on 30 June served to purchase additional time. None the less, the emerging indicators of what the new Administration's policy might be give cause for concern to some observers of the Middle East scene.

Secretary of State Alexander Haig's delaying tactics in going out to the Middle East rather than face the problem of which Middle East leaders – and in what sequence – to invite to an unprepared Washington were astute. His trip will have provided him with a privileged tourist's insights into the attitudes of key countries he was visiting for the first time as the principal guest. But the predominantly geo-political lens through which he views the Middle East (along with the rest of the world) can only heighten concern. Without as yet having scrutinized the contents of the Middle East box (including, *inter alia*, the Palestine problem and the Arab–Israeli conflict), Mr Haig proposes to wrap it in a 'strategic consensus' between the Israelis and the Arabs in the face of the USSR.

* Essay first published in *Foreign Affairs*, Vol. 59, No. 5, (July 1981), pp. 1050–1063.

A number of separate events during the spring indicated a discernible direction in Administration attitudes. On Mr Haig's trip, Egyptian President Anwar Sadat's agreement to the participation of an American contingent in the Sinai buffer zone meshed with Mr Haig's expectations about a 'strategic consensus', as Sadat would have intended. Then in Jerusalem Mr Haig appeared to swallow Israeli Prime Minister Menachem Begin's line concerning Israel's 'rescue mission' in Lebanon against the 'brutal' Syrians. (The Syrians were, after all, protégés of the Soviets, so it all seemed to fit.) At the same time, in Washington, National Security Adviser Richard V. Allen was conceding on network television that the Palestine Liberation Organization (PLO) could be described as a 'terrorist organization' and that the Israelis were justified in their 'hot pursuit' of Palestinians in Lebanon, even though the Israelis had long ago abandoned this strategy for what they prefer to call 'preemptive retaliation'. Meanwhile at the United Nations there was to be a self-imposed US silence on Israeli colonization of the Occupied Territories, now in high gear.

Presumably to offset all this, the Saudis were to get the hardware they had been asking for. Washington's expectations would seem to have been that the emplacement of the Airborne Warning and Control System aircraft (AWACs) and the American personnel to go with them would in time constitute a *de facto* incorporation of the Saudis into the 'strategic consensus'. Another expectation would seem to have been that in return for the hardware the Saudis would underwrite a Camp David formula for Palestinian autonomy with only cosmetic changes. If this exercise in divining is not too far off the mark, the Reagan Administration, while ostensibly waiting for the outcome of the Israeli elections, may already have on its hands a policy for Palestine and the Arab–Israeli conflict but, like the gentleman in the French play, without knowing it.

II

All this appears to indicate that the Palestinian issue has been shelved by the Reagan Administration. Therefore, it is necessary at this juncture to take a hard look at what is actually at stake in the non-resolution of the Palestine problem and the Arab–Israeli conflict.

US policy toward the Palestine problem and the Arab–Israeli conflict has been an amalgam of three main variables: the geo-political, the domestic and the regional. The geo-political variable involves concepts of the national interest and images of other powers, principally the USSR. The regional variable involves readings of the political map of the Arab world (or any other region in question). The domestic variable (in the form, for example, of inter-institutional competition, public opinion and electoral considerations) influences the two others. Policies whether geo-political (towards the USSR) or regional (towards the Arab world, or any region in question) reflect the mix between these three variables. If one variable, say, the domestic, is paramount, the resulting foreign policy could be irrelevant or worse. Likewise, what role is assigned to the geo-political and regional variables and the manner in which the two are integrated are primary considerations. Also, if the reading of the regional political map is faulty the resulting policy will be counter-productive in both regional and geo-political terms. The lower the importance attached (for whatever reason) to even a correct reading of the regional political map, the likelier the irrelevance – or worse – of the regional and *therefore* the geo-political policies.

It is the contention of this article that the mix of these three variables in the formulation of US policies towards the Palestine problem and the Arab–Israeli conflict has gone consistently awry since the late 1940s. Sometimes the domestic, at others the geo-political, and just as often the two together have been allowed to play paramount roles, at the expense of the regional variable. If the forebodings expressed in the preceding section are not unduly alarmist it looks as if we are in for more of the same.

A first remedial step is to upgrade the regional variable from the status of a poor cousin to that of a peer in relation to the other two. But this may not be all that is required. There may be regions of the world (and the Arab world could be one of them) where the regional variable, if only at certain moments, needs to be given particular attention. To compensate for the inferiority hitherto accorded this cardinal component of US policy, the regional aspect should be promoted to the rank of 'Regio-politics'. With a capital 'R', Regional expertise (on the Arab

world and elsewhere) might have a fairer chance of competing
with the godfather of foreign policy, Geo-politics. This is not a
plea for empathy. States are by definition in chronic short supply
of this commodity. It is a plea for policies towards the Arab
world (and other regions on this globe) that are more in touch
with the regional facts of life.

III

The Arab world is a baffling political universe. One explanation
is that it is literally an infant in terms of the age of older states'
systems. The West European states' system, it will be recalled,
has been evolving for more than a millennium. In spite of its
infancy the Arab world shares a common political resonance.
This is true in a sense of the whole world today. But what
distinguishes the Arab world from the global setting is the
intensity of its transnational resonance and of its impact, both
negative and positive, across the sovereign frontiers of individual
Arab states. To be sure, what echoes within this area of
resonance is often a protracted cacophony. Yet beneath the
confused signals there is a logic of sorts. This is the continuing
struggle between centripetal and centrifugal forces. The former
are grounded in the ideologies of pan-Arabism and pan-Islamism
and their non-doctrinaire versions, which take the form
of sentiments, cultural solidarity, interpersonal contacts and
enlightened self-interest. The latter stem from the more restrictive perspectives of individual states, ruling élites and leaders,
and ethnic, sectarian and tribal sub-national forces.

Within the Arab world six issues dynamically interact: (1) the
Palestine problem; (2) the Arab–Israeli conflict; (3) domestic
change and instability; (4) oil policies; (5) inter-Arab relations;
and (6) relations with the outside world.

It would be ludicrous to maintain that the non-resolution of the
Palestine problem and the resulting perpetuation of the
Arab–Israeli conflict are responsible for all developments (or
those adverse to the West) in all the other 'fields' listed above.
But it would be sloppy 'Regio–politics' to fail to assess their
significance. The issue is particularly alive today because a tacit
assumption of the non-centrality (whatever that may mean) of

the Palestine problem seems to be a major premiss of the new American Administration's policy toward the Arab world.

Given all the other tensions outside the immediate area of the Palestine problem and the Arab–Israeli conflict it would seem highly desirable to get these two out of the way – by working towards a solution. What makes the Middle East and its environs so explosive today is precisely this unprecedented coincidence between the non-resolution of the Palestine problem and the occurrence of so many other dilemmas in contiguous areas.

IV

A brief look at how the Palestine problem has in fact interacted in recent history with the other 'fields' provides a useful perspective.

The Palestine problem and the Arab–Israeli conflict.   That the Arab–Israeli conflict derives from the non-resolution of the Palestine problem should be self-evident. The Arab states' political and economic confrontation with Israel as well as all the Arab–Israeli wars since 1948 are essentially the result of this non-resolution. For reasons that will be given later, it would be rash to generalize from the example of Sadat.

The Palestine problem, domestic changes and instability.   Change and domestic instability in the Arab world preceded the emergence of the Palestine problem and will presumably be around after its resolution. But the rapidity and extent of change, and the intensity of the cultural backlash against it, are relatively recent phenomena in the Arab world. Since 1948 incumbent Arab regimes have been at the receiving end of monumental demands from internal opposition forces and regional rivals bent on delegitimizing them in the name of Palestine. In the new circumstances of rapid change and regional turbulence, the non-resolution of the Palestine problem could constitute the bushels of straw that could break the backs of some Arab regimes.

The Palestine problem and oil policies. Since the mid 1930s, when Palestinian guerrillas first attacked the Iraq Petroleum Company pipelines in Mandatory Palestine, the *threat* to interrupt oil

supplies, *armed attack* on oil installations, *disruption* in the flow
or transport of oil and the *imposition of embargoes* have been –
with the singular exception of the recent Iraqi–Iranian conflict –
exclusively connected in the Arab world with the non-resolution
of the Palestine problem and the perpetuation of the Arab–Israeli
conflict. Chapter and verse are easy to cite.

Possible future threats to Arab oil fall broadly into the
following categories: (1) direct assault by the USSR; (2) attacks
against installations, pipelines, shipping, etc., by Palestinian and
non-Palestinian extremist groups; (3) embargoes imposed by
radical Arab incumbents, already in place for reasons unconnected with the Palestine problem; (4) embargoes imposed by
radical/conservative Arab regimes during a future Arab–Israeli
war; (5) embargoes imposed by radical/conservative Arab regimes
in despair at the consolidation of the Israelis' hold on the
Occupied Territories and East Jerusalem or in the event of large-
scale Israeli operations in Lebanon; (6) embargoes imposed by
radical regimes after the overthrow of conservative ones;
(7) seizure of the oil installations by opposition forces in radical
or conservative regimes; (8) war between two oil-producing Arab
countries or between an oil-producing and a non-oil-producing
one; (9) war between an oil-producing Arab country and a non-
Arab country other than Israel; (10) blowing up of oil installations in anticipation of Israeli seizure; (11) bombing of oil
installations by Israel in a future Arab–Israeli war; (12) blowing
up of installations in anticipation of seizure by the US Rapid
Deployment Force to forestall some or all of the above.

A detailed analysis of this list would indicate that many if not
most of these threats could be generated directly or indirectly by
the non-resolution of the Palestine problem.

The Palestine problem and inter-Arab relations. Many centrifugal forces in the Arab world operate independently of any
ramifications of the Palestine problem. A list enumerating
'purely' inter-Arab conflicts would be a long one. But from the
US point of view these conflicts do not adversely involve the US
image or interests quite in the same way, if at all, as do inter-
Arab tensions related to the Arab–Israeli conflict.

Given the dynamics of the Arab area of resonance, the oil-rich
Arab countries do not constitute a cohesive sub-system in any
meaningful political sense within it. Both their affiliation with the

West and their conservative regimes make these states particularly vulnerable to the pressure of the Palestine problem both domestically and in their inter-Arab relations. This pressure has been a major cause of polarization among the Arab states as a whole. Its most destabilizing effect has been the outbidding tactics, both offensive and defensive, that the Arab states have used against each other in the name of Palestine.

The outbidding process has taken place not only between radical and conservative regimes but also between conservative regimes (e.g., Hashemite Iraq and Saudi Arabia in the 1950s) and between the radicals themselves. By and large the conservatives have been at the receiving end, but sometimes they have gone on the offensive against the radicals (e.g., Jordanian and Saudi Arabian castigation of Nasser for hiding behind the United Nations Emergency Force in 1966–7). In imposing the 1973 embargo the conservatives were demonstrating to Arab public opinion that they were second to none in their espousal of the cause of Palestine. The agony of Lebanon (reminiscent of Spain in the 1930s) is the most poignant example of the spillover effect of the non-resolution of the Palestine problem into inter-Arab relations.

A point can be made that, notwithstanding the foregoing, the Palestine problem has been the principal 'unifying' factor in inter-Arab politics and that its resolution would give momentum to centrifugal forces. At worst the fervent proponents of Arab fragmentation might perhaps be persuaded to endorse a Palestinian settlement if only with their own objective in mind. And yet it is a moot point whether a polarized Arab world is in anybody's interest – though Nasser once told this writer that in his view the USSR and the United States were equally opposed to Arab unification.

The Palestine problem, the Arabs, the United States and the USSR. The Palestine problem and Arab–Israeli conflict have had the following broad effects on Arab relations with the West and the USSR: (1) They have resulted in the deepening and perpetuation of Arab political alienation from the West – an alienation which admittedly had historico-cultural roots older than the Palestine problem and was also a product of the Arab experience of European colonialism in general. Western, and particularly American, sponsorship of Israel and a perceived unwillingness to solve the Palestine problem largely counter-balanced the positive effects of decolonization on Arab–Western relations. With West European colonial disengagement completed, the onus of the non-resolution of the Palestine problem was shifted increasingly to the United States. (2) At the same time, the attractiveness of Soviet military and diplomatic help has increased in proportion to American backing of Israel. In fact, the Palestine problem provided the main Soviet entrée into the Arab world, affording Moscow the opportunity to champion the most popular Arab cause at the expense of the West. (3) While the fundamentally nationalist ideology of even the most radical Arab regimes has set limits on Soviet influence, and while disillusionment with Soviet help has developed in many countries, the non-resolution of the Palestine problem has supplied the most powerful motivation (and rationalization) for continued reliance on the USSR. And while the Arab cultural backlash in its nationalist and religious manifestations has involved 'repudiation' of both East and West, the emotional and intellectual balance of Arab public and élite opinion remains in favour of the USSR. (4) Western military support of Israel has led to Soviet military support of the Arabs. The vicious circle this established has reinforced the Arab emotional and intellectual tilt in favour of the Soviets, especially with the younger generations.

Since the early 1950s the non-resolution of the Palestine problem has been the single most important factor frustrating Western attempts to co-opt the Arab countries into an overt Western military alliance against the USSR. Such is the moral of the collapse of both the Baghdad Pact (and with it the Hashemite dynasty of Iraq) and of the Eisenhower Doctrine. The 'strategic consensus' sought by Mr Haig would seem to be the contemporary version of these ill-fated attempts. Its chances of success are no brighter; its impact on its Arab adherents is likely to be no less catastrophic.

V

From the perspective of Washington the Arab world can be looked at in several ways: as intermediate space between the United States and the USSR;[1] as a universe inhabited by three-dimensional indigenous peoples whose political evolution and orientation are important in themselves as well as being relevant to the global balance of power including security and access to oil. A third perspective, not necessarily mid-way between the foregoing, is characterized by a reluctance (for whatever reason) to face the regional reality and a tendency to resort to 'alibi' solutions. Built into this third perspective is a propensity to veer towards the first perspective.

In framing policy, one must define the real challenges facing American statesmanship in the Arab world. They are: how to get on with the radical Arabs; and how not to undermine the conservative Arabs. An American policy whose components are, first, pursuit of a 'strategic consensus' and second, the simultaneous downgrading of the Palestine problem will prove highly counter-productive with regard to both challenges.

Quite simply, the general Arab mood since World War II has become less and less conducive to the incorporation of Arab countries into either superpower's military network. Sadat, like Iraq's Nuri Said in the 1950s, is a freak. Sadats do not grow on trees, not even in the lush valley of the Nile. In the Arab world (as elsewhere) nationalism is the bulwark vis-à-vis both Moscow (*in spite of* Soviet sponsorship of the cause of Palestine) and Washington (largely *because* of American sponsorship of Israel). In the post-Nasser era a potentially crucial but little-noticed development has been the increasing tendency of radical and conservative regimes to align themselves with each other across the ideological barrier (for example, Jordan and Syria in the mid to late 1970s, the ongoing relations between Iraq and Jordan and Saudi Arabia on the one hand, and Iraq and Syria on the other). Another equally significant development has been the tendency of both radicals and conservatives to put some distance between themselves and their respective superpower sponsor (Iraq and the USSR; the conservatives generally and the United States) and to edge toward the other superpower (Jordan and Kuwait and the USSR; Iraq and the United States).

This increasing political diversification reflects the political self-confidence that comes from the economic power of both the conservative and the radical (e.g., Iraq) oil-producing countries; disillusionment with both superpowers; and the burgeoning nationalism stemming from mass politicization, Islamic resurgence, and cultural backlash. This phenomenon of political diversification is in the long-term interest of regional stability. The main question facing Washington is how to harness it in that direction. With some imagination, this can be done.

The beginning of wisdom would be to downgrade the 'strategic consensus' concept from a hackneyed grand design aimed at establishing a substitute focus for the adversaries on either side of the Arab–Israeli cleavage, to the level of a unilateral signal by Washington to Moscow of American purposefulness in the Indian Ocean environment. Simultaneously, the moderate policies of the Arab conservatives on the Palestine problem and on oil policy, as well as their perceived affiliation with the United States, should be seen to bear demonstrable fruit. This could be in the shape of the supply of the requested US military hardware (AWACs, etc.) but primarily in meaningful progress on the Palestine problem. This would vindicate moderate policies, and enhance the influence of the conservatives with the radicals. To press on towards the grand design of a strategic consensus while downgrading the Palestine problem and shilly-shallying on the military hardware is the unfailing recipe for inter-Arab polarization and outbidding, the undermining of moderation, and the erosion of the prestige and the legitimacy of the conservatives – developments that preclude any progress in the resolution of the Palestine problem.

To be sure it could be argued that polarization could be turned against the radicals. The chances are that such polarization would boomerang against its Arab and Western architects. It could be further argued, as a variation on the theme of the marginality of the Palestine problem, that its solution would likewise have a marginal effect in terms, for example, of improving the chances of establishing the 'strategic consensus'. True enough, but then the thesis in this article has not been that a Palestinian solution would result in an Arab *démarche* at Foggy Bottom in favour of the Rapid Deployment Force.

VI

No one knows what an Arab world bereft of the Palestine problem would look like, but there are excellent reasons for trying to find out. For Israel a settlement of the Palestine problem will mean the end of war. For the Palestinians a sovereign Palestinian state on the West Bank, in the Gaza Strip, and in East Jerusalem in coexistence with Israel – the terms on which the PLO would settle – means a haven from their Diaspora and a repository for their vast potential for constructive achievement. The endorsement by Fatah, the mainstream PLO group, of a settlement along these lines will isolate and contain the Palestinian and Arab dissidents. Such a settlement would remove a primary source of instability throughout the Arab states' system. It could improve the prospects for functional inter-Arab regional cooperation. Agitation on behalf of Palestine would markedly decline. The interruption of oil supplies resulting from such agitation will lose its rationale, while that resulting from an Arab–Israeli war will be precluded. The continual Arab–American confrontation over Palestine in international forums will end. The incentive for Arab acquisition of nuclear weapons to match Israel's will become less cogent. Such Arab military dependence on outside powers as has been generated by the Arab–Israeli conflict will significantly diminish. Superpower collision in the Middle East will lose a hitherto ever-present catalyst.

VII

On the other hand, it is not difficult to see why Israel and Sadat's Egypt might not be altogether averse to alternative scenarios that could be envisaged in the event of non-resolution and the concurrent pursuit of the mirage of a 'strategic consensus.' They would hope to enhance their ostensible usefulness to Washington in an environment of confrontation with the Arab radicals, the PLO, and the USSR. This would divert attention from the obduracy of the one and the failures of the other in the wake of Camp David.

The rationale for American coyness about moving forward on a settlement could be reduced to three arguments: (1) the PLO and the radical Arabs are unwilling to contemplate a reasonable and honourable settlement; (2) the same is true for the USSR; (3) what might be described as the Cohabitation Argument – the removal of Egypt through Camp David from the Arab–Israeli military equation – makes it possible to live with the new status quo.

Israeli arguments against a sovereign Palestinian state on the West Bank, in the Gaza Strip, and in East Jerusalem in coexistence with Israel have been examined elsewhere by this writer.[2] But the PLO is excluded from peace negotiations on the grounds that it is a terrorist organization. This is hypocritical and unadult. Like every liberation movement in history the PLO has used terrorist tactics. Most of the PLO's terrorist tactics are, in fact, variations of those introduced into the Middle East in the 1930s and 1940s by the Irgun Zvai Leumi before the establishment of the state of Israel. Israel and the PLO are at war with one another and war is terror. Some leading civilized nations in the world have within living memory used 'terrorist' tactics on the most horrendous scale. Of all liberation movements in recent history the PLO has been among the most viable in genuineness of motivation, grassroots appeal, organizational structure, and international support and standing.

The PLO is likewise ruled out of court because of the provisions in its Covenant which deny the legitimacy of the state of Israel and call for the liberation of 'the whole of Palestine.'[3] One way of looking at the Covenant is to view it as a gratuitous tract of hate against an altogether innocent party. Another is to see it in relation to the evolution of the Palestine problem and the tribulations of Palestinian disinheritance and statelessness. Nevertheless, whatever its background the Covenant is maximalist, unrealistic and no basis for a settlement.

The Palestine National Council (PNC), the highest PLO authority, has met twelve times since the adoption of the present Covenant in 1968. If the resolutions adopted by successive PNCs are read in sequence, a movement away from maximalism and in the direction of accommodation is unmistakable. This movement is noticeable on four levels: (1) from explicit emphasis on the objective of the liberation of the 'whole' or the 'entire' soil of Palestine to the discarding of these adjectives; (2) from explicit reliance on 'armed struggle' as the only means for the achievement of liberation to increasing expressions of the need for political activity in addition to this 'armed struggle', and of readiness to attend international peace conferences as well as to meet with 'progressive' Jewish elements from both inside and outside Israel; (3) from repeated statements about the 'secular democratic state' over the whole of Palestine as the ultimate objective to an increasing de-emphasis of this objective; and (4) from repeated and vehement rejection of a 'political entity' or a 'ministate' in the post-1967 Occupied Territories to an implied though conditional acceptance of such a state. It remains to make explicit what is implied in this movement. That is the task of quiet diplomacy.

The Arab countries that are pivotal for a solution of the Palestine problem are the radicals: Syria and Iraq. Neither Jordan nor Saudi Arabia could sponsor a solution unacceptable to both or either of these two. Damascus and Baghdad are the ideological capitals of pan-Arabism, and in fact much of the tension between them is over its leadership.

The quintessence of Camp David is: *Egypt* first. Neither Syria's President, Hafez al-Assad, nor Iraq's President, Saddam Hussein – much less Saudi and Jordanian Kings Khalid and Hussein – could appear to be putting *their* respective countries ahead of Palestine. The greater leeway enjoyed by Sadat stems from the political culture of Egypt. This has three main strands: Egyptianism, Islam and Arabism, *in that order*. This writer belongs to a post-1948 generation which spent two decades of its adulthood wooing Nasser's Egypt into the Arab fold in order to balance Israel's overwhelming superiority over the eastern Arabs. Nasser elevated the Arab component of Egypt's policy partly as a result of his own self-image as the champion of pan-Arabism.

Sadat's worldview stood Nasserism on its head. The immediate circumstances of his accession to power were conducive to that end. With honour satisfied by the 1973 War, Sadat led his countrymen back towards their basic ethos: Egyptianism. The basic ethos of the Arabs east of Suez, however, is Arabism, with Islam close behind in the case of Saudi Arabia. That is why Camp David, with its present content and form, is unrepeatable on the other fronts.

If Syria, Iraq and the PLO have a veto among Arabs over a Palestinian settlement, the Saudi role is no less indispensable. The cornerstone of Saudi diplomacy in the post-Nasser era has been the effort to forge a moderate inter-Arab consensus on the Palestine problem, oil policies, regional disputes and international relations in general. Intrinsic to this Saudi diplomacy has been bridge-building with the radicals, Syria and Iraq, and Fatah. No other Arab capital is on speaking terms with as many Arab (and Muslim) capitals as Riyadh. This makes the Saudis the ideal interlocutor between the Arabs (and Muslims) and the West. The greater the prestige of Saudi Arabia in the Arab world, the greater the impact of its moderating influence.

The contours of a settlement on Palestine acceptable to the radicals emerge from the inner deliberations and the published communiqué of the Baghdad Summit of November 1978. Their gist is a sovereign Palestinian state in coexistence with an Israel contained within the 1967 frontiers and Israeli withdrawal to these boundaries in the Golan. This consensus is not dead but hibernating. What is implicit in it should be made explicit. This, too, is the task of quiet diplomacy. A tripartite US–Israeli–Egyptian strategy to polarize the Arab world is tantamount to sabotaging this burgeoning consensus – the *sine qua non* of an honourable and peaceful settlement of the Palestine problem.

The assumption that the USSR has no interest in a Palestine settlement may or may not be true. What is unquestionable is that the USSR will wreck a solution composed and orchestrated exclusively by the United States. The thrust of the top Soviet leadership's advice to the PLO has been along the lines the PLO will now accept. The mercurial nature of Arab regimes with regard to Moscow may have generally sunk into Soviet political consciousness and the Soviets may by now be aware that all Arab regimes are fundamentally nationalist. Further, the Soviets may not relish being dragged to the brink of confrontation with the United States by a runaway ad hoc Arab military coalition – a likely eventuality should no solution of the Palestine problem materialize. They may not relish the prospect of an Arab client being humiliated in a future Arab–Israeli war, nor view with equanimity the Arab trend toward the acquisition of nuclear weapons.

Given all these considerations, the attractions for the Soviet Union of a role as co-guarantor of a settlement as a peer with the United States may not be insignificant. Such a settlement might even fit into a broader global framework of trade-offs and linkages. And even if the Soviets were to wax oil-thirsty in the 1980s, an agreed quota (in the fullness of time) of Middle East oil within some such general context might be preferable to the risks of making a dash for the oil wells in the face of an over-alert United States. Nor should the face-saving function of Soviet endorsement of a moderate settlement be dismissed. This could be invaluable for both the PLO and the Arab radicals vis-à-vis Arab public opinion.

That the Camp David status quo is something the United States can live with is the most dangerous illusion. There is in fact no such status quo. Within the Camp David framework Israeli colonization policies in the Occupied Territories have been changing the situation on the ground so rapidly that before long the physical basis of a Palestinian settlement will have been removed for all time. No Arab regime (including Egypt) can be reconciled to the permanent loss of the Occupied Territories. Israeli retention of the West Bank, the Gaza Strip, and East Jerusalem *as well as* the Golan maximizes the probability of Arab reaction. The religious ferment in the region could reconfirm Jerusalem's credentials as a catalyst for crusades. Continued public silence by Washington on Israel's colonization policies is no asset to the United States in the worlds of Arabdom and Islam. It reinforces the already formidable Israeli constituency against the evacuation of the Occupied Territories.

Israel could badly bloody the PLO again and again but the prospects of the PLO's extirpation are slight. The confrontation in Lebanon between Syria and the PLO, on the one hand, and the Maronite Phalangists and Israel, on the other, is a probable flashpoint for a fifth Arab–Israeli war. In such a war Israel might march into more than one Arab capital. What it cannot do is control the reverberations. Islamism and Arabism are still powerful forces in Egypt. In the circumstances, mounting pressures could still summon a conscience-stricken Egyptianism from its present limbo. There is no *deus ex machina* in a Labour victory in the Israeli elections. The Labour leader, Shimon Peres, will at best be a hostage of his coalition partners and his Hashemite daydreams.

VIII

The Europeans cannot deliver Israel or the PLO. They don't have to. But there are things that urgently need to be done which the United States cannot and the Europeans can undertake – with an American cautionary yellow light. The Europeans could constructively focus attention on the two principles of 'reciprocity' and 'coexistence' – the leaven for a *modus vivendi*. They could draw out the PLO and the Arab radicals on what they have been implying. They could elicit from Israel responses, however guarded, about what in the circumstances it might contemplate. Should the Europeans collectively ascertain the preparedness of this or that protagonist to exchange reciprocal assurances on the basis of coexistence, this should be welcome news. The United States might find the information worthy of building on.

A new hierarchy of priorities could thus emerge. All this fuss about a 'strategic consensus' might fall into perspective. Even the AWACs issue might be seen in a different light from both Washington and Riyadh. This could finally render progress on the core issue of Palestine more feasible given the realities of the domestic political setting in the United States.

Notes

1 The *reductio ad absurdum* of this outlook is best illustrated in the proposition, 'Let the Russians have the influence, and let us [the United States] have the oil.' See Miles Ignotus, 'Seizing Arab Oil,' *Harper's*, March 1975, pp. 45 ff.

2 See 'Thinking the Unthinkable: A Sovereign Palestinian State', this volume, pp. 97 ff.

3 The Covenant uses such phrases as: 'elimination of the Zionist presence in Palestine' (Article 15); 'entire illegality of the United Nations partition of Palestine in 1947 and the establishment of Israel there' (Article 19); 'since the liberation of Palestine will involve the destruction of the Zionist and imperialistic presence therein . . .' (Article 22).

CHAPTER 4

Towards Peace in the Holy Land*

I

The uprising that began in December 1987 in the territories Israel has occupied for over twenty years ranks as the fourth major attempt by the indigenous inhabitants of Palestine to stem the Zionist colonization of the country. First was the rebellion of 1936–9 against Britain's policy, exercised under its League of Nations mandate, for a Jewish National Home; then came the resistance to the 1947 UN General Assembly resolution to partition Palestine, which developed into a civil war before the regular war that broke out when the British left on 15 May 1948. Third, from 1964–5 onward, came the rise among the Palestinian Diaspora of the Palestine Liberation Organization (PLO) and guerrilla movements against the status quo.

Today, in contrast to the three earlier instances, the Palestinians on the West Bank of the Jordan River and in the Gaza Strip are face to face with their perceived dispossessors, with no third party or geographic distance intervening. While the Israelis wield all state powers, the chief weapons of the Palestinians are the stones of the countryside. If the areas of Israel proper and those in the Occupied Territories already colonized, requisitioned or annexed are subtracted from the total area of Mandatory

* Essay first published in *Foreign Affairs*, Vol. 66, No. 4, (Spring 1988), pp. 771–89.

Palestine, the Palestinians in the Occupied Territories today stand on no more than 15 per cent of the soil of the country.

In a statement read out at a Jerusalem hotel on 14 January 1988, which might be called the Jerusalem Programme, leading representatives of the uprising outlined their aspirations and demands for lifting the oppression of the occupation and achieving 'real peace' between Israel and the Palestinian people.

A certain Masada-like poignancy attaches to this latest manifestation of the Palestinian collective will, and with it a legitimate claim to the attention and concern of the outside world.

II

The Palestinian national identity had already begun to take shape at the beginning of World War I. It crystallized during the British Mandate (1918–48) in the resistance to Zionism. The notion that the Palestinians were a people, and merited a national state of their own, was evident to those members of the United Nations, including the United States, that voted in 1947 for the partition of Palestine. Since the beginning of the Palestinian Diaspora in 1948 the sense of Palestinian nationality has been vastly strengthened; the rise of the PLO only gave expression to an existing reality.

For four decades since the establishment of Israel, the Palestinians have been pushed and pulled together by a multitude of shared experiences which have created a sense of national community rare in the Middle East and the Third World: it has transcended geographic dispersion, village, clan and sectarian loyalties, as well as the pressures of Arab host governments and Israeli occupiers. Endowed with skills surpassing those of most Arab peoples, the Palestinians long ago crossed the threshold of nationhood, and, like so many other peoples in history, are irreconcilable to living in a limbo of permanent statelessness. It is this, rather than any brilliance in the leadership of Yasser Arafat, which has frustrated all attempts to foist an illegitimate leadership upon the Palestinians or fob them off with substitutes for a sovereign place under the sun. It is this which constitutes the umbilical cord between the Palestinians of the Occupied Territories and the Diaspora.

The Palestinians have more than tripled in number, from 1,300,000 in 1948 to 4,500,000 today, and their rate of increase is not declining. In the Gaza Strip alone they number some 600,000 and are destined there to reach 900,000 by the end of the century. All the psychological and physical pressures bearing down on them the last twenty years to leave the Occupied Territories have failed. The Palestinians under occupation have drawn the obvious lesson from the fate of their countrymen who left in 1948 and 1967. Even for those who want to leave, the absorptive capacity for Palestinians in the Arab countries has been strained to the limit: Lebanon and Syria no longer qualify as havens for Palestinians; Jordan's King Hussein is already obsessed with the nightmare of a massive Palestinian influx into his country. Egypt hardly has standing room for its own people, and opportunities in the countries of the Persian Gulf have been circumscribed.

Some Israeli leaders contemplate a policy of thinning out or expelling the Palestinians. But to where? Northward into the Shi'ite heartland of Lebanon or across the Golan Heights toward Damascus? Southward into Sinai? Eastward across the Jordan River? Even hardliners in Israel might balk at the first two suggestions, and the third is also problematic. It was one thing to drive out a civilian population amid the confusion of large-scale military operations, as happened in 1948; it would be another to do so in an environment where no fighting by regular armies was taking place. It was one thing to drive refugees across the river from their camps in the Jordan Valley in the wake of the retreating Jordanian army, as happened in 1967; it would be another to uproot the inhabitants of the towns and villages of the highlands. Even before the recent events in the Occupied Territories, Palestinian conduct in Lebanon in the face of siege and bombardment showed that Palestinian civilians do not panic as readily as they did in 1948.

The extraordinary courage displayed in the Occupied Territories since December 1987, especially by Palestinian youth, is but one indicator of the resistance an Israeli policy of mass expulsion would face. It is therefore reasonable to assume that the bulk of the Palestinians in the Occupied Territories will remain *in situ*, and that they will increase in number, even as the acreage at their disposal continues to dwindle with Israeli foreclosures and their political frustrations mount in the absence of a general settlement. Given the resonance between the Palestinians inside and outside the Occupied Territories, continued denial of Palestinian nationhood is unlikely to lead to the diminution of its intensity or the moderation of its expression. It would therefore seem that, just as Israel is a reality which the Palestinians and the PLO must accept, Palestinian nationhood is a reality which Israel must accept. As Israel is here to stay, the Palestinians are here to stay too.

III

Over the years the Palestine problem has generated concentric circles of expanding conflict. From the early 1880s to 1948 the conflict was preponderantly between the Jewish community of Palestine and the indigenous Arab Palestinians. From 1948 to 1967 the conflict was preponderantly between Israel and the neighbouring Arab countries. In the period since 1967 the struggle has grown to new dimensions despite the Egyptian–Israeli peace treaty some ten years ago. Even a cursory look at this last period would reveal the adverse – and often bizarre – effects of the persistence of this conflict on regional stability, Western interests and super-power relations.

The rise of Middle Eastern radicalism, for example, is not altogether unconnected with the continued non-resolution of the Palestine problem. Libyan leader Colonel Muammar al-Qaddafi, like most of his Arab contemporaries, was suffused in his youth with anger at the perceived injustices suffered by the Palestinians. The rise of the radical PLO in the mid 1960s was as much a revolt against moderate Arab regimes and their Western sponsors as against Israel. The PLO strategy of seeking bases in the Arab countries for operations against Israel led to the destabilization of Jordan in 1970–1 and contributed to the disintegration of Lebanon. It took the PLO's operations from Lebanon against Israel and Israel's scorched-earth strategy against southern Lebanon (which was designed to pit its Shi'ite inhabitants against the PLO) to make a new breed of Shi'ite militants receptive to Ayatollah Khomeini's message and install Iranian-style fundamentalism on Israel's northern borders. The oil embargo of 1973, with all its consequences, was motivated by the Arab perception of American support for Israel during the Middle East war of that year.

The Israeli hope of dealing a death blow to Palestinian nationalism by the military destruction of the PLO led to the 1982 invasion of Lebanon; for the first time, Israel laid siege to and occupied an Arab capital. The perceived opportunity afforded by the departure of the PLO from Beirut induced the United States (with not a little encouragement from Israel) to assume the anachronistic task of reconstructing Lebanon around the Maronite Christian minority, in colossal disregard of the other Lebanese sects and the heritage of the ancient city of Damascus next door. The result was the tragic loss of American and other lives and the first military skirmish in history between America and Syria, in which two American planes were shot down and an American pilot was taken prisoner.

The bizarre chain of events only grew longer. Lebanon's central institutions broke down totally, creating an ideal environment for anarchy and the unfettered pursuit of vengence through the taking of American and other Western hostages. Eventually the trail led to White House preoccupation with the release of hostages and to the scandal of the Iran–Contra operation.

Israel's need for the mass immigration of Jews to offset Palestinian demographic growth supplies part of the motivation for focusing international attention on the plight of Soviet Jewry. This issue impinges on US–Soviet relations and figured prominently during General Secretary Mikhail Gorbachev's December 1987 visit to Washington. The powerful opposition of the American Jewish establishment towards US arms sales even to moderate Arab countries affects the credibility of the United States with these Arab regimes, as well as the viability of their pro-Western orientation; it drives some of them to seek alternative sources of supply in Moscow, further weakening Western influence.

With competitive support from the two superpowers the arsenals of Israel and some Arab radical countries have grown exponentially. A nuclear alert was declared by the United States in 1973, in response to a threatened Soviet intervention at a time of heightened Arab–Israeli tension. Meanwhile, we have growing reminders that Israel has crossed the atomic, if not the thermonuclear, threshold, while evidence of biological warfare capabilities in the region also mounts.

The likely harvest of human and material devastation in a future Arab–Israeli war is a cogent argument for the need to defuse the Palestinian problem from which the conflict between Israel and the Arab states derives. This need is all the more compelling because of the increasingly religious aspect that the struggle for Palestine is assuming.

Religious undertones have always been present in the Palestine conflict. To be sure, Herzlian Zionism has remained explicitly secular in orientation despite the implicit premiss of Divine Right in Zionist polemics. Palestinian opposition was primarily motivated by the political objectives of Zionism, even though some religious fears were voiced among Palestinians concerning the Muslim sanctuaries of Jerusalem and Hebron. Even after the creation of Israel and the expansion of the conflict to include the Arab states, Arab reaction did not assume a Muslim colouring *per se* – and this despite the historical analogy uppermost in the Arab mind, of Israel as the reborn Crusader kingdom of mediaeval times.

The reason for the secular thrust of Arab reaction was the vigour of pan-Arab ideology as preached in the 1950s and the 1960s by the Baath Party from Damascus and Baghdad and the Arab National Movement from Beirut, and the adoption of this ideology by Gamal Abdel Nasser until his death in 1970. Pan-Arabism posited the existence of one multi-state Arab nation to which the peoples of the individual Arab states belong. The components of the nation are a common language and history, and shared sentiments and interests.

As opposed to pan-Arabism, pan-Islamism stressed the unity through faith of all Muslims, whether Arab or not. Religious fundamentalism has been precipitated in the Arab world in the last two to three decades by a number of developments and factors, not least being the growth of Jewish fundamentalism in Israel and the Occupied Territories. There is also the continuing grinding poverty of tens of millions, despite the oil wealth; there is the profligacy of the life-styles of the rich and powerful, coupled, especially in Egypt, with claustrophobic demographic pressures. A newly educated and relentlessly growing army of university graduates has emerged with few economic opportunities and little knowledge of the West. Some Arab rulers are perceived as subservient to the United States, particularly in matters pertaining to Israel. And Israel is perceived as enjoying an intolerable freedom of action throughout the Arab world, as when, for example, it launched air raids on Baghdad and Tunis in 1981 and 1985, respectively.

Ultimately, secular pan-Arabism failed to achieve a convincing semblance of unity, and the *raison d'état* of individual Arab states conflicted to the point of causing internecine disputes; these Arab countries seemed powerless in the face of continued Israeli occupation of Palestinian, Syrian and Lebanese territory.

These are the circumstances in which the appeal of Ayatollah Khomeini resounds. His appeal is not restricted to Shi'ites, but extends to the Sunni masses and intellectuals, inasmuch as his rallying cry is not Shi'ism but Islam, and the targets of his attacks include both the great powers and the Arab dynasts. His constant reference to the liberation of Jerusalem is as effective as it is deliberate.

Religious fundamentalism is both a reactive and assertive phenomenon in the face of challenge and failure. It is partly a search for a bulwark against engulfment by alien values, partly a protest against tyranny whether foreign or indigenous, and partly a revolt against underdog status and frustrated expectations. The context in which religious fundamentalism has taken hold in the Arab world is wider than the Arab–Israeli conflict, but that the conflict exacerbates the pace and intensity of fundamentalism's evolution is undeniable.

Palestinians both inside and outside the Occupied Territories have been affected by this change in the political climate. The competition between Muslim fundamentalist groups and PLO sympathizers under occupation (which, ironically, was encouraged by Israeli intelligence authorities) has been replaced by growing solidarity and operational coordination between the two groups.

This is in part an index of the general shift in the Middle Eastern political mood away from secularism, but it is also a response to the paramount necessity of closing ranks in the face of escalating Israeli pressures. It is not too difficult to understand

why, at times of great adversity or challenge, believers might seek a
deux ex machina in Allah. The immediate and omnipresent
stimulus for such a trend in the Occupied Territories lies in the
biblical pronouncements, posturings and conduct of the Gush
Emunim – the spearhead and the hated symbol of Jewish
fundamentalist wilfulness, particularly in the ancient quarters
adjoining the Muslim sanctuaries of Jerusalem and Hebron. It is
perhaps no exaggeration to say that the Palestine problem and
the Arab–Israeli conflict may have already crossed the threshold
of their metamorphosis into a twenty-first-century version of the
Crusades.

IV

Within living memory, the United States was looked upon by
Arab public opinion as the most friendly and trustworthy
Western power. Unlike Britain or France, which took control of
much of the region after World War I, the United States was
unencumbered by any legacy of imperialism or conflict with any
Arab people. But with the assumption by the United States of its
new global responsibilities at the end of World War II, this idyllic
state of affairs was unlikely to persist, and it did not.
Nevertheless the depth of alienation from the United States of
contemporary Arab public opinion (among both the masses and
the intellectuals), even in moderate states with friendly official
relations with Washington, has elicited little concern in the West.
This alienation is a grave harbinger of things to come.

What strikes one most about this state of affairs is its sheer
gratuitousness: two of the principal objectives of the United
States in the Middle East – access to Arab oil and the prevention
of Soviet domination of the area – do not necessarily militate
against cordial Arab–American relations.

No Arab state wants to see the area dominated by either the
United States or the Soviet Union; geographic proximity to
Russia argues the prudence of cultivating the friendship of the
more distant superpower. Pan–Arab parties have been locked in
often mortal combat with the local communist parties, and even
in radical Arab countries these parties live at the state's
sufferance. The Soviet penetration that has occurred in the

Middle East cannot be dissociated from the failure to resolve the Arab–Israeli conflict and the Arab need to balance American support of Israel with support from the Soviet Union. Similarly, with oil, the Arabs need American and Western markets no less than the West needs Arab oil. The most disruptive political impingement so far on the supply of oil to the West has been a result of American policy toward Israel.

For four decades now the Arab world has pondered the nature and motivation of this policy. Probably no other topic has been discussed at greater length in Arab political literature or debate. Three principal hypotheses have emerged: (1) US policy in the Arab–Israeli conflict is the reflection of unchangeable American cultural and religious values; (2) the American pluralistic political system gives leeway to competing groups, including the powerful pro-Israel lobby; (3) as a capitalist, imperialistic system the United States is intrinsically inimical to the interests of the Arabs.

The Arab circles most concerned for the future of Arab–American relations have clung to the second hypothesis; we have come under harsh attack for the naïveté of our implicit faith in the possibility of a change for the better in American policy. We have long argued the need to distinguish between harsh-sounding election promises and the policies subsequently pursued, and have stressed the learning potential of political incumbents and the existence of an institutional memory and regional expertise in the State Department and other American agencies which tend to balance domestic political calculation. The experience of the Reagan Administration – even in a second term when reelection was not a factor – systematically knocked down each of our arguments. To be sure, the Administration's Middle East diplomatic initiative of September 1982 gave momentary demonstration of the goodwill of the United States, but unfortunately this effort soon petered out.

The effect of all this on the consciousness of Arab intellectuals has been a direct identification of the United States with Israel: when Israel confiscates, colonizes or invades, it is the United States that is seen to be behind these actions. Not only does this threaten to eliminate the United States as a disinterested third party which can mediate, referee and act as a court of appeal, but for Arabs it casts the United States in the same mould as the enemy. The pervasiveness of these perceptions is not annulled by the comfort taken by some Arab rulers in the presence of American warships on the horizon or AWACs aircraft overhead.

A deep emotional alienation from the United States is developing in the Arab world, buttressed by a hardening conviction that the US government is structurally incapable of being fair. The stereotyping of the Arab in US popular culture and politics grows apace, giving little incentive to American leaders to be more forthcoming toward the Arab world. It is not altogether a coincidence that US citizens have been specifically targeted by radical Arab groups in these last few years.

A major assumption of American policy has been that a strong Israel is more likely to make concessions towards a peace settlement. With both Egypt and Iraq neutralized and Syria bogged down in Lebanon and at loggerheads with the PLO, Israel is as near the zenith of its military might as it will probably get. Yet the essence of even the Israeli Labour Party's position would seem categorically to preclude accommodation to the minimal demands of the Palestinians and the substance of the consensus forged at the Fez Summit of the Arab League in September 1982: a sovereign Palestinian state within the 1967 frontier, in binding, internationally guaranteed coexistence with Israel, a solution which could be fashioned in such a way as to eliminate any threat to the security of Israel, as I have already argued.*

To the best of my knowledge, the farthest the Labour Party seems willing to go would be the creation of Palestinian 'enclaves' in the Gaza Strip and the West Bank. These enclaves, separated from one another by Israeli settlements and suburban blocs as well as by various military enclosures, would amount to 60–70 per cent of the Gaza Strip and about 40 per cent of the West Bank. The Jordan River would constitute the international frontier behind which the Israeli army would remain in control. Municipal or quasi-municipal functions would devolve to local Palestinian representatives in these enclaves, but internal security would remain in Israeli hands. Jordan would be invited to 'co-police' the

---

* 'Thinking the Unthinkable: A Sovereign Palestinian State', and 'Regio-Politics: Towards a US Policy on the Palestine Problem'. This volume, pp. 82–104 and 105–20.

enclaves with Israel and presumably to extend its citizenship to all the inhabitants. This attenuated and selective Jordanian presence would be the justification for calling the arrangement a 'territorial compromise'. Face-to-face talks with a Jordanian delegation containing local Palestinians virtually chosen by Tel Aviv would negotiate this settlement at an otherwise ceremonial international conference.

This, to the best of my understanding, is the essence of the Jordanian option to which the United States and the Labour Party of Israel seem wedded, as at once a conduit, a repository and final destination. Strategically it would absolve Israel of acknowledging a Palestinian nationhood, past or present, embracing the Occupied Territories and the Diaspora, with all the attendant political, juridical and moral implications. Tactically it would keep the PLO, symbol of Palestinian nationhood, out of the peace process, drive a wedge between the PLO and Jordan, present a 'conciliatory' Israeli face to the outside world, and throw the burden of rejectionism and 'missed opportunities' on the Palestinians.

This Jordanian option is but a latter-day version of an almost hallowed tradition for solving the Palestine problem over the heads of the Palestinians. Theodore Herzl established the tradition in his talks in 1898 with Kaiser Wilhelm II. Chaim Weizmann followed the pattern in his dealings with Lord Balfour (1917) and with Emir (later King) Faisal in 1919. Throughout the 1930s Zionist leaders persisted on this course via non-Palestinian pan-Arab leaders in Damascus, Beirut, and Amman. Like the Balfour Declaration fifty years earlier, UN Resolution 242, passed in 1967, made no reference to the Palestinians, while the Camp David accords settled their future without their participation. With impressive monotony the same recipe is tried again and again despite the catastrophic consequences that each attempt brings in its train, and the cumulatively invalid arguments heard at each juncture.

Even *full* Jordanian sovereignty over the West Bank (including East Jerusalem) during the period between 1949 and 1967 was not viable. The alleged dichotomy between the Palestinians in the Occupied Territories and those in the Diaspora is in the eye of the beholder; I argue that the bonds between those Palestinians are as intimate and indestructible as the bonds between Jews inside and outside Israel. No West Bank or Gaza 'leader' anointed by the United States or Israel could look his compatriots in the eye, much less negotiate away their birthright. Far from stabilizing Jordan, the Jordanian option would strike at the very roots of the regime. It would involve it in mortal combat with all factions of the PLO and pit it against last-ditch Palestinian resistance in the Occupied Territories. Nor would the détente between Amman and Damascus survive such developments. Syria's Hafez al-Assad may encourage Jordan to isolate Yasser Arafat for his own tactical reasons, but no conceivable consideration of ideology, self-interest or prudence would lead him to implement the Jordanian option. As the senior statesman of the Arab world, King Hussein must know this, and his sound political instincts will lead him to the obvious conclusion.

V

The sad events in the Occupied Territories since December 1987 confirm this analysis. And while it is too early to say what new leadership (if any) will emerge, certain assessments can be offered with reasonable assurance.

There is evidence of an extensive organizational infrastructure emerging at the grassroots, an intermeshing of formal and informal groups of the kind described in classical writings on revolutions. The activist leadership seems to be typically diffuse, anonymous, decentralized and non-pyramidal, with heavy representation from the younger urban, rural and refugee camp generations in relatively equal proportions. A new psychology seems to have gripped the bulk of the population, partly induced by the anniversaries falling in 1987–88 (the twentieth of the occupation and the fortieth of the establishment of Israel), partly by the immobilism of the Israeli political scene, the ultra-hawkish stance of Prime Minister Yitzhak Shamir, the perceived indifference of Washington and the loss of momentum in the peace process. The November 1987 Arab League summit in Amman seemed preoccupied with the Iran–Iraq war, and the PLO leadership was locked in its perennial crisis of relations with Assad and Hussein.

Within this psychology, three new elements can be singled out.

Factional and ideological differences among Palestinians (e.g., the business sector versus the radicals, secularists versus fundamentalists, some PLO factions against others) are being overcome. These differences had hitherto impaired the effectiveness of resistance but now seem to have been subsumed under a national consensus of unprecedented scope and cohesion.

A barrier of fear has been broken. This is the result of a sense of immunity acquired incrementally over two decades against the worst the occupation could do. Well over half of the entire adult male Palestinian population of the Occupied Territories must have seen the inside of an Israeli prison. In the extended family networks that prevail in the Territories only a minority will not include a relative who has been manhandled, humiliated, injured, imprisoned or exiled, or had his or her home demolished. When every detail of one's daily personal, social, economic and professional life is governed by one or more of the 1210 ukases (of competing absurdity) issued so far by the military governors of the Occupied Territories, one's response is bound to be a deepening contempt for the system and its keepers – as a necessary condition for surmounting one's fear of them.

Finally, we see growing awareness of the need for self-reliance, or rather a compelling realization that in the last analysis salvation is self-generated. This phenomenon should be familiar to Jews in particular. For too long the Palestinians in the Occupied Territories have waited for St George to come from across the border. For too long they have seen themselves as minor actors (if actors at all) in the shaping of their own destiny. That the Occupation has succeeded in activating the moral outrage of the population is self-evident.

The flavour and weight of this occupation, the motivation and forces behind the current uprising, and the thrust of the population's aspirations may be gathered from the Jerusalem Programme – the statement read out at a press conference in January at the National Palace Hotel in Jerusalem by a spokesman for the 'Palestinian National Institutions and Personalities from the West Bank and Gaza Strip'.

The statement contains a long political preamble and fourteen specific points. Three deal with the immediate crisis: the release of those recently arrested, 'especially the children', the return of four Palestinians deported amid wide criticism, and the lifting of the siege of the refugee camps. Five points deal with human rights: they call on Israel to adhere to the Fourth Geneva Convention; to release people under administrative detention and house arrest and facilitate the reunion of families; to cease the demolition of houses; to initiate formal inquiries into the behaviour of soldiers, settlers and security men who have 'unduly caused death or bodily harm to unarmed civilians'; and to grant the political freedom of meetings and conventions including 'free municipal elections' under a neutral authority.

Two points address religious fears: the curtailment of 'provocative activities' in the Old City of Jerusalem and the preservation of the status quo of the Muslim and Christian holy sites. Two others address the loss of land and water: they call for the cessation of settlement activity and land confiscation and the release of land confiscated, as well as the rescinding of measures 'to deprive the territories of their water resources'. Two address taxation issues: the cancellation of the Israeli value-added tax and all other direct taxes, and the release of 'monies deducted from the wages of labourers' inside Israel, in the absence of commensurate social services. The statement also calls for the removal of restrictions on building permits, industrial projects and agricultural development programmes, including the digging of artesian wells. Discriminatory trade policies are also addressed: either the free transfer of industrial and agricultural produce from the Occupied Territories into Israel should be permitted or 'comparable restrictions' should be placed on such produce entering the Territories from Israel.

The political preamble states the obvious, that the occupation cannot last for ever, and that 'real peace' can be achieved only through the recognition by Israel of Palestinian national aspirations to which the uprising is committed. These include 'the rights of self-determination and the establishment of an independent state on our national soil under the leadership of the PLO as our sole, legitimate representative'. Continued occupation will lead to further violence, bloodshed and the deepening of hatred. The only way 'to extricate ourselves from this scenario,' the preamble states, is an international conference with the participation of 'all concerned parties including the PLO as an equal partner' as well as the five permanent members of the Security Council 'under the supervision' of the two superpowers. 'To prepare the atmosphere for the conference', Israel is called upon to comply with the demands outlined.

If this statement represents the uprising's demands (and the indications are that it does indeed) no one could accuse the Palestinians under occupation of not knowing what they want; nor do the leaders of the uprising seem to be grooming themselves as substitutes or proxies for the PLO.

The tone of the Jerusalem Programme is firm but sober. There are no maximalist territorial demands or flamboyant formulations about an unrealizable democratic secular state. The aim is clearly a negotiated peace with Israel on a nation-to-nation basis. Perhaps the most interesting demand of the Jerusalem Programme is for the removal of restrictions on political contacts with the PLO, to allow for 'participation of Palestinians from the territories in the proceedings of the Palestinian National Congress in order to ensure a direct input into the decision-making process'. Such input is more likely to be in favour of pragmatism than not.

VI

Despite Arab disarray and the tumultuous fortunes of the PLO since 1982, the Arab and Palestinian stance today is more propitious for an honourable and viable settlement than ever before. The pity is that neither the Israeli nor the American government yet seems able to see this, or if either does, it has yet to find the way to nurture and build upon it.

In the first place, the resolutions of the September 1982 Arab Fez Summit remain a remarkably forthcoming, collectively articulated Arab peace plan, enunciated at the level of the heads of state (only Qaddafi absented himself). Sceptics are invited to compare the resolutions with, say, the pronouncements of the 1967 Khartoum Summit to see the political light-years travelled by the Arab countries in the direction of pragmatism. There was absolutely no precedent for the Fez Summit in collective Arab diplomacy. Its orientation was unmistakably conciliatory toward a peaceful, non-transitional and guaranteed settlement on the basis of coexistence with Israel within the 1967 frontiers. There is still nothing like it on the Israeli side at such an authoritative and comprehensive level. Likewise, the PLO position as fashioned under Arafat's leadership has evolved within the framework of the Fez resolutions and reached a new level of refinement during the PLO–Jordanian talks of January–February 1986.

I was but a marginal and informal participant in those talks, but my distinct impression was that they broke down not because Arafat was averse to accepting Resolution 242, negotiating with Israel or denouncing terrorism – the three conditions set by Washington and relayed by Amman. Arafat specifically accepted Resolution 242 alongside 'other pertinent UN resolutions'. He specifically mentioned the Israeli government as a party with whom he was willing to negotiate a peaceful settlement within the context of an international peace conference and on the basis of his February 1985 accord with King Hussein. He reaffirmed his denunciation of operations outside the Occupied Territories and Israel.

There was one fundamental sticking point: Amman absolutely insisted (presumably at the behest of Washington) on a take-it-or-leave-it basis, that acceptance of Resolution 242 should be 'without trimmings', i.e., with no qualifications whatsoever. This raised the obvious question of the quid pro quo, which, Arafat was told, was US acquiescence in the participation in a joint Jordanian–Palestinian delegation to the international conference of Palestinians who were not themselves PLO officials but were approved by the PLO. 'What about Palestinian self-determination?' the PLO asked. This, Amman replied, was a matter between Jordan and the PLO. Would that it were! In the circumstances Arafat asked that in return for accepting the three conditions, Amman should obtain assurances from Washington (not Tel Aviv) about Palestinian self-determination on the basis of the Jordanian–PLO accord of February 1985. Amman could not see its way to doing that – hence the breakdown of the talks.

Is it really so outrageously perverse of Arafat to have balked at unilateral, unconditional, unreciprocated recognition of Israel, which the Israeli government itself has not solicited and has declared its intention to reject? Or is his perversity more in his hesitation to place his hope blindly in a UN resolution that does not even mention his people by name, to stop resistance to Israeli occupation and to give up PLO presence at the peace conference? Is he so lamentably wrong to hesitate to forget all

UN resolutions favourable to his cause, to delegate Palestinian representation to Amman, and to throw himself upon the *noblesse oblige* of Tel Aviv and the empathy of Washington?

The eighteenth meeting of the Palestine National Congress (PNC) held in April 1987 in Algiers demonstrated, with the return to the fold of the Popular Front for the Liberation of Palestine and the Democratic Front for the Liberation of Palestine, the fundamental solidarity between the central Palestinian factions that constitute the PLO, isolating the dissident factions sponsored by Syria. The admission for the first time of the representatives of the Palestine Communist Party to the PLO Executive was counter-balanced by the admission of two specifically Muslim representatives to the General Council, thus broadening the popular base of the PLO. The Abu Nidal group was denied admission to the various PLO bodies. The eighteenth PNC meeting confirmed Arafat's status as *primus inter pares*.

The PNC position on Resolution 242 was a retreat from Arafat's specific but qualified acceptance of it during his talks in Amman. But the Congress's rejection of the resolution was reasoned rather than categorical, on the grounds that 242 considered the Palestine problem as a 'question of refugees' and ignored the 'inalienable national rights' of the Palestinian people. On the other hand, the PNC reaffirmed support of the 1982 Fez Summit peace plan and called for the development of relations with 'the democratic forces in Israel' which are against 'Israeli occupation and expansion'. Equally significant, because of the presence of the Popular Front and the Democratic Front, was the Congress's readiness to participate in an international peace conference 'on a footing of equality' under the aegis of the United Nations, with the participation of the permanent members of the Security Council and 'the concerned parties in the region', i.e., Syria and Israel. The distinctive relations between the Palestinian and Jordanian peoples were re-emphasized, as was 'confederation between two independent states' as the principle for future relations between Jordan and a Palestinian state in the Occupied Territories. In sum, the Algiers PNC meeting left the door open for peaceful negotiations while specifically acknowledging the need for a constitutional link with Jordan.

Between the PNC meeting in April and the Amman Summit in

November 1987, several initiatives were undertaken to reduce the tensions between the PLO and Damascus. This was partly necessitated by the festering wounds in Lebanon, but largely by the need dictated by common sense to coordinate with the 'concerned party' of Syria before any international conference. One early result of these initiatives was the absence of a PLO-Syrian confrontation at the Amman Summit; another has been the lifting of the siege of the Palestinian refugee camps in Lebanon.

My impression as a participant in these initiatives is that while the gap in perceptions between Damascus and the PLO is considerable, both parties are equally keen to bridge it. A *rapprochement* between the PLO and Damascus is a *sine qua non* for serious Arab preparation for peace talks. Of the three Arab core parties to the conflict (Syria, Jordan and the PLO), Syria is the senior coalition member. This is a function of its geographic position, history, traditional role and its military strength and preparedness. As to whether President Assad is committed to peace talks, the answer is that he is a signatory to the Fez Summit peace plan but, like many others, is very sceptical about the outcome of the negotiations with an Israel that is so preponderant militarily and enjoys perceived unlimited and unconditional American backing. Can anyone credibly blame him for this?

The West has misinterpreted the significance of the Amman Summit's preoccupation with the Iran–Iraq war and the green light it gave for the resumption of relations with Egypt. This summit was a special session, summoned specifically to address the Gulf War. No regular Arab summit has been convened since 1982 because of tensions between Syria and the PLO and between Syria and Iraq.

The true significance of the Amman Summit, therefore, is that it was held with the presence of Assad, Arafat and Saddam Hussein of Iraq, and that it paves the way for a regular summit meeting to address the Arab–Israeli conflict – a necessary preparatory step to the peace talks. Egypt's 'return' may increase its military, political and economic role in the Gulf countries, but it does not necessarily enhance its role or credibility in the decisions that have to be taken collectively by the three main Arab parties in the conflict: Syria, Jordan and the PLO.

VII

For several years now much time and energy have been expended on the issue of an international conference versus direct talks. This has been at the expense of any crystallization of substantive principles for the resolution of the conflict. There is little difference between direct talks with or without the umbrella of an international conference if such a conference is purely ceremonial. It is difficult to see what attraction a ceremonial international conference would have to the Syrians, the PLO or, for that matter, the Soviets. Conferences, qua conferences, do not solve conflicts. Surely the key to a successful international conference (ceremonial or not) and even to direct talks is intensive, high-level albeit quiet pre-negotiations with and between all the principal protagonists (Syria, Israel, Jordan and the PLO) with maximal persuasiveness exerted by the superpowers on their respective friends.

In the light of historical experience accumulated since the Balfour Declaration, the recent uprising in the Occupied Territories and the configuration of power in the Arab world, the building blocks of what seems to me an honourable and pragmatically just settlement would appear without equivocation to be the following:

- the withdrawal of Israeli forces from southern Lebanon and the Golan Heights to the international frontiers, with demilitarization of the evacuated areas under UN supervisory observers and contingents stationed therein;
- the territorial partition of Mandatory Palestine along the 1967 frontier;
- a Palestinian state on the West Bank and Gaza Strip (linked by a non-extra-territorial road) living in peaceful coexistence alongside Israel. This Palestinian state would be in confederation with Jordan and precluded from entering into military alliances with other countries, whether Arab or not;
- the designation of West Jerusalem as the capital of Israel, East Jerusalem as the capital of Palestine. Extra-territorial status and access to the Jewish Holy Places would be assured, and a Grand Ecumenical Council formed to represent the three monotheistic faiths (with rotating chairmanship), to oversee

inter-religious harmony. Reciprocal rights of movement and
residence between the two capitals within agreed-upon limits
would be negotiated;
- an agreed limited return of 1948 Palestinian refugees to Israel
  proper and their unrestricted right of return to the Palestinian
  state. Those unable or unwilling to return would be compensated;
- agreement that the Jewish settlements existing in the Occupied
  Territories in 1948 would remain under Palestinian law, the
  others to be evacuated but not dismantled;
- explicit reciprocal recognition between Israel, the PLO,
  Jordan and Syria;
- Arab summit and Islamic summit guarantees of the settlement
  as the *point finale*;
- superpower and great power guarantees (inside and outside
  the UN Security Council) with sanctions;
- an interim transitional period of fixed and limited duration.

Important sectors of Israeli public opinion, not only on the left
of centre but at the centre itself, favour a settlement that might
be acceptable to most Palestinians. They are aware of the
dangers of indefinite domination of another people, but this is
not the thrust of popular Israeli sentiment nor of the thinking of
the Israeli leadership. The Israeli scorpion is determinedly
uncognizant of the Palestinian fellow creature in the same bottle.
Paradoxically, a Palestinian state in the Occupied Territories
within the 1967 frontiers in peaceful coexistence alongside Israel
is the only *conceptual* candidate for a historical compromise of
this century-old conflict. Without it the conflict will remain an
open-ended one between the maximalist concepts of Zionism and
those of its Arab and Muslim hinterland, whatever palliative
measures are taken in the meantime.

One would have thought the Jewish genius capable of grasping
effortlessly the need for an honourable and viable settlement in
light of the geographic, demographic and ideological realities of
the Middle East. Even archaeology adds its imperative plea in
the form of the debris of so many past regional empires. The path
to integration into a region would not seem to be via emphasis on
extraneousness and escalating dependence on the outside. The
breaking of bones is no passport to peace.

CHAPTER 5

The United States and the Palestinian People*

Preface

The belated decision by the Reagan Administration to open talks with the PLO has moved the United States a step closer to dealing with the substance of the Palestine problem. The decision has created both an opportunity and a risk. The opportunity now exists for a long overdue revaluation of American policy towards the Palestinian people. The risk is that of repeating policies similar to those which have hitherto prevented the United States from directly addressing the needs and internationally recognized rights of the Palestinian people.

Past American policies have failed to respond to Palestinian interest in a peace settlement. They have applied a double standard to Palestinian and Israeli violence, and they have been based upon an unthinking and unreasonable presumption that an independent Palestinian state would necessarily be a threat to Israel's security. In the observations which follow, I wish to focus upon these issues. The first section will examine the revolution in Palestinian political attitudes that took place at the meetings of the Palestine National Council in Algiers in November 1988. Following this, I wish to analyse the realities of Palestinian and Israeli violence in the Middle East, outline a proposal for the creation of a Palestinian state as part of a peace settlement that

---

* Essay first published with the title 'At a critical juncture' as a Center for Contemporary Arab Studies Report, Georgetown University, Washington, D.C., March 1989.

would guarantee Israel's security, and survey the options facing the Bush Administration.

I

The Algiers Declarations: A Palestinian Turning Point

To formulate a policy on a conflict as deeply rooted as the Palestine problem in isolation from its historical genesis and evolution is as productive as treating a major illness without studying the patient's case history. Yet this was the hallmark of the Reagan administration's approach. The most impressive testimony to this was offered by the decisions to dismiss out of hand the pronouncements of the Algiers PNC and soon afterward to deny Chairman Arafat a visa to the US.

Two historic documents emerged from the Algiers PNC: the Declaration of Independence and the Political Statement. The first was approved unanimously. The second received overwhelming support, the voting being 250 in favour, 39 against, with 10 abstentions.

The most significant aspect of the vote was that it established a new norm. On earlier occasions, those who found themselves in the minority would walk out or leave the organization in dissidence. This time, after prolonged deliberations, the minority groups agreed to abide by the majority rule. In the words of George Habbash, the leader of the Popular Front for the Liberation of Palestine: 'I have serious reservations whether moderation and concessions will get you anywhere. I hope I am wrong. If I be proved right I expect Arafat to return to us and confess his failure. If I be proved wrong I shall be the first to apologise to you all.'

The Declaration of Independence has three major themes: (1) the persistence of Palestinian identity through the ages and the passionate attachment of Palestinians to their soil, of which the intifada is the latest manifestation; (2) the legitimacy of a Palestinian state; and (3) the characteristics and policies of the state to be.

Politically, it is the Declaration's discussion of the issue of legitimacy and of the characteristics and policies of the future state that is most significant.

There are declared to be three sources of legitimacy of a Palestinian state: *natural right, historic right* and *international legitimacy*. It is the Declaration's discussion of international legitimacy that is most crucial.

The international legitimacy of the Palestinian state is said to derive from Article 22 of the Covenant of the League of Nations formulated in 1919, the Treaty of Lausanne of 1923 and United Nations General Assembly Resolution 181 of 1947 calling for the partition of Palestine.

The reference to Article 22 is to its fourth paragraph, which states that 'communities formerly belonging to the Turkish Empire have reached a stage of development where their existence as independent nations can be provisionally recognized'. The Treaty of Lausanne formalized the separation of the Arab provinces from the Ottoman Empire. But it is the reference to the 1947 UN partition resolution that is startling.

Here is how the reference occurs:

> In spite of the historic injustice to the Palestinian people, which resulted in its dispersion and in depriving it of its right of self-determination following the United Nations General Assembly resolution 181 of 1947, this resolution which partitioned Palestine into two states, one Arab and one Jewish, continues to provide the conditions of international legitimacy to safeguard the right of the Palestinian Arab people to sovereignty and national independence.

There is no fudging or hypocrisy here. The 1947 partition resolution is described as unjust, but accepted in spite of its injustice. And it is accepted in full knowledge that its acceptance cannot be partial or selective. The components of partition are specifically stated to be an Arab state and a Jewish state.

The ideological implications are enormous. If the 1947 partition resolution is a source of the international legitimacy of a Palestinian state, then it is the source of international legitimacy of the Jewish state. The moral barrier rooted in the deep-seated Palestinian sense of the injustice of partition which has hitherto inhibited its acceptance is breached. Acceptance of partition is proclaimed by the Declaration, in spite of its perceived injustice.

There has been absolutely no precedent for this in the history of the Palestinian national movement since the idea of partition was first propounded by the British in 1937. The first intifada, the Great Rebellion which erupted in 1936, reached new peaks of intensity and continued well into 1939 precisely because of the 1937 British partition proposal. Thousands of Palestinians died resisting the 1937 proposal and many thousands of others were wounded or exiled. The second Palestinian intifada of 1947–8 was against this selfsame resolution mentioned by the Declaration of Independence. Many more thousands of Palestinians died resisting it at the time and afterward. The very *raison d'être* of the PLO before the 1967 war was to resist partition.

The revolutionary nature of the PNC's acceptance of partition is self-evident to anyone with an elementary knowledge of the historical background. Nevertheless it would be pertinent to compare this acceptance with the provisions of the 1968 PLO Covenant.

Article 2 of the Covenant states:

Palestine with the boundaries it had during the British mandate is an indivisible territorial unit.

Article 19 states:

The partition of Palestine in 1947 and the establishment of the state of Israel are entirely illegal regardless of the passage of time; they were contrary to the will of the Palestinian people and to their natural right in their homeland, and inconsistent with the principles embodied in the U.N. Charter, particularly the right of self-determination.

Article 20 states:

Judaism, being a divine religion, is not an independent nation. Nor do Jews constitute a single nation with an identity of its own. They are citizens of the states to which they belong.

The contradiction between the Declaration and these provisions is not one of nuance. It is diametric and total. The other politically significant theme in the Declaration concerns the policies of the future state. The Palestinian state is:

committed to peaceful coexistence and will act with all other states and peoples to establish permanent peace based on justice and respect of rights to enable the human capacity for construction to blossom, and to encourage competition for the embellishment of life and the abolition of fear of what tomorrow holds . . .

The Palestinian state:

believes in the peaceful resolution of international and regional conflicts according to the U.N. Charter and U.N. resolutions. It rejects all threats of force, violence, or terrorism, and their use against its own territory and political independence, or the territorial integrity of any other state.

It is striking that nowhere in the Declaration of Independence is there any reference to the 1968 Covenant.

The crucial section in the Political Statement, the other major document to emerge from the Algiers PNC, is the one entitled 'Resolutions in the Political Field'. This contains three major themes within the framework of the Declaration of Independence. The themes in the two documents are remarkably consistent with one another, and should be considered as an integrated whole. The themes of the Political Statement pertain, first, to the final status of the settlement; second, to the specific terms of the settlement; and third, to the means of achieving the settlement.

The final status is defined as 'a comprehensive political settlement of the Arab–Israeli conflict and its crux, the Palestinian people'. Later it is described as 'a comprehensive political settlement, and the realization of security and peace for all, with their mutual acceptance and consent'. Later still, 'the Security Council should formulate and guarantee arrangements for the security and peace of all the affected states in the area including the Palestinian state'. And 'the future relationship between the two states of Jordan and Palestine should be on a confederal basis as a result of the free and voluntary choice of the two peoples'.

These details in the Political Statement reinforce the sections in the Declaration of Independence just quoted concerning peaceful coexistence, permanent peace, and the rejection of force. They indicate that the desire for an end to the conflict is a strategy and not an interim tactic. This is confirmed, as we shall see, by the acceptance of Resolutions 242 and 338.

The specific terms of the settlement (the second major theme in the Political Statement) are identical with those spelled out in the 1982 Fez Summit Peace Plan: withdrawal to the 1967 frontier including East Jerusalem, removal of settlements established since 1967, solution of the refugee problem according to UN resolutions, freedom of religious practice in the Holy Places, and a transitional period of limited duration for the Occupied Territories under UN supervision.

The means of achieving the settlement (the third and last major theme in the Political Statement) are repeatedly described as peaceful and political, and 'within the framework of the U.N. Charter, the provisions and principles of international legitimacy, the norms of international law and the resolutions of the U.N.'.

While the intifada is encouraged as an expression of the natural right of peoples to self-defence and resistance to foreign occupation, the Political Statement declares its 'rejection of terrorism in all its forms, including state terrorism'. It reaffirms the 1985 Cairo Declaration against operations outside Israel and the Occupied Territories and it affirms its acceptance of UN General Assembly Resolution 40/61 of 9 December 1985. This resolution was adopted by the General Assembly without a vote, which indicates that the US refrained from calling for a vote to register its opposition to or abstention from it. The resolution affirms the right of people to self-determination and to resist foreign domination but the bulk of its text is devoted to combating terrorism. The resolution registers deep concern at 'the worldwide escalation of acts of terrorism in all its forms which endanger or take innocent human lives, jeopardize fundamental freedoms and seriously impair the dignity of human beings'. It condemns 'as criminal all acts, methods and practices of terrorism wherever and by whomever committed'. It 'deeply deplores the loss of innocent human lives'. It also deplores 'the pernicious impact of acts of international terrorism on relations of cooperation among states'.

The chief instrumentality toward a peace settlement, according to the Political Statement, should be 'an effective international conference' with 'the participation on an equal footing of the permanent members of the Security Council and *all* the parties to the conflict in the area, including the P.L.O.'.

Attendance of the conference is accepted on the basis of Resolutions 242 and 338, which are specifically mentioned. Three other bases for attendance are added. The first is the principle of the non-acquisition of territory by war. The second is the principle of self-determination in accordance with the UN Charter, and the third basis consists of UN resolutions pertinent to the Palestinian problem.

Let us see what PLO acceptance of Resolutions 242 and 338 amounts to in itself. Let us then see how the addition of the three bases affects PLO acceptance of Resolution 242.

The core demand of Resolution 242 is 'termination of all claims or states of belligerency and respect for and acknowledgement of the sovereignty, territorial integrity, and political independence of every state in the area and their right to live in peace within secure and recognized boundaries free from threats or acts of force'. It also calls for 'guaranteeing the territorial inviolability and political independence of every state in the area through measures including the establishment of demilitarized zones'. Resolution 338 calls for implementation of Resolution 242 through negotiations under UN supervision. It should be noted that Israel is not specifically mentioned in either Resolution 242 or 338.

By accepting Resolution 242, the PNC surely accepted its language as just quoted. This acceptance is not in a vacuum. It is in consonance with the principles enumerated in the Declaration of Independence as underlying the policies of the Palestinian state. It is in harmony with the principles of the final status of the settlement as propounded in the Political Statement itself. In other words, the principles underlying Resolution 242 are affirmed again and again in other parts of both the Declaration of Independence and the Political Statement.

But do the three other bases added to Resolution 242 for attendance of an international conference vitiate acceptance of Resolution 242?

The principle of the non-admissibility of the acquisition of territory by war (the first of the bases) is specifically spelled out in the preamble of Resolution 242. It cannot be at variance with the resolution.

The principle of self-determination (the second basis) is specifically based on the UN Charter. The UN Charter has a short preamble and 21 chapters. Respect for 'the principle of equal rights and self-determination of peoples' occupies pride of place in the second of four paragraphs of Article One of Chapter

One. The UN Charter is singled out in the preamble of 242 as the fountainhead of the resolution. The principle of self-determination derives from the same fountainhead. Its application by the PNC is conceived within the context of the acceptance of the principle of partition. The principle of partition by definition acknowledges the legitimacy of Israel, which is the fundamental premiss of Resolution 242. The addition of self-determination to Resolution 242 as a basis for attending the international conference cannot in this context reasonably be construed as vitiating acceptance of the resolution.

The addition of 'U.N. resolutions pertinent to the Palestine Problem' (the third added basis) might seem at first sight to warrant complaint. But the phrase does not say '*all* resolutions'. At the same time, the only UN resolution mentioned in the Declaration of Independence is the 1947 partition resolution, and no UN resolutions are referred to in the Political Statement that are at variance with Resolution 242. Indeed, it is contrary to the PNC intent to vitiate acceptance of Resolution 242. This acceptance is conceived not only for the purpose of attending the international conference but also for indicating that the frontiers sought for the Palestinian state are those of 1967 and *not* those of 1947. This point is confirmed by the reference to withdrawal to the 1967 frontiers in the terms of the settlement spelled out by the Political Statement. No demand is made for an Israeli withdrawal from territories other than those that were occupied in 1967.

To sum up: the goal, as defined by the Declaration of Independence and the Political Statement, is peaceful coexistence and guaranteed permanent peace on the basis of partition along the 1967 frontier. The means of achieving this are negotiations at an effective international conference.

Such a goal and such means are again in diametric and total variance with the goals and the means spelled out in the 1968 PLO Covenant. Thus the *goal* in the Covenant is variously described as the 'liberation of Palestine', the 'retrieval of Palestine', the 'liberation and retrieval of Palestine', or 'the total liberation of Palestine'. These phrases occur in ten of thirty-three articles of the Covenant. Article 21 specifically rejects 'all solutions substituted for the total liberation of Palestine'.

The *means* in the Covenant are variously described as 'armed struggle', 'armed revolution' or 'liberation war'. These phrases occur in five of thirty-three articles of the Covenant. Article 9 defines armed struggle 'as the only way to liberate Palestine'. It continues, 'Thus armed struggle is the overall strategy, not merely a tactical phase'. Article 21 rejects 'all proposals aiming at the internationalization of the problem'.

Finally in the combined 15,000 words of the Declaration of Independence and the Political Statement, the two-word phrase 'armed struggle' occurs not once.

If all this was missed by the Tel-Avivologists of Foggy Bottom when the Declaration and Political Statement were issued, they deserve a resounding F− grade, by the laxest professional criteria. If they understood it all (which is more likely) and nevertheless recommended the humiliating punishment of denial of a visa to the architect of a Copernican Revolution in Palestinian decision-making, they deserve an A+ on the scale of partisanship for the Israeli cause.

In the words of Isabella in *Measure for Measure*:

> O, it is excellent
> To have a giant's strength; but it is tyrannous
> To use it like a giant
>   Man, proud man,
> Drest in a little brief authority
> Most ignorant of what he's most assured
> Plays such fantastic tricks before high heaven
> As make the angels weep.

II

The US and Middle East Terrorism: A Double Standard

In approaching the problem of violence in the Middle East, the United States government has applied a double standard in judging Israeli and Palestinian actions. Nowhere was this more apparent than in the explanations given by Secretary of State Shultz in November when, despite the PNC's peace initiative, he denied Arafat a visa to address the United Nations General

Assembly in New York. The justifications offered by Shultz were misleading, insensitive, disingenuous and defamatory.

First, they were *misleading* because they conveyed the impression that Arafat in person and his movement, Fatah, had been involved in acts of violence against Americans. The Reagan administration knew – as did members of previous administrations – that since 1973, Arafat has consistently cooperated with the US in safeguarding the lives of Americans in the Middle East and protecting American institutions there.[1] It was Fatah who looked after the security of the American University of Beirut and more indirectly of the American Embassy in Beirut. It was Fatah who escorted the American ambassador on his visits to South Lebanon and often warned of impending attacks against American diplomats in Lebanon and elsewhere in the Middle East. It was Fatah who facilitated the safe evacuation by the Sixth Fleet of 263 Westerners trapped by the civil war in Lebanon in 1976. The first batch of American hostages were released by Teheran at least partly at the urging of Arafat. Indeed, Arafat intervened so strenuously on behalf of the American hostages that his own relations with the Iranian revolutionary regime were in consequence severely strained. When, in 1982, some 3000 Americans were trapped in the hell of the siege by Israel it was Arafat who ensured that not one of them came to harm and who supervised their safe evacuation. Terrorists would have kept them there as the ideal buffer against Sharon.

It is no secret that Arafat himself is on the hit list of some extremists, precisely because of what is seen as his orientation toward the United States. Several of his diplomats have been assassinated for the same reason. That he would renege on the 1973 arrangements even while transforming PLO policies towards a dialogue with Washington is inherently implausible.

The accusations made by the State Department were *insensitive* because they turned a blind eye to the violence inflicted upon the Palestinians in the Occupied Territories. They also implied that support of the intifada was tantamount to terrorism.

Twenty-six 'injuries and usurpations' were listed in the American Declaration of Independence to justify the revolution against the King of England. Here are twenty-six not incomparable Israeli 'injuries and usurpations' in the Occupied Territories that could be cited by Palestinians: seizing our land, stealing our water, deporting our citizens, maiming our mayors, smashing our bones, killing our teenagers, blowing up our houses, threatening our expulsion, closing our schools and universities, imposing armed settlers on us, giving them free rein, arresting us in thousands, denying us elections, detaining us without formal charge or trial, closing our newspapers, harassing and physically abusing our detainees, discriminating against us in courts, imposing endless curfews, maligning our nation, restricting our travel, assassinating our leaders, curtailing our trade, refusing us political organization, opposing the return of our compatriots, claiming our patrimony, and threatening our Holy Places.

Did Secretary Shultz really need to be asked, 'Hath not a Palestinian hands, organs, dimensions, senses, affections, passions? Is he not fed with the same food, hurt with the same weapons, subject to the same diseases, healed by the same means . . . as a Christian is'?

The accusations of terrorism made against Arafat when he was denied a visa were *disingenuous* because they implied general abhorrence of violence when the expressed abhorrence was transparently selective.

It is no secret that former members of the Irgun and Stern Gang are among the élite of the Likud, the dominant party in Israel's government, for which Secretary of State Shultz always advocated the most generous American support. The Irgun and Stern Gang played a pioneering role in the use of the political strategy of terrorism in the Middle East, and were the first to introduce many contemporary terrorist tactics into the conflict over Palestine.

Here, in chronological order, is a list of twelve major tactics of modern terrorism and the dates of their first introduction into the conflict over Palestine by members of the Irgun or Stern Gang, and in one case by the Hagana, which was the military organization of the Jewish Agency for Palestine.[2] Four of the twelve incidents, it should be noted, took place outside the borders of Palestine and are thus also early instances of international terrorism.

1 *Grenades in cafés*: first used against Palestinians in Jerusalem, 17 March 1937.[3]

2 *Delayed-action, electrically timed mines in crowded market places*: first used against Palestinians in Haifa, 6 July 1938.[4]

3 *Blowing up a ship with its civilian passengers still on board*: first used in Haifa, 25 November 1940. Although the action was politically aimed at the British, the ship in question, the *Patria*, had 1700 Jewish refugees on board.[5]

4 *Assassination of a government official outside Palestine for a reason related to the Palestinian–Zionist conflict*: first used against the British in Cairo, 6 November 1944.[6]

5 *Taking of hostages to put pressure on a government*: first used against the British in Tel Aviv, 18 June 1946.[7]

6 *Blowing up of government offices with their civilian employees and visitors*: first used against the British in Jerusalem, 22 July 1946.[8] The toll was ninety-one dead and forty-six wounded.[9]

7 *Blowing up of embassy outside Palestine with a booby-trapped suitcase*: first used against the British Embassy in Rome, 31 October 1946.[10]

8 *Booby-trapped car parked alongside buildings*: first used against the British in Sarafand (east of Jaffa) on 5 December 1946.[11]

9 *Whipping of hostages as a reprisal for government actions*: first used against British in Tel Aviv, Natanya and Rishon-le-Zion, 29 December 1946.[12]

10 *Letter-bombs sent to politicians outside Palestine*: first used against Britain when twenty letter-bombs were sent from Italy to London between 4 June and 6 June 1947.[13]

11 *Murder of hostages as a reprisal for government actions*: first used against the British in the Natanya area on 29 July 1947.[14]

12 *Postal parcel-bomb sent outside Palestine*: first used against the British in London, 3 September 1947.[15]

If this be considered ancient history, here is a recent development. On 12 September 1988, John Kifner reported in the *New York Times* that two Israeli gentlemen, Yehoshua Zeitler and Meshulam Markover, had told Israeli television the previous night that, as members of the Stern Gang, they and two other members of the Gang had on 16 September 1948 assassinated the UN peace mediator in Palestine, Count Folke Bernadotte, and his French aide, Colonel Serot.

The information is important because the leadership of the Stern Gang was vested in the Central Committee, and the Central Committee was composed of three men: Yitzhak Yizernitsky (later Yitzhak Shamir), Israel Sheib (later Israel Eldad) and Nathan Friedman Yellin (later Nathan Yalin Mor).

When, after the TV appearance of Zeitler and Markover, Shamir's office was asked about their confessions, a spokesman said that 'the Prime Minister had played no role in the assassination; the group [i.e., the Stern Gang] had officially disbanded six months before.'

The spokesman's denial does not tally with the information published by Dan Kurzman (no enemy of Israel) in his book *Genesis 1948*.[16] According to Kurzman, who based his account on extended personal interviews with Shamir, Eldad and Yalin Mor, the decision to murder Bernadotte was taken on Friday, 10 September 1948 at a meeting of the Central Committee attended by these three gentlemen in Yalin Mor's apartment on Ben Yehuda Street in Tel Aviv. Zeitler, who made the recent TV confession, had himself driven Eldad to this meeting from Jerusalem and waited for its outcome in the car. It was at this meeting on 10 September, according to Kurzman, that a decision was taken to set up a phantom organization with the Hebrew name Hazit Moledet, or Fatherland Front, to assume *public* responsibility for the murder. Count Bernadotte and Colonel Serot were assassinated six days later. It is interesting that Zeitler and Markover made their TV confession not on 16 September 1988, the fortieth anniversary of the murder of Bernadotte, but on 11 September 1988, the fortieth anniversary almost to the day of the meeting in Ben Yehuda Street.

The earlier information from Kurzman and the recent confessions of Zeitler and Markover leave little room for doubt about Shamir's role. Counter-terrorists at the State Department should perhaps take note when Shamir next applies for a visa to the US. Needless to say, the *New York Times* did not find a letter I wrote with this information to be news fit to print.

Finally, the double standard exhibited when Arafat was denied a visa was *defamatory*. The grisly tally of the casualties of the conflict since the emergence of the PLO in the 1960s shows that for every Israeli killed at least thirty Palestinians have been killed, that the ratio of the military to the civilians among the

Israeli dead is 1:1 and among the Palestinian dead 1:5.[17] And yet Secretary Shultz singled out the Palestinians by talking about the 'blight of terrorism that afflicts their cause'.

In his selective condemnation of Palestinians, Secretary Shultz was not holding the scales of justice high aloft. He was sitting on one of them, and he knew it.

III

A Palestinian State and Israeli Security

The most important substantive issue now faced by the United States in its relations with the Palestinian people is the irreducible Palestinian demand for an independent state.

The most common argument heard in the United States against a Palestinian state is that it poses a threat to the security of Israel. Ten years ago I maintained, as I still maintain, that no such threat is posed.[18]

I proposed at the time and still propose that some variant of the Austrian model be applied in the case of the future Palestinian state. The state would thereby voluntarily and irrevocably give up, under Security Council guarantee, the option of entering into a defensive or military alliance with any outside party, whether Arab or non-Arab. It would therefore rely for its defence not so much on itself or on the Arab countries as on the guarantee of the Great Powers. This would naturally entail a threshold of Palestinian armed forces in quantity and quality that was congruent only with necessary state functions and internal security.

Two other safeguards could be added: (1) a multinational force responsible to the Security Council could be deployed in the Jordan Valley to act as a reserve to help the Palestinian government in the maintenance of law and order; and (2) UN observers could be stationed at all main points of entry.

An additional component would of course be Arab collective endorsement. For what we are talking about is a comprehensive peace involving withdrawal from the Golan and therefore the accommodation of Syrian demands, and withdrawal from South Lebanon and therefore the accommodation of Lebanese Shi'ite demands, in addition, of course, to a confederal arrangement with Jordan.

Such a settlement would create a psycho-political environment totally different from the current one. One of the difficulties of assessing a post-settlement environment is precisely our tendency to transpose to it features of the current one.

Before we look at the putative threats posed by a Palestinian state to Israel let us remember two factors.

1 No matter how changed the psycho-political environment after the settlement, geographical realities will remain the same. The Gaza Strip will remain separated from the West Bank, cut off by land from the world, its access from the sea dominated by Israel. The West Bank will remain cut off from the sea and surrounded by Israel from the north, west and south. Both the Gaza Strip and the West Bank will remain utterly accessible to Israel within minutes.

2 This utter accessibility will remain a function of the local and regional balance of power, which will remain crushingly in favour of Israel.

But what are the arguments regarding the threat posed by a Palestinian state to Israel?

There would seem to be two main arguments: (a) that a Palestinian state is bound to be radical and a radical state is bound to expose Israel to a whole spectrum of threats; (b) that the retention of the West Bank and Gaza Strip in peacetime is necessary for the defence of Israel in the event of a future Arab invasion.

The assumption that a Palestinian state will be radical in its policies is highly questionable. Its government is bound to be a coalition of the intifada and Diaspora leaderships. This will be a seasoned veteran leadership with no illusions about what is and what is not possible. They would be only too aware of the cost and sacrifices suffered to achieve statehood. They would have a vested interest in not embarking on or encouraging suicidal policies that would provoke renewed Israeli occupation.

But even if a radical group did seize power, the worst it could do would be very limited and containable and it would be more than likely that such a group would be ousted by Palestinian public opinion sooner rather than later.

But what is the worst a radical group could do? It could call upon the Soviet Union or a Soviet-sponsored country to establish a base in the Palestinian state or send heavy arms to it. The chances that the Soviet Union or a Soviet-sponsored country would do such a thing are nil. There would be no conceivable gain for Moscow to renege on its obligations as a guarantor of the settlement and to expose itself to certain humiliation at the hands of Tel Aviv. Given the geographical realities described, there would be no way of sending heavy equipment without immediate discovery and the activation of the sanctions mechanisms that would be built into the settlement.

The radical group could try to involve an Arab country in the same way. But the same constraints that apply to Moscow would apply to any Arab country, with the additional deterrent that the Arab country would expose itself to Israeli retaliation.

The radical group could decide to launch an all-out attack against Israel with the forces available to it. Given the miniscule forces the Palestinian state would have in comparison to Israel's, even if such an attack could get underway before its very early detection, it would be crushed within hours, bringing about the downfall of the group.[19]

The radical group could initiate continuous small-scale attacks against Israel. These would activate the sanctions mechanisms of the agreement, justify Israeli retaliation and sooner rather than later arouse Palestinian public opinion against the group, forcing it to resign or desist.

The argument that the retention of the West Bank and the Gaza Strip is needed as a security measure in the event of an Arab invasion is also highly questionable.

We are talking about a comprehensive settlement involving the PLO, with collective Arab endorsement and the neutralization of Arab irredentism. One would assume that the chances of an Arab war against Israel would be enhanced by the continued occupation and colonization by Israel of Arab land and not by the termination of this occupation.

But even in the unlikely event of a post-settlement future Egyptian or Syrian government reneging on the settlement, the presence in such a scenario of a Palestinian state along the lines we described cannot hamper Israel's ability to deal with the Syrian or Egyptian threat. Should the Palestinian government be reckless enough to have colluded with the Syrian or Egyptian governments or both, then Israel would have a clear *casus belli* and the ability to gobble up the Palestinian territories in no time.

The worst-case scenario is of Iraq's serried tank divisions suddenly lumbering up the Eastern slopes of the Judaean hills. But how will they get there?

The shortest distance between Baghdad and the Israeli frontier via Rutba, Mafrak and Irbid is 580 miles – some five times the distance between the Suez Canal and Israel. The other routes via Mafrak and then Jerash or Amman are both about 680 miles each, six times the distance between the Suez Canal and Israel, or about the distance between Paris and Berlin. The terrain throughout is open, vulnerable, vegetationless desert – ideal burial ground for tanks to the side which enjoys mastery of the skies, as Israel does. This terrain can be and is kept under constant surveillance by Israel through a combination of devices: on-site intelligence at source and in transit, friendly intelligence and satellites, incessant Israeli overflights in Saudi and Jordanian airspace, the Israeli Hawkeye AWAC system, long-range drones, radar, and very soon the Israeli satellite Offek.

The mass movement of tanks in such an environment cannot escape early detection, giving ample time for Israeli mobilization and aerial interception with conventional and less conventional weapons. A Palestinian state in the West Bank and the Gaza Strip would in no way hinder or diminish Israel's ability to detect, intercept or mobilize for a hypothetical Iraqi invasion. Jewish settlements in the Golan and the Palestinian Occupied Territories cannot defend Haifa and Tel Aviv in the missile, chemical and nuclear warfare of the future. A Palestinian state will not prevent Israel from reaching the high ground of the West Bank next door long before the Iraqi tanks hundreds of miles away could get there.

IV

The New Palestinian Diplomacy

The policy propounded by the Algiers PNC was not the result of a Pauline revelation. It was the product of intensive Palestinian soul-searching and of a long drawn-out trend towards pragmatism in the resolutions of successive PNCs, which has been noted by observers for a decade and a half and now dramatically brought to culmination by the sacrificial courage of the intifada and the statesmanship of Yasser Arafat. On the basis of a mature reading of local, regional and international realities, the Algiers PNC formalizes Palestinian conceptualization of the conflict as a non-zero sum game. Its decisions were a conquest of the self, for the self – a triumph of compassion for one's people over hatred of one's enemy. It thus opened wide the gate towards a historic reconciliation while spelling out its irreducible minimum condition of statehood. It offers an integrated cluster of ideas on which an infrastructure of peace can be built through quiet and purposeful dialogue, preferably with Israel, but otherwise with Washington.

The Algiers PNC does not view the conflict as resembling an industrial dispute (as some tend to do) where a little give here and a little give there will bring about reconciliation. A vital core demand is involved on each side and is non-negotiable. This is the continued communal and national survival of each protagonist. An outcome that concedes this to one side but denies it to the other will not work.

After forty years of ghostly wandering in No Man's Land and twenty-one years of occupation, the Palestinians want to start living and stop dying. They want to start laughing and stop crying. They want to breathe Palestinian oxygen, plough Palestinian soil, watch Palestinian skies, hear Palestinian accents. They want their own, their very own nest, hole, perch or haunt. They want to turn this into a badge of identity, a centre of pride, a symbol of dignity and a refuge of last resort. The site of their state can only be in their ancestral land. The harvest of historic reconciliation can grow only in the soil of the conflict itself.

The Palestinians long ago crossed the threshold of nationhood. Their fortitude is geologically constituted. Time will not erode it and brutality will not domesticate it. The Palestinians are not becoming fewer but more numerous. They are not becoming less but more mobilized.

Whatever Washington's responses, the PLO leadership should not be deflected from the course it has set itself, a course dictated by its own highest national interest. The very panic in certain circles at the prospect of PLO moderation indicates the soundness of the Algiers pronouncements.

The PLO should reaffirm the principles it propounded in Algiers and should build upon them to enlarge, consolidate and formalize the circles of Arab and international consensus in their favour. An emerging universal Arab consensus in support of the Algiers principles, including Syria, Iraq and Egypt, is the first pillar on which Palestinian diplomacy should base itself; the second is the deepening international empathy outside Israel and the US administration.

It is important that PLO leadership should persevere on its chosen course. Even with Arafat addressing the UN in New York and the US in dialogue with the PLO, the road to statehood is long, hard and uphill all the way. To declare a state is one thing, to establish it another.

V

The Bush Administration: Critical Decisions

Three options face the Bush administration:

1 to follow in the footsteps of the Reagan Administration with a negative attitude to the Palestinian demand for self-determination;

2 to introduce only cosmetic changes in the Reagan Administration's policy;

3 to conduct a thorough revision of US policy towards the Palestinian people.

To adopt either of the first two options would continue to deepen Arab alienation from the US, further undermine the prestige and credibility of regimes friendly to the US, and confirm the Arab perception of American partisanship for Israel and hostility to the Arabs. The inevitable result would be to fan the flames of fundamentalism, play into the hands of radical forces, sow the seeds of the next Arab–Israeli war and set the US and the Arab world on an inevitable collision course.

This may sound alarmist. But there are very real dangers. All the ingredients are there. American policy in the Middle East for almost all of the past eight years has been a shambles. A severe crisis of confidence in Washington's good faith pervades every single Arab capital. Saudi Arabia's switch to Britain and China for her arms purchases was only the tip of the iceberg.

The rudderless ship of American Middle Eastern diplomacy, guided by the absurdly reductionist compass of counter-terrorism, has spent years throwing its ballast overboard – its extensive regional expertise, its collective institutional memory and all the insights of the Law of Causation into human affairs – only to relapse into a diagnostic paralysis.

Paradoxically, at the same time a wide window of opportunity beckons. The Soviet attitude on the Middle East is more conducive to a peaceful settlement than ever before and the voice of Western Christendom rings out in the pronouncements of His Holiness Pope John Paul II. Meanwhile the political map of the Arab world is rapidly changing before our very eyes with Hussein's formal disengagement from the Occupied Territories, the Algiers PNC, Syria's coy acknowledgement of Mubarak's successive conciliatory moves, Iraq's less belligerent tone toward Syria and mounting calls for the reinstatement of the annual Arab summit.

The change in the Arab scene is noticeably in the direction of a consensus around the principles of the Algiers PNC. The chances are that an Arab summit will formalize the collective Arab endorsement of these principles. The resultant new collective Arab position on the Arab–Israeli conflict and the Palestinian problem will be significantly more advanced than the last one forged at Fez in 1982. It will be more advanced because the Fez Summit did not mention Resolution 242 specifically and referred only very indirectly to the 1947 partition resolution. Such a new Arab position would be truly pathbreaking. But to recognize the opportunity for real Middle East peace that it affords requires minds that are open and eyes that can see.

The reappraisal of American policy, if it takes place, will have to pose hitherto unposable questions and scrutinize hitherto hallowed premises and assumptions: is a stronger Israel necessarily more prone to peace? Is Israel really interested in an exchange of land for peace? Is Israeli withdrawal from Sinai a guide to Israeli intentions in the Occupied Territories? Is a Palestinian state with proper safeguards really a danger to Israel? Is American public opinion really hostile to the establishment of such a state if it produces a peaceful settlement? Is it in the US interest to view the middle East through the prism of Tel Aviv? Is it in the US interest to appear so closely identified with Israel? Is it a liability for the US to appear to be fair-minded?

It would be foolish to forecast whether the Bush Administration will be disposed to conduct some such appraisal, and if it is, whether it will be disposed to follow up on its findings and invest the sustained high-level effort and the enormous political capital needed to bring matters to fruition.

It can only be hoped that the counsels of common sense and self-interest will prevail and that sooner rather than later there will be some echo in the policy towards Palestinians of this great and unparalleled republic, of the self-evident truths that men are created equal, that they are endowed by their creator with certain inalienable rights and that among these are life, liberty and the pursuit of happiness.

APPENDIX

Notes on Israeli and Palestinian Casualties

There are no systematic surveys either of the Israeli military and civilian death toll since the rise of the PLO in the mid sixties, or of the number of Palestinian (and Lebanese) combatants and civilians killed by Israel during the same period. Enough data, however, exist on which to base the ratios of Israeli to Palestinian casualties given in the preceding discussion.

1 Israeli Civilian Dead

1.1 Baruch Leshem, an Israeli journalist and former police official, concluded after personally examining the annual Israeli police records for the seventeen years 1965–81 that the total number of Israeli civilians killed by the PLO during these years in Israel and the Occupied Territories was 282. His findings were published in the Hebrew-language weekly *Anashim* in July 1982.[20]

1.2 Meron Benvenisti and his co-authors of the *West Bank Handbook* give the total number of Israeli civilians killed by the

PLO in Israel and the Occupied Territories during the eighteen years 1968–85 as 383.[21]

1.3 I have estimated the total number of Israeli civilians killed by the PLO or by Palestinians in Israel and the Occupied Territories in the two years 1986 and 1987 at 32. This estimate is the result of the addition of the numbers of Israeli civilian dead reported by the *New York Times*, the *Washington Post* or the *Boston Globe* to have been declared by Israel during these two years.

Add the 10 Israeli civilians (including some armed settlers) killed by Palestinians since the beginning of the intifada (*New York Times*, 9 December 1988), and the total number of the Israeli civilian dead in the three years 1986–8 is 42. If we take the higher Israeli figure given by Benvenisti and his co-authors as accurate, and add to it 11 Israeli civilians given by Leshem as having been killed in the three years 1965–67 (*not* covered by Benvenisti and his co-authors), the total of Israeli civilians who died at the hands of the PLO and Palestinians for the years 1965–88 is 436.

2 Israeli Military Dead

2.1 In the same issue of *Anashim* quoted above, the weekly reports that it asked the Israeli Ministry of Defence for figures of the Israeli military killed by the PLO during the seventeen years 1965–81. An Israeli Defence Forces (IDF) spokesman, Danny Wiener, supplied *Anashim* with the figure of 285.

We also have official Israeli statistics for four years of this period which seem to tally with Wiener's data. The IDF spokesman revealed that 156 Israeli soldiers were killed from the end of the June 1967 War until September 1970 as a result of 'incidents along the Jordan border, mostly carried out by the terrorists'.[22]

2.2 In his book *Operation Peace for Galilee*, written with the cooperation of the IDF, with whom he had close relations, Richard A. Gabriel gives the number of Israeli military killed by the PLO during the 1982 invasion of Lebanon as 113, of whom 25 were killed in South Lebanon and 88 in the siege of Beirut.[23]

2.3 Using the same sources and criteria that I used in calculating the Israeli civilian dead in 1.3 above, I estimate the

Israeli military killed by the PLO or Palestinians in Israel, the Occupied Territories and outside them in the six years 1983–8 at 34. Add this to the totals given by Wiener and Gabriel, and the total of Israeli military killed by PLO or Palestinians from 1965 to 1988 is 432.

3   *The Palestinian (and Lebanese) Civilian Dead*

If we take the Palestinian and Lebanese civilians killed by Israel *only* since the October 1973 War the following picture emerges:

3.1   from the October 1973 War until the first Israeli invasion of Lebanon in March 1978, the number of Palestinian and Lebanese civilians killed by Israel in Lebanon alone is estimated at 2000.[24]

3.2   The Palestinian and Lebanese civilians killed by Israel *during* its 1978 invasion of Lebanon were estimated at 'up to several thousand' by the *New York Times* (editorial, 17 April 1978) and at more than 2000 by *Time* (3 April 1978).

The extent of the devastation caused to the civilian population by Israel may be gauged from a UN report which put the number of 'completely destroyed' houses in South Lebanon at 2500 and those partly destroyed at 5200.[25]

3.3   Between March 1978 and the second invasion of Lebanon in June 1982, Israel greatly escalated its air, sea and land strikes against Palestinian targets in the country. Following one massive three-minute air raid on 17 July 1981 against PLO administrative offices in a densely populated quarter of Beirut, the death toll had risen by 21 July 1981 to 300 civilians in addition to 800 wounded (*New York Times* and *Boston Globe*, 18 July and 21 July 1981).

3.4   The numbers of Palestinian and Lebanese civilians killed by Israel reached unprecedented levels *during* the 1982 invasion. For these statistics, we have two authoritative Lebanese sources: (1) a field survey carried out by the Arabic daily, *al-Nahar*, whose findings were published on 1 September 1982; and (2) the report compiled for the Lebanese government by a special task force of security personnel organized for this purpose.[26]

Al-Nahar, independent and Christian-owned, ranks as perhaps the most credible newspaper in the Arab world. Its survey was based 'on the records of hospitals, clinics, the Civil Defence Agency and first aid stations, as well as on the statistics compiled by the Lebanese security services'. The paper considered its figures to be on the conservative side because

> scores of the dead could not be transported to mortuaries and were buried in collective graves, while the bodies of many others were shattered into so many fragments that the remains could not be collected together. In some cases, bodies were cremated on the spot for health reasons, while in other cases the victims were burned to ashes in buildings shelled with incendiaries by the Israelis.

The Security Services' report was compiled by selected members of 'the Beirut police, the national police, the internal security forces and Military Intelligence'. Its tallies were the result of 'cross-checking reports from municipal authorities, hospitals, local police stations and *mukhtars* – local officials who report such things as deaths and inheritances'.

It is worthy of note that the statistics of both surveys were compiled under the aegis of a central Lebanese government favourably disposed towards Israel and cool if not hostile to the Palestinians and the PLO. The organizers of both surveys had little incentive to pander to the PLO or provoke the Israelis, if only because of the massive Israeli military presence in the country.

Al-Nahar's statistics are of Arabs (Lebanese, Syrian, Palestinian, military or civilian) killed by Israel during the period between 4 June 1982 and the end of August 1982. They do not include Israeli casualties. The statistics are divided by *region* as follows: (1) Tyre: 2195; (2) Sidon: 5376; (3) Beirut's southern outlying suburbs: 933; (4) the Shouf mountains to the western Beq'aa: 3806; (5) Beirut: 5515. The total is 17,825 dead.

One way of calculating the number of Syrian and PLO combatants in this total is to use the IDF to PLO, and IDF to Syrian 'kill-ratios' formulated by Richard A. Gabriel in the book cited above. On the basis of 'casualty lists released by the IDF, corollated [*sic*] with the days and places on which battles were fought', Gabriel reached the conclusion that the IDF kill-ratio against the Syrians was 1:4 in favour of the IDF, 'which is to say that for every Israeli soldier killed, at least four Syrian soldiers died'. The IDF kill-ratio against the PLO was better still at 1:6.5, 'which is to say that for every Israeli soldier, 6.5 PLO died'

(p. 182). Gabriel also informs us that according to his research, the IDF lost 255 dead fighting the Syrian army and 113 fighting the PLO (p. 182).

Multiplying the numbers of Israeli dead respectively by the two kill-ratios gives us about 1020 Syrian military killed and 734 PLO combatants dead, or a total of 1754 Syrian and PLO combatants killed. If we subtract this from the *al-Nahar* total of 17,825 (which Gabriel strongly but implausibly disputes), we get a total of 16,071 Lebanese and Palestinian civilian dead.

Al-Nahar distinguishes the *Lebanese* civilian dead in all the four regions covered by its survey *outside* Beirut. The figures are: (1) Tyre: 470; (2) Sidon: 1239; (3) Beirut's outlying southern suburbs: 346; (4) the Shouf to the West Beq'aa: 458. This makes a total of 2513 Lebanese civilian dead *outside* Beirut for the period from 4 June to the end of August 1982.

Considering that the total for all the dead of *all* Arab nationalities *outside* Beirut according to *al-Nahar* is 12,310 (17,825 − 5515 = 12,310) the percentage of this total made up by Lebanese civilians dead outside Beirut (2513) is 20.4 per cent. Apply the same percentage to the total of all the dead of *all* Arab nationalities *inside* Beirut (20.4 per cent of 5515), and the result is 1125 Lebanese civilians dead inside Beirut. Add this to the Lebanese civilian dead outside Beirut (1125 + 2513 = 3638) and subtract this total from 16,071 (the grand total of Lebanese and Palestinian civilian dead in the five regions covered by the *al-Nahar* survey) and the result is 12,433 Palestinian civilians dead in the five regions in the period between 4 June 1982 and the end of August 1982.

The Security Services' report re-confirms the figure of 12,310 Arab war dead in the four regions outside Beirut. But it adds 1200 bodies of war dead that were found after early September in mass graves for victims of Israeli bombardments dug in Beirut by the PLO. This would raise the *al-Nahar* total of dead inside Beirut to 6715 (5515 + 1200) and the overall *al-Nahar* total for the five regions from 17,825 to 19,025. The report does *not* include in this new total the Palestinian civilian victims of the 16–18 September 1982 massacre (conservatively put at more than 1000) at the Sabra and Shatila refugee camps perpetrated by the Phalangists in the presence of IDF forces surrounding the camps.

The report further states that 84 per cent of the 6715 dead in

Beirut were civilian and that one-third of these were 'younger than 15 and a quarter over the age of 50'.

3.4   Since 1982, and particularly since 1983, the Israeli army has been engaged in fighting against Lebanese Shi'ite resistance forces, as distinct from the PLO. I have, therefore, restricted my tally of casualties from 1983 to 1988 to Palestinian civilians and military personnel killed by Israel.

Using the same sources and criteria I used in 1.3 and 2.3 above to calculate the Israeli civilian and military dead for the period 1983 to 1988, I estimate the number of Palestinian civilians killed in refugee camps in Lebanon during this period as a result of Israeli attacks at about 382.

Add to this statistic some 390 Palestinian civilians killed by Israelis in the Occupied Territories from the beginning of the intifada until 9 December 1988, and the result is a total of 772 Palestinian civilian dead inside and outside the Occupied Territories.

3.5   The total of Palestinians killed according to the above estimates is over 15,000. This total is reached even if we (1) exclude any Palestinian civilians killed between 1965 and 1973, and (2) consider only 50 per cent of the 2000 Lebanese and Palestinian civilians killed between 1973 and 1978 to be Palestinian civilians; (3) consider only 50 per cent of over 2000 Lebanese and Palestinian civilians killed in the 1978 invasion of Lebanon to be Palestinian civilians; (4) consider only the victims of one single air raid (that of 17 July 1981) between March 1978 and June 1982, and estimate Palestinian civilian dead in this air raid to have been only 150 (see 3.3 above); (5) take only the lower figure of 12,433 Palestinian civilian dead based on the *al-Nahar* survey and exclude the higher figure of the Lebanese Security Services report cited above; (6) exclude the Sabra and Shatila victims; and (7) assume that none of the wounded civilians died of their wounds (*al-Nahar* gives the figure of 30,103 Arab wounded only for the period 4 June 1982 to the end of August 1982). If we make all these exclusions and assumptions, the result is a fairly conservative statistic of 15,355 Palestinian civilians killed in the period 1973–88 (i.e., 2000 Palestinian civilians between 1973 and 1978; 150 from 1978–82; 12,433 from the *al-Nahar* statistics; and 772 Palestinians killed between 1983 and 1988, including the casualties of the intifada).

4 *Palestinian Combatant Deaths*

If we accept Gabriel's estimate that the IDF killed 6.5 members
of the PLO for every Israeli soldier killed by the PLO, and apply
it to the number of IDF personnel killed by the PLO in the
period 1965–88 (a number which we have estimated at 432), we
obtain a total of 2824 as the approximate number of PLO
combatants killed by the Israelis during this period. This averages
out at 100 per annum.

Such an annual average does not seem implausible in the light
of specific data released by the IDF for a twenty-month period of
very intensive operations against the PLO in Lebanon between
5 June 1979 and February 1981. During this period, 52 land, sea
and air operations were carried out against PLO targets in
Lebanon, resulting in 160–180 PLO combatants killed.[27]

5 *Summary*

The 1:1 ratio of military to civilian dead in Israeli victims of PLO
violence is borne out by the totals estimated in sections 1 and 2
above.

If the total Israeli civilian dead are about 436 (see section 1
above) and an incomplete list of Palestinian civilian dead is about
15,000 (see 3.5 above), the 1:30 ratio is borne out.

If the total of Palestinian combatants dead is about 2824 and
the total of Palestinian civilians dead (in an incomplete
computation) is about 15,000, a ratio of at least 1:5 of Palestinian
combatant to civilian dead is borne out.

Notes

1 Henry Kissinger, *Years of Upheaval* (Boston: Little, Brown and
   Company, 1982), pp. 626ff. See also David Ignatius, 'P.L.O.
   Operative, Slain Reputedly by Israelis, Had Been Helping U.S.',
   Washington Post, 23 January, 1979.
2 The statement that these are the first instances of the use of the
   different tactics is based upon years of historical research that I have
   conducted into the Mandate period using hundreds of primary and
   secondary sources.

3 United Kingdom, *Report of His Majesty's Government in the United Kingdom of Great Britain and Northern Ireland to the Council of the League of Nations on the Administration of Palestine and Trans-Jordan for the Year 1937* (Colonial 146). The report was published in London by His Majesty's Stationery Office in 1938. The reference is to p. 6.

4 Commenting on this 'new tactic' and 'great surprise', the official Hebrew history of the Haganah, *Sefer Toldot Ha Haganah* (Tel Aviv: Zionist Library and Marakot, 1954–1972) has this to say:

> The new tactic involved placing a delayed-action mine in crowded Arab meeting places. This tactic was the fruit of the planning of a number of young ETZEL [i.e., Irgun] leaders. The device would be hidden in a kerosene container, a milk can or a large vegetable basket. It would be filled with bits of scrap metal and screws and explosives. A timing mechanism would set off the electrically-operated detonator. (Chapter 43, p. 812)

5 The incident caused the death of 252 Jewish illegal immigrants (the ship carried 1700 Jewish immigrants) and British police personnel, according to the British Mandatory Government's publication *A Survey of Palestine* (Jerusalem: Government Printer, 1946), Vol. I, p. 61. For the circumstances, the rationale, and the explanation of the 'miscalculation' in overestimating the ability of the ship to withstand the explosion, see the account by one of the perpetrators, Munya M. Mardor, *Strictly Illegal* (London, 1957), pp. 56ff.

6 The British politician in question was Lord Walter Moyne, British Resident Minister in the Middle East. For Prime Minister Yitzhak Shamir's direct involvement in Moyne's assassination and for his general 'philosophy' of assassination, see Nicholas Bethel, *The Palestine Triangle* (London: André Deutsch, 1979), p. 187 and pp. 277ff.; and Dan Kurzman, *Genesis 1948* (London: Valentine, Mitchell and Co., 1972), pp. 555ff.

7 See R. D. Wilson, *Cordon and Search* (Aldershot: Gale and Polden, 1949), p. 55. Wilson, the official historian of the Sixth Airborne Division in Palestine, describes the incident as 'a new development in lawlessness'. The individuals kidnapped were five British officers. See also *Supplementary Memorandum by the Government of Palestine* (Jerusalem: Government Printer, 1947), p. 12.

8 This is the notorious King David Hotel incident described in detail in Thurston Clarke's *By Blood and Fire* (London: Hutchinson, 1981). In the blurb for the book, Dominique Lapierre (co-author of *Oh Jerusalem*) describes the event as 'the first massive terrorist political action of modern history'. See also R. D. Wilson, *op. cit.*, pp. 63ff.

9   Of the 91 dead, there were

> [twenty-one] first-rank government officials, 13 soldiers, three
> policemen, and five members of the public. The remaining 49 were
> second-rank clerks, typists and messengers, junior members of the
> Secretariat, employees of the hotel and canteen workers. By
> nationality there were two Armenians killed, one Russian, a Greek,
> an Egyptian, 28 Britons, 41 Arabs, and 17 Jews. (Thurston Clark,
> *op. cit.*, p. 294)

The mastermind behind the attack was Menachem Begin, the future
Prime Minister of Israel.

10   Nicholas Bethel, *op. cit.*, p. 289.

11   R. D. Wilson, *op. cit.*, p. 259. This was probably the first use
anywhere of this device. On this occasion, two were killed and 28
injured.

12   The victims were a British army major and three British non-
commissioned officers. See *Supplementary Memorandum, op. cit.*,
p. 24; R. D. Wilson, *op. cit.*, p. 87; Nicholas Bethel, *op. cit.*,
p. 291.

13   The first batch of eight letter-bombs arrived in London on 4 June
1947. The bomb was made of 'powdered gelignite placed between
two pieces of cardboard with a pencil battery to fire a detonator'.
One of the letter-bombs was addressed to Sir Stafford Cripps,
Minister at the Board of Trade, and another to Mr John Strachey,
Minister of Food. All were intercepted by Scotland Yard, whose
investigations indicated that this was 'another attempt by Jewish
terrorists to intimidate responsible people in this country' (*The
Times*, 5 June 1947, p. 4). Three more letter-bombs were intercepted on 5 June. One of these was addressed to Mr Ernest Bevin,
Foreign Secretary, another to Mr Anthony Eden, former Foreign
Secretary, and the third (incorrectly addressed) to Mr Arthur
Greenwood, Minister Without Portfolio (*The Times*, 6 June 1947,
p. 4). On 6 June, nine more letter-bombs were intercepted. The
contents of each were said to be capable of 'making a hole in a steel
plate' (*The Times*, 7 June 1947). On 9 June, two Jews were arrested
by the Belgian police trying to smuggle six letter-bombs addressed
to prominent people in Britain (*The Times*, 10 June 1947). The man
who made these bombs was Yaacov Eliav, who was the bomb
expert of the Stern Gang, as he himself acknowledged to the *Sunday
Times* of London (24 September 1972). The leadership of the Stern
Gang was vested in a triumvirate, one of whom was Yitzhak
Shamir, the present Prime Minister of Israel.

14   The victims were two British NCOs, Martin and Paice, kidnapped
on 12 July 1947. On 31 July, they were found 'hanging from a

eucalyptus tree. . . . The area for some distance round was mined and as one of the bodies was cut down, it exploded, having been booby-trapped. In this explosion, a British officer was severely wounded' (R. D. Wilson, *op. cit.*, p. 132). Menachem Begin, as leader of the Irgun, gave the order to hang the two NCOs. For his defence of his action, see Bethel, *op. cit.*, p. 338.

15 The parcel-bomb in question was addressed to a Brigadier in Intelligence at the War Office, according to the *Sunday Times* of London (24 September 1972). It exploded in a London district post office at Howick Place, Victoria Street, injuring two postmen (*The Times*, 4 September 1947, p. 6). According to the *Sunday Times* (24 September 1972), 'The British Intelligence had no doubt its origin was Palestinian [i.e. from Palestine]. For several months earlier there had been persistent reports from field intelligence that the Irgun or Stern were planning a bombing campaign in Britain.' This incident is probably the first instance anywhere of the use of the tactic for political purposes. Earlier in this century an unbalanced Swede, Martin Eckenberg, who was also a gifted chemist, is supposed to have invented the device, though he used it to settle personal accounts with Swedish businessmen who incurred his displeasure. Eckenberg died in a London prison in 1910. On 3 May 1948, a parcel-bomb addressed to Roy Farran in Britain was opened by Rex Farran, his twenty-five-year-old younger student brother. Rex Farran's stomach was torn to pieces and he died. Roy had been a member of an anti-terrorist British army squad in Palestine. The Stern Gang and its triumvirate leadership, one of whom was Yitzhak Shamir, was responsible for the incident (Bethel, *op. cit.*, p. 348; *Sunday Times*, 24 September 1972).

16 Dan Kurzman, *Genesis 1948, The First Arab–Israeli War*, (New York: World Publishing Company, 1970), pp. 555–57.

17 For detailed estimates, see the Appendix.

18 See Walid Khalidi, 'Thinking the Unthinkable: A Sovereign Palestinian State', *Foreign Affairs*, Vol. 56, No. 4 (July 1978), pp. 695–713; 'Regio-Politics: Toward a U.S. Policy on the Palestine Problem', *Foreign Affairs*, Vol. 59, No. 5 (July 1981), pp. 1050–63; and 'Toward Peace in the Holy Land,' *Foreign Affairs*, Vol. 66, No. 4 (Spring 1988), pp. 771–89. (All this volume, pp. 82–104, 105–20, 121–40.)

19 The idea that two or three lightly armed brigades, which is what the strength of the Palestinian state's army is likely to be, would constitute a military or security threat to Israel is ludicrous. 'The military preponderance of Israel in relation to the Palestinians is a factor of a thousand to one', according to a former Israeli Foreign

Minister, Abba Eban. (Abba Eban, 'The Threats are from Within', *Jerusalem Post* international edition, 3 December 1988, p. 8.) According to the latest estimates, Israel fields an active army of 141,000 and has a reserve army of 504,000. In addition to 3850 main battle tanks and 400 reconnaissance tanks, it has 10,300 armoured personnel carriers, 1361 towed and self-propelled artillery pieces, 677 combat-ready aircraft, 200 helicopters, 3 submarines, and 59 patrol and coastal combatant naval craft, not to mention a whole spectrum of missiles, air defence, surveillance and anti-tank systems. There are, moreover, 'recent unconfirmed reports' that 'up to 100 nuclear warheads have been produced and that these may include some enhanced radiation (neutron) weapons'. (International Institute for Strategic Studies, *The Military Balance, 1988–89*, London, 1988, p. 103.)

20 *Anashim*, 12–18 July 1982, p. 8. See also B. Michael's Hebrew article, 'A Note on Numbers and Wars', in *Haaretz Supplement*, 16 July 1982, p. 15.
21 *The West Bank Handbook* (Jerusalem: Jerusalem Post, 1986), p. 221.
22 'I.D.F. Spokesman', *Basic Facts: The I.D.F. and the Security of Israel* (Tel Aviv: Israel Defence Forces, April 1982), p. 109.
23 Richard Gabriel, *Operation Peace for Galilee* (New York: Hill and Wang, 1984), p. 182.
24 *Time*, 27 March 1978, p. 26.
25 Report of the UN High Commission for Refugees, 'Affected Villages in South Lebanon Visited by U.N. High Commissioner for Refugees, May 19, 1978'.
26 *Washington Post*, 2 December 1982, p. A24.
27 'I.D.F. Spokesman', *The Lebanon Border* (Tel Aviv: Israel Defence Forces, December 1981), pp. 107 ff.

CHAPTER 6

The Half-Empty Glass of
Middle East Peace*

Looking around the Middle East and the world scene, one is struck by an extraordinary constellation of circumstances that seem conducive to a just and durable solution of the Palestine problem and its derivative, the Arab–Israeli conflict.

Globally, there is the steady convergence between the two superpowers on the resolution of regional conflicts; the virtual end of the cold war; the growing Soviet flirtation with Tel Aviv accompanied by the relative cooling of relations with Damascus; and the mounting universal concern, in spite of the distractions of the collapse of Eastern European communism, for the tribulations of the Palestinians under prolonged occupation and at Israeli brutality in the suppression of the intifada.

Regionally, the most remarkable development has been the steady crystallization, since the early 1970s, by the mainstream PLO leadership of a pragmatic solution of the Palestinian problem accommodating the concepts both of Israeli statehood and Palestinian sovereignty – a crystallization that found its culmination in the declarations of the PNC held in Algiers in November 1988 and later in the successive statements of Arafat.

A second, no less remarkable, regional development was the parallel evolution of a collective pragmatic interstate Arab posture reflecting and deriving from this Palestinian process. This Arab posture has been successively expressed in the Fahd Plan in 1981, the Fez Summit in 1982, and the Casablanca Summit in

* Essay first published in the *Journal of Palestine Studies*, 19, 3 (Spring 1990).

1989. At the Fez Summit in 1982, the Arab heads of state, for the first time since 1947, collectively endorsed the concept of guaranteed peaceful relations with *all* states in the Middle East. At the Casablanca Summit in 1989, the Arab heads of state, for the first time since 1947, collectively endorsed the concept of partition (a two-state solution) and for the first time since 1967, collectively endorsed UN Security Council Resolution 242.

Also, in spite of (or is it because of?) the continuing confrontation between Saddam Hussein and Hafez al-Assad, and despite Iraq's emergence from the war with Iran with the military upper hand, Baghdad has been a staunch supporter of Arafat's moderate pragmatic policy. This has removed the outbidding competition over the Palestine problem in Iraqi–Syrian relations (at least from the Iraqi end) which in the past has been a serious obstacle to the development of a collective pragmatic inter-Arab approach.

Last but not least, the Egyptian–Israeli peace treaty has survived the Israeli raids on Iraq (1981) and Tunis (1985), the annexation of the Golan (1981), the carnage of Lebanon (1982), and the smashing of countless bones in the Occupied Territories since December 1987. Not only has the peace treaty survived, but Egypt has been readmitted to the Arab League, is a founding member of the recently formed quadripartite Arab Cooperation Council, and has resumed diplomatic relations with Syria.

In Israel, the military balance of power with its Arab neighbours stands more in its favour today than at any other time since its establishment. Militarily, Egypt, the largest Arab power, is neutralized. Iraq, the second most powerful Arab country, is preoccupied with demobilization and post-war reconstruction, with its confrontation with Syria, and with its need to face eastwards to deter possible Iranian revanchism. Syria is militarily isolated from Cairo and Baghdad, deeply mired in Lebanon, and unable to persuade Moscow to endorse its armament demands beyond a level of barely credible deterrence. Jordan, small as its armed forces are, has severed all administrative and legal links with the West Bank. In addition to all this, there is the steady evolution of Israel's nuclear, thermonuclear, neutron, chemical, biological, satellite, warhead, and delivery capabilities.

In the United States, literacy in foreign affairs has returned to the White House after an eight-year sabbatical, and the new administration has from the outset had its dirty work done for it (whatever former Secretary Shultz's motives may have been) in the opening of the US–PLO dialogue.

And yet, surveying this extraordinary constellation of propitious circumstances, one is nevertheless driven to conclude that the glass of Middle East peace is half-*empty*.

Whence this pessimism? It derives from two sources: a deeply pessimistic assessment of the mind-set of the incumbent Israeli leadership, and the sanction given by Washington to the Israeli government's twenty-point initiative of 14 May – henceforth the Shamir Plan.[1]

The Shamir Plan

Shamir's plan, formalized by the Shamir government, envisions five sequential stages:

Stage I. 'First and foremost, dialogue and basic agreement by the Palestinian Arab inhabitants of Judea and Samaria and the Gaza district [*sic*][2] . . . on the principles constituting the initiative.' The dialogue is to take place with Israel. Jordan and Egypt may take part if they so wish.

Stage II. Once the inhabitants agree to these principles, 'immediately afterwards' would begin 'preparations and implementation of the election process'. During this stage 'there shall be a calming of the violence in Judea, Samaria and the Gaza district.'

Stage III. An election held 'in an atmosphere devoid of violence, threats, and terror', takes place for 'a representation' of these inhabitants.

Stage IV. Immediately afterwards this representation will conduct negotiations for a five-year transitional period of 'self-rule'. This representation will be 'the self-governing authority' during the five-year transitional period (the interim agreement).

Stage V. Three years after the start of the transitional period, negotiations will begin between Israel and Jordan, with the participation of the elected Palestinian representation, on the permanent solution. The transitional period will last until the signing of a peace treaty with Jordan. Only at this last stage will issues of substance pertaining to the permanent solution be raised.

The main points to note in all this are fairly obvious.

(a) The Palestinian negotiating side is to come exclusively from the Occupied Territories.

(b) The principal Arab protagonist at the crucial stage V is Jordan – the main thrust of the plan being a bilateral treaty between it and Israel.

(c) The duration of stages I–IV is not specified. The transitional period, although ostensibly limited to five years, automatically becomes open-ended since its duration is linked to the signature of the treaty with Jordan and since it is not explicitly stated that such signature must occur *within* or at the end of the transitional period.

(d) The intifada will have to end before elections.

(e) The sequence of stages has to be inaugurated 'first and foremost' by Palestinian 'basic agreement on . . . the principles constituting the initiative'.

Further light is thrown on these principles in three introductory sections of the plan, carrying, respectively, the titles 'General', 'Basic Premises', and 'Subjects to be dealt with in the peace process'.

The first section ('General') spells out the following concurrent objectives:

- termination of the state of war with the Arab states;
- 'a solution for Judea, Samaria, and Gaza district';
- peace with Jordan;
- resolution of the 'problem of the residents of the refugee camps' in Judea, Samaria, and the Gaza district.

The second section ('Basic Premisses') spells out the assumptions on which the initiative is based, as follows:

- direct negotiations on the basis of Camp David;
- opposition to 'an additional [*sic*] Palestinian state in the Gaza district and the area between Israel and Jordan';
- refusal to negotiate with the PLO;
- 'no change in the status of Judea, Samaria, and the Gaza district other than in accordance with the basic guidelines of the government.'

Under the third section ('Subjects to be dealt with in the peace process') four subjects are enumerated:

- strengthening and extending the peace with Egypt on the basis of Camp David;
- ending the state of war between the Arab states and Israel;
- resolving the 'problem of the residents of the refugee camps' in Judea, Samaria, and the Gaza district;
- holding the elections.

What are the 'basic guidelines of the government' referred to under 'Basic Premises' and in the context of which the principle of no change in the status of the Occupied Territories is mentioned? These include provisions for a coalition government balanced between its two major partners in such a way as to accord each partner veto power over policy decisions. Thus, in the absence of agreement by these partners on a substantive change in the status of the Occupied Territories (a most unlikely eventuality), current policies are bound to be maintained.

Two additional issues, while not specifically addressed in the plan, loom large in this regard: settlement, and East Jerusalem. The basic guidelines call for the establishment of eight settlements in the government's first year (1989), with each additional settlement after that requiring the approval of the Treasury (i.e., of the Labour Alignment, whose leader, Shimon Peres, is Finance Minister). Elaborating on this, Shamir had this to say in his speech explaining his plan to the Likud Central Committee on 5 July 1989: 'The government's basic guidelines state that the existence and development of the settlements established by the various Israeli governments will be guaranteed. . . . there are differences of opinion on this matter between us and our friends in the US. Yet the settlement activity will continue.'[3]

Concerning East Jerusalem, the position of the Israeli government is well known: united Jerusalem is the eternal capital of Israel, one indivisible city under perpetual Israeli sovereignty. This militates against the participation in the envisaged elections of the Palestinian inhabitants of East Jerusalem who constitute the largest and most sophisticated Palestinian urban concentration in the Occupied Territories. In his 5 July speech, Shamir took pains to point out that the policy on united Jerusalem precluded the participation of the Palestinians of East Jerusalem in the elections, and that the policy was an integral part of the basic guidelines of the government.

The above items in combination constitute the principles of the Shamir Plan. It is these principles that the Palestinians must 'first and foremost' agree to at the outset of stage I before the other four stages can follow. Further light may be thrown on Shamir's attitude from the fact that all these principles were consolidated in the Likud platform, which Shamir himself read out at the meeting of the Likud Central Committee on 5 July 1989. This platform further states that 'Likud representatives are obliged to work in the Cabinet and the Knesset according to this platform'. On ending the intifada as a precondition of implementing his plan, Shamir stated on 5 July: 'The implementation of the initiative . . . will never materialize as long as violence continues.'

Three references are made in the plan to the Camp David Accords and one to Security Council resolutions 242 and 338. Shamir, of course, had opposed Camp David when it was formulated, but here is his latest interpretation in this country of the Accords in an interview with Leslie Stahl on 'Face the Nation', 19 November 1989:

Shamir: We have some differences of view with the United States . . . The Americans believe that the end solution has to be something in the spirit of land for peace.
Stahl: Camp David.
Shamir: It's not Camp David.
Stahl: Land for peace?
Shamir: Excuse me, it's not Camp David.
Stahl: Land for peace?
Shamir: In our opinion, we have to resolve the conflict, but the territories are part of our national heritage.

On this point, Shamir stated in his speech to the Likud Central Committee: 'I cannot conceive any territorial component in the permanent solution which may, at the end of the process, be acceptable to us and our neighbours.'

As to Resolution 242, Shamir's interpretation consistently has been that it is inapplicable to negotiations with Jordan because it has been exhausted by the withdrawal from Sinai. To be sure, at

the start of negotiations for a permanent solution the Palestinians
'shall be entitled to present for discussion all subjects'. On the
other hand, at the Central Committee meeting Shamir declared:
'The IDF and the security forces will be in the area. They will
constitute the guarantees that the negotiations on the implementation of the initiative will be conducted exclusively along the
path acceptable to us.'

What is extraordinary in all this is that Shamir's declared
objective in the plan is to lasso Jordan into signing a peace treaty
based on what is in essence the Jordanian Option Resurrected à
la Likud. Except that in the Labour prototype, an Israeli–Jordanian
condominium of sorts was to be instituted in selected areas of the
Occupied Territories (separated from one another by settlement
blocs and other Israeli-controlled areas), thus giving Jordanian
'presence' a territorial bouquet.

Does Shamir really expect Jordan to agree to his version when
it rejected Labour's? He could be bluffing. But he may also be
relying on the implicit threat contained in one of the 'Basic
Premisses' (now incidentally endorsed by Labour), namely
Israel's opposition to 'an additional [sic] Palestinian state in the
Gaza district and the area between Israel and Jordan'.

To be sure, the Labour Alignment and Likud do not see eye-
to-eye on all the details of a desirable settlement. Labour most
probably still aspires to revive its own version of the Jordanian
option. The Alignment is almost certainly responsible for the
references to Security Council resolution 242 in the Shamir Plan.
It is more chary of alienating world opinion and particularly the
US administration. It is less finicky with regard to the status of
the Palestinian delegates. Nevertheless, Labour is the joint
sponsor of the Shamir Plan which, therefore, represents the least
common denominator between the two components of the
current Israeli government.

The Likud Mind-Set

What we have here is a mind-set. For Shamir, there are Arabs in
what he calls Judea, Samaria, and the Gaza 'district'. There is no
Palestinian people.

For Shamir, there are *residents in the refugee camps* in what he calls Judea, Samaria, and the Gaza district. He seems loath even to bestow upon them the honorific of 'refugee'. And, of course, he has no cognizance of the 1,411,000 registered Palestinian refugees in the twenty-three refugee camps of Lebanon, Syria, and Jordan[4] – not to mention the unregistered ones.

For Shamir, there is no Palestinian territory. The West Bank and Gaza Strip, 92 per cent of whose people are Palestinians, for him is not Palestinian territory. For Shamir, there was no Palestine, although when he first set foot in it in 1935, only 5 per cent of it, as he well knows, was Jewish-owned while the Jews constituted less than one-third of the population, most of whom, like himself, were recent immigrants. For Shamir (and now apparently the Labour Alignment, given its endorsement of the plan) the only Palestinian territory that exists is east of the Jordan.

For Shamir, there is no Palestinian Diaspora. If there is a Diaspora, it is of no interest to him. For Shamir, there is no connection historically, logically, or in the chain of human causation between the establishment of Israel and the Palestinian Diaspora. Indeed, for Shamir there is no Palestinian problem.

In a speech on 5 October 1981, in New York, he said:

> It is important to understand the 'Jordan is Palestine' aspect and that the conflict is not and never was between Israel and a stateless people. . . . If it [the conflict] is perceived in this light, you have on the one hand a Palestinian–Jordanian Arab state and Israel on the other. Then the problem is reduced to a territorial conflict between these two states.

Et voilà!

For Shamir, as he told the Likud Central Committee, 'the terrorist organizations have not budged one inch from their despicable path'. For him, it mattered not at all that Arafat turned the Palestinian National Charter on its head, that he accepted 242 with 'no trimmings' at the behest of the State Department. Or that he accepted partition (a two-state solution) which no Palestinian leader had ever done since partition was first proposed in 1937. Arafat had caused the Palestine National Council not only to accept partition but to declare partition as a source of legitimacy of the Palestinian state, explicitly mentioning 'the Jewish state' in the same context. He repeated the American catechism concerning Israel's right to exist and Resolution 242 word for word, letter for letter, down to 'renouncing' terrorism with all the implications of the initial 'r' instead of an initial 'd'. But for Shamir, 'the terrorist organizations have not budged an inch from their despicable path'. For Shamir there is no possibility of change in PLO attitudes. For Shamir, even if there were a positive change, it is of no relevance to him. And this is so because the mind-set we are looking at is the manifestation *par excellence* of the solipsism of nationalism. All national movements pass through greater or lesser solipsistic phases. In Shamir, vintage solipsistic Zionism is personified. With such a mind-set it is difficult to conclude that Shamir is in hot pursuit of peace. But by the same token, it is possible to understand why Shamir (to quote John Le Carré in a different context) experiences such 'withdrawal symptoms' at Arafat's 'peace threats'.

This mind-set has very deep moorings in the evolution of Zionism since World War I. One has to dig through three geological layers to get through them. The deepest layer involves the foundation of Revisionist Zionism, in 1925, by Vladimir Jabotinsky. Revisionist Zionism rejected the interpretation of the British Mandate over Palestine given in 1922 by Winston Churchill (no anti-Zionist), then British Colonial Secretary. Churchill had declared the Balfour Declaration to be applicable to Palestine (i.e., Cis-Jordan) but not to Trans-Jordan (i.e., the East Bank of Jordan).

The World Zionist Organization (WZO) under Weizmann accepted this, while Revisionist Zionism under Jabotinsky wanted to revise the Mandate (hence its name) so that Zionism could establish a Jewish majority on both banks of the River Jordan. But the dispute was not at bottom over the territorial extent of the Jewish state. The WZO had its own territorial ambitions east of the Jordan, which it had submitted at the Versailles Congress in 1919. The dispute was a function of a clash between two domineering personalities, Weizmann and Jabotinsky, over tactics and timing and the role of the imperial sponsor, Britain.

The conflict between the WZO and Revisionist Zionism continued to fester and escalate, increasingly acquiring Left/Right ideological dimensions until 1935, when Revisionist Zionism institutionalized itself in a new organization: the New Zionist Organization (NZO).

Thenceforth there were two transnational Zionist organizations: on the one hand, the WZO, and on the other, the NZO. Just as the WZO had its labour federation, the Histadrut, the NZO now established its own labour federation, the National Workers' Organization. Just as the WZO had its underground army/militia, the Haganah, the NZO now created its own militia, Haganah B. The resultant of this split was the virtual evolution of two yishuvs (i.e., Jewish communities) in Palestine: the official pro-WZO yishuv and the dissident pro-NZO yishuv.[5]

The second layer emerges in 1935 when the NZO militia, Haganah B, developed into the Irgun Zvai Leumi (National Military Organization). The Irgun Zvai Leumi, Irgun for short, developed its own strategy for the implementation of the Revisionist territorial goals of the NZO – a strategy best exemplified by the insignia it adopted: a rifle across Palestine and Jordan with the Hebrew words *Raq Kach*: 'Only Thus'.

The Irgun introduced into Palestine the idea of placing electrically detonated mines in marketplaces. In about twenty such incidents in the period September 1937 to July 1939 the Irgun translated its insignia into deed, killing or maiming at least 500 Palestinian civilians.[6] One of its militants was Itzhak Yzernitsky, who arrived in Palestine in 1935 at the age of twenty from what is now Byelorussia. One of his first alleged exploits after joining the Irgun was to blow up a WZO kiosk for the collection of contributions to the Haganah in 1938.[7]

The third layer involves a group which broke away from the Irgun in 1939. Because of the war with Hitler, the Irgun had decided on a truce with Britain for the duration of the war. But one Irgunist group dissented. Its leader was Abraham Stern, also known as 'Yair' (the Illuminator). Stern/Yair summarized his principles in a manifesto issued in 1939 under the Hebrew title 'Ikarei ha Tehiyyah' ('The Principles of the Revival'). It outlined three fundamental doctrines for the new dissident movement 'Lohmei Herut L'Israel' ('Fighter for the Freedom of Israel'), Stern Gang for short. These doctrines were:

- Eretz Israel is the land between the brook of Egypt and the Euphrates, as stated in Genesis 18:15;

- the Third Temple must be rebuilt;
- the Palestinians must be 'transferred', i.e., expelled.[8]

Stern/Yair was killed in 1941 by the British police. He was succeeded by a triumvirate at the centre of which stood Itzhak Yzernitsky, later Yitzhak Shamir.

It is not, however, only a matter of cumulative historical conflict and ideological lineage. The rift between Labour and Revisionist Zionism is also about pride of place on the tablets of history and posterity. Major themes in the still-ongoing Labour–Revisionist polemic concern who in the past did what to whom and who contributed more to the creation of the Jewish state in 1948. In 1933, for example, the Labourite Chaim Arlosoroff, the brilliant head of the Political Department of the Jewish Agency, was gunned down in Jerusalem by Jewish assassins. Labour accused the Revisionists, who of course denied the charge. Fifty years later, in 1982, Menahem Begin, wincing from renewed Labour charges of Revisionist responsibility, formed a commission of inquiry to refute these accusations.

As to the relative contributions of each side to the creation of Israel, who, Likud polemicists still ask, defied the British in the 1940s? (Answer: the Irgun and Stern Gang.) And who joined the British in a 'hunting season' against their compatriots? (Answer: the Haganah, i.e., Labour – the reference being to Haganah collaboration with British security forces in the mid 1940s against members of the Irgun and Stern Gang.) And again, who panicked the British to terminate their Mandate, thus paving the way for the creation of Israel? Each side claims its tactics were responsible. And each side, seemingly oblivious of the official Israeli version of the Palestinian Exodus in 1948 as having been triggered by orders from the Arab leaders, to this day claims its tactics performed the other 'miracle' of emptying 400 villages and a score of towns of their Palestinian inhabitants in 1948.

The conflict runs very deep because so much is at stake: the present and future leadership of Israel, and therefore of the WZO, and therefore of the organized Jewish communities throughout the world. In addition to all this there is for Shamir the question of self-image which haunts every politician. What is his ranking going to be in the Zionist pantheon?

Herzl founded Zionism; Weizmann got the Balfour Declarations; Ben-Gurion established and consolidated Israel; Begin knocked Egypt out of the Arab military coalition. What is left for Shamir to do? Surely not give up the West Bank and Gaza Strip?

'Points' and 'Assumptions'

The Politics of 'Points'

Seldom since mediaeval times, when scholars (Talmudic, Quranic, or Scriptural) burnt the midnight oil piling commentary upon text, has a diplomatic document generated as many exegetical glosses as has Shamir's twenty-point plan: Mubarak's ten points on Shamir's twenty, Arens's comments on Mubarak's points, Baker's five-point framework on the Mubarak and Arens points, the 'assumptions' of Israel, Egypt, and the PLO about Baker's five points, etc.

Actually the idea of holding elections in the Occupied Territories as the *launching pad* for 'a peace process' was, according to Rabin, originally his.[9] It seems also coincidentally to have occurred in a report by a pro-Israeli think tank in Washington authored, among others, by subsequent members of Baker's inner circle of Middle East advisers.[10] The disengagement of Hussein from the Occupied Territories in July 1988 and Arafat's successive peace moves culminating in the opening of the US–PLO dialogue brought the idea to maturity in Rabin's mind. The intifada proffered the opportunity and the decisive incentive. Rabin read in the intifada a profound if non-apparent disillusionment with the PLO. He divined that it augured a shift in the balance between the Palestinians under occupation and those in the Diaspora in favour of the former. Like the wrestler who uses his foe's weight against him, he planned to exploit the potential of divergence in interest and strategy that he expected to occur between the new leaders of the intifada and the Diaspora leadership. This divergence he hoped to harness and channel via his elections idea in the direction of favourable outcomes.

Shamir was alarmed by Secretary Baker's remarks in mid

March 1989 that Israel may have to talk to the PLO, but he was also encouraged by Baker's scepticism about an international conference and his preference for 'a more measured approach'. Sensing an opening and wishing to preempt the PLO, he brought with him to Washington in late March a skeletal proposal to launch a 'political negotiating process' via elections. The US was charmed and promised help. Shamir returned home and by 14 May his proposal had blossomed into his twenty-point plan.

Within a week of the announcement of Shamir's plan, Baker addressed AIPAC on the Arab–Israeli conflict. He considered the Shamir Plan 'an important and positive start', which deserved 'a constructive Palestinian and broader Arab response'. While in no way minimizing the difficulties ahead, he thought it possible to reach agreement 'on the standards of a workable election process'. And it was, therefore, high time 'for serious political dialogue between Israeli officials and Palestinians in the territories [sic]'. In other words, Baker agreed to sponsor a peace process launched via the vestibule of local elections and within the general context of Shamir's plan with all its constraints.

To be sure there were important areas of divergence between Baker's thinking and Shamir's. It was in his speech before AIPAC that Baker called upon Israel 'to lay aside once and for all the unrealistic vision of a greater Israel – forswear annexation. Stop settlement activity – reach out to the Palestinians as neighbors who deserve political rights.' He indicated that the 'successful outcome of the process' would 'in all probability involve [Israeli] territorial withdrawal and the emergence of a new political reality.'

Even before Baker's speech and as early as the first week in March 1989, Washington had publicly made clear that there would be no substantive discussion in the US–PLO dialogue pending US exploration with Israel of the prospects of activating the peace process. It was about this time, and before Shamir took his plunge, that Baker was paradoxically signalling to Israel that it might have to talk to the PLO.

Although Washington did try to sell the election idea directly to the PLO, its preference once it had in principle endorsed the Shamir Plan was clearly to bypass the PLO in favour of Egypt, which had been assigned a role in Shamir's plan specifically for this purpose. From Washington's viewpoint, bypassing the PLO had the merit of gratifying both Egypt and Israel while allowing itself to continue to avoid substantive discussions (e.g., on the permanent settlement) with the PLO. Egypt, trusted ally at peace with Israel, could be counted on to cooperate in keeping the focus of the discussions on the elections themselves. Suddenly the entire process hinged on Egypt's ability to persuade the PLO to give the green light to the Palestinians in the Occupied Territories to enter into dialogue with Israel on the elections proposal, a signal without which the Shamir Plan (itself designed to knock the PLO out) would be stillborn.

In his balancing act against Hafez al-Assad and given his personal predilection for Egypt (he speaks Arabic with an Egyptian accent), Arafat had greatly contributed to the rehabilitation of Egypt in Arab and Palestinian public opinion and had championed Egypt's return to the Arab League. His hope was to use Egypt as a lever against both Israel and the US, but he may not have quite foreseen the extent to which Egypt (which had its own agenda) could also become a conduit for pressures from these two. In any event, the outcome of all this was Mubarak's ten points, first formulated in July and made public in early September.[11]

These were crafted ostensibly as questions addressed by Egypt to Israel to flesh out the details of the Shamir Plan, but they simultaneously outlined Mubarak's own terms for its acceptance.

The input of the US in the formulation of these points, as much by osmosis as more directly, is unquestionable. Also unquestionable is Arafat's input, although the finished product reflects more the converging pincer pressures from Washington and Cairo than his own preferences.

Mubarak's Ten Points

Structurally and substantively, the ten points reflect the thrust of American diplomacy – the holding of the elections as the immediate towering priority. Thus seven of the ten points are connected with the elections: participation of East Jerusalemites (point 1), freedom to campaign (point 2), international supervision (point 3), Israeli commitment to accept the results (point 4), Israeli army withdrawal from polling stations (point 6), no entry to non-resident Israelis on polling day (point 7), a two-month preparatory period (point 8). Of these, point 1 has important political implications since it raises the issue of the status of East Jerusalem.

Otherwise the political hub of the ten points is point 5. This requests Israel's commitment that the elections lead 'not only to an interim phase but also to a final settlement and that all efforts from beginning to end will be based on the principles of solution according to the U.S. conception, namely Security Council resolutions 242 and 338, territory for peace, insuring security of all states in the region, including Israel, and Palestinian political rights.' Saliently absent is all mention of the PLO, the Palestinian state, the international conference and the right of return – massive concessions which delineate the outermost circumference of Arafat's elasticity at this stage. Two more points remain. In point 9 Mubarak seeks prior US and Israeli guarantees 'of all the above [sic] points', i.e., points 1 to 8. Point 10, which as may be expected is printed *below* point 9, deals with the vital issue of 'the halt of settlements'.[12] Question: Is it covered by the US guarantees?

If, when squabbling together as children and having sent one another to Coventry, we needed to communicate before reconciliation, we would ask the wall of the room (a neutral intermediary) to convey our message and vice versa. Since the unveiling of the Shamir Plan, a diplomatic adult (?) version of this ploy has been in operation because of Washington's preference to discuss the Shamir Plan with the PLO via Egypt. Thus the line of communication has run from Washington to Cairo to Tunis to Cairo to Washington to Tel Aviv and then all the way back to Washington. As texts displaced and obfuscated one another in bewildering sequence and the need for secrecy often ordained that the latest authorized version be conveyed only by word of mouth, a Byzantine climate of mutual suspicion was created feeding the inherent paranoia of all concerned. It was against this background that Baker produced his five points, themselves kept secret for a full two months until being released on 6 December.

Meanwhile the focus of deliberation began to shift from Shamir's plan and Mubarak's ten points to a specific suggestion by Mubarak to host in Cairo the opening dialogue between the Palestinians and Israelis proposed in the Shamir Plan. This, of course, immediately raised two issues: 1) Which Palestinians? and 2) What agenda? From the Israeli viewpoint, the answer was plain enough: no PLO involvement whatsoever, direct or indirect, in naming the Palestinian delegation or its membership, and the restriction of the agenda exclusively to the question of the elections on the basis of the plan.

Baker's Five Points

Supporting the idea of a dialogue in Cairo, what Baker tried to do in his five points was to provide 'wriggle room' (a favourite phrase at Foggy Bottom with Baker's Middle East advisers) ostensibly evenhandedly to all the protagonists.[13] Thus, on the issue of naming the delegation (point 2), the US 'understands' that 'Egypt cannot substitute itself for the Palestinians and will consult with Palestinians on all aspects of that dialogue.' The Palestinians referred to remain unspecified, but it hardly requires clairvoyance to identify them. Likewise, the US 'understands' in point 3 that Israel will attend 'only after a satisfactory list of Palestinians' has been drawn up, leaving it room to boycott the dialogue with impunity without quite according it veto rights.

On the agenda issue (point 4), the US 'understands' that Israel will come to the dialogue '*on the basis* of the Israeli government, 14 May, initiative' [i.e., the Shamir Plan] and that the Palestinians will be '*prepared to discuss* elections *and* the negotiating process *in accordance with* Israel's initiative' (emphasis added). The US 'understands *therefore* that the Palestinians would be free to raise issues that relate to their opinions on how to make elections *and* the negotiating process succeed' (emphasis added).

Point 5 comprised an invitation to Egypt and Israel to send their foreign ministers to Washington 'to facilitate this process', i.e., to name the Palestinian delegation on behalf of the Palestinians and agree on an agenda for the Cairo dialogue. The Washington meeting is to launch the Cairo meeting which is to launch the ship of peace.

Baker's five points almost brought down the Israeli government, with Likud critics insisting that the US meet certain conditions to prevent this sellout to the PLO, and Labour dismissing Likud fears and threatening to walk out of the government if 'conditions' were demanded of Washington. By the first week of November, and after casting a shadow on Shamir's planned visit to Washington, the delayed Israeli response came in the form of an acceptance based on six 'assumptions': negotiations only with residents from the territories approved by Israel, no negotiating with the PLO, focus of talks to be only the elections proposal, the US and Egypt to declare their support of Camp David [compare Shamir's view of Camp David above], the US publicly to support Israel's position in the event another party deviated, and one meeting to take place in Cairo whose results would determine whether the talks would continue.

The PLO followed suit with 'assumptions' of its own. As will have been inferred, the PLO had serious misgivings about the direction the peace process was taking. But it was not opposed to elections in the Occupied Territories, nor was it opposed to a dialogue with the Israeli government. Indeed, far from opposing such a dialogue, it was anxious that the Israeli delegation to it be a political and not a technical one, and that a PLO delegation attend. But it could not agree either to a dialogue restricted to discussing the elections alone or to one on the basis of the Shamir Plan. It requested that there be no prior conditions, and that the agenda be open. This would enable each side to raise the issues it wanted, including elections, Mubarak's ten points, and Baker's five points. It could not concede to Israel, or anybody else, the right to name the Palestinian delegation. This was its own prerogative, although it did offer to discuss 'specifications' (not names) of the Palestinian delegates that would be acceptable to all, and it agreed to the US proposal that the 'outside' delegates be *recent* deportees unassociated with 'terrorist' activities. It argued that the US had already accepted the concept of an open agenda in a major policy statement by former Secretary of State Shultz on 16 September 1988[14] and at a tripartite Swedish–American–Egyptian meeting on 16 September 1989 held at the Egyptian Foreign Ministry. At this latter meeting, it was also the PLO's understanding that there was agreement on the PLO's right to name the Palestinian delegation and that the dialogue would be under international sponsorship. The PLO was anxious for this sponsorship because it envisaged the Palestinian–Israeli dialogue as a preparatory step towards convening an international peace conference under UN auspices. This conference was in conformity with Security Council Resolutions 242 and 338, which the US had been urging the PLO to adopt. It would be attended by the five permanent members of the Security Council, whose guarantees for a final peace settlement the PLO was eager to obtain.

These views were transmitted to Washington via Ambassador Pelletreau in Tunis and Cairo. But since, as we have seen, Washington's pretense is that the official dialogue on the peace process is not with the PLO but with Cairo, and since Cairo would attempt to mediate the PLO position to make it acceptable to Washington, it is to be assumed that Cairo conveyed its own version of the PLO position. If this is the case, we do not know how many of the PLO's views Cairo officially adopted. Thus, the US response to Cairo's message was most probably a response to an Egyptian text rather than to that of the PLO. We do know, however, that on 6 December the State Department announced receipt of 'positive' responses from both Israel and Egypt which also included 'certain views and positions' (polite for 'assumptions', itself polite for 'conditions') conveyed by the two countries. This sets the stage for the Washington trilateral meeting.

The US and the Shamir Plan

Overlooking the Mind-Set

If Shamir's mind-set, faithfully reflected in his plan, leaves little room for optimism, one's sense that the glass is half-empty is reinforced by the sanction the plan has won from Washington. The Shamir Plan has in effect become Baker's, despite the divergence of opinion between the two over many of its aspects.

Baker seems to have calculated that a plan proposed by Shamir and endorsed by the Labour Alignment enjoyed unique advantages over any originating from Washington itself or the Labour Alignment alone. Thus, Shamir could always be reminded of his parentage, the pro-Israeli US Congress would be less prone to subvert a plan based on 'free elections', and Washington would have ample opportunity to exert its influence at more than one halting station along the way. Also, the 'measured pace' of the plan meshed in with the tautological philosophy that informs the thinking of Baker's small inner circle of Middle East advisers, namely that diplomacy succeeds only when the time is ripe for it to succeed.

What seems to have been overlooked is the texture of Shamir's mind-set and his ability to frustrate, both on the spot and via Washington's permeability, the potential of progress perceived by Baker's advisers in the very dynamics of an ongoing peace process. Against all evidence Baker seems to think that Shamir's attitude is not a matter of principle but of incertitude regarding Palestinian intentions. In the opening remarks of his AIPAC speech, he not only accepts at face value Shamir's self-designation ('I am a man of principle but I am also a pragmatist'), but seems to assume the two of them were birds of the same feather. According to Baker: 'We understood each other to be pragmatists, guided by principle' – hence the title of Baker's speech, 'Principles and Pragmatism', was directly taken from Shamir's mouth. That these were not merely the blandishments of a wily diplomat is suggested by Baker's subsequent remarks, namely that he 'understood Israel's caution, especially when assessing Arab attitudes'. True, Arab attitudes were changing, as witnessed by Egypt's commitment to peace and 'evolving Palestinian attitudes', but 'much more needs . . . to be demonstrated that such a change is real'. Nevertheless, the change could not be ignored 'even now', and this is where Shamir was invited to demonstrate his expertise in 'the right mix of principles and pragmatism'. It is difficult to imagine what institutional file Baker drew upon in this assessment of the veteran Stern Gang and Mossad leader. The fact that Shamir is, as it were, to the left of Sharon does not make him a centrist. When Shamir says, 'Not one inch of territory', he is as sincere as a devout Muslim attesting that Muhammed is the Prophet of God. Shamir's 'not one inch . . .' is an article of faith rooted in the bedrock of Revisionist Zionism. When Begin bargained with Sadat on Sinai he was in effect saying: 'I keep the other occupied territories and you take Sinai.' Shamir is *not* bargaining for the same reason that Begin *did* bargain – because he too wants to keep these other occupied territories. That is what his plan is all about.

Many of the flaws of Shamir's plan will already have been

inferred, but a closer look at some of these is in order in the light of Washington's endorsement (albeit conditional) of the plan.

The Transitional Period and Israeli Settlement Activity

There is no quarrel with the concept of a transitional period leading to a final settlement. One cannot leap from the present situation to a final settlement in one go. The concept of a transitional period was endorsed by the Arab heads of state as early as the 1982 Fez Summit.

The key issue in the concept of a transitional period is its function. What central purpose is the transitional period supposed to serve? According to Baker, the transitional period 'will allow the parties to take the measure of each other's performance, to encourage attitudes to change and to demonstrate that peace and coexistence are desired'.

If this indeed is the purpose of the transitional period, it is to be wondered how this could be achieved in the absence of a halt to Israeli settlement and the concomitant land seizure.

It is true that Baker did call in his 22 May AIPAC speech for a stoppage of 'settlement activity', but Shamir knows, and Baker knows, that US policy, which in consonance with the Geneva Conventions considered the settlements illegal from 1967 through the Carter administration, has, since the beginning of the Reagan administration, considered them 'not illegal' – Reagan pronounced them as such on 2 February 1981 within ten days of his inauguration. Thus, the very least that Baker could do to give credibility to his call for the stoppage of settlement activity (not to mention his call on Israel to abandon notions of greater Israel and to forswear annexation) is to reaffirm the illegality of the settlements.

The Palestinians are the world's experts on Israeli settlement, having been at the receiving end of Zionist colonization since the early 1880s. For the Palestinians, Israeli settlement is the relentless process that led to their dispossession and replacement in the period culminating in 1948. It is the same relentless process, that after a hiatus of twenty years and since 1967, has been dispossessing and replacing them in East Jerusalem, the West Bank, and the Gaza Strip. Except that the pace since 1967 has been faster, and the methods more brutal (direct seizure instead of purchase) because Israel enjoys a monopoly of power in the Occupied Territories and flaunts it.

Thus, by 1988 at least 55 per cent of the West Bank lands and 30 per cent of the lands of the Gaza Strip had already been seized by Israel. This phenomenon of Israeli settlement and the concomitant land seizure in the Occupied Territories is a throwback to earlier colonial eras – Israel being the only country in the world today still expanding its frontiers and settling its citizens in the conquered lands. In the circumstances, to put the onus of reassuring the other side on the *Palestinians*, cliff-hanging from the residual rump of their patrimony and waiting for the final shove, is as unconscionable as it is grotesque.

But whence the wherewithal for all this settlement? Grants from the US government to Israel for the period 1952–89 totalled $53 billion, a perennial Marshall Plan.[15] Concurrently, Israel has received an average of $500 million per annum in tax-deductible contributions from American Jews. It is these funds that have enabled Israel to spend in the period 1967–88 $2.4 billion on settlement activity in the West Bank and the Gaza Strip.[16] It is these funds that have enabled it to allocate $2.6 billion[17] to the master plan for the Year 2010 (prepared in 1983 by the Israeli Ministry of Agriculture and the Settlement Department of the World Zionist Organization) whose objective is to settle 800,000 Jews in the West Bank.[18]

This is what Raanan Weitz, the retired chairman of the Jewish Agency Settlement Department, has to say about the link between US funds and settlement activity in the Occupied Territories.

> U.S. law prohibits the use of American Jewish money in the territories but American Jews tolerated the establishment of a separate WZO Settlement Department that could devote Israeli funds to the West Bank – funds that wouldn't be available were it not for American UJA [United Jewish Appeal] money making up the shortfall. A legal fiction, in other words. It encouraged Begin and Sharon to direct money we could not afford. And the American government was just as inconsistent. They oppose the occupation but instead of enforcing their view by applying pressure as they have a right to do, they keep granting massive aid. This relieves pressure so Israel can pour millions into the territories.[19]

Continued settlement activity is the single most lethal threat to the prospects of Israeli–Palestinian coexistence. The halting of settlement activity is the single most reassuring test of Israeli peaceful intentions. The threat has been immeasurably compounded by the planned mass emigration of hundreds of thousands of Soviet Jews to Israel in the wake of the restrictions imposed on their entry to the US *as a result* of pressures from Israel. Israel has already made no secret of its intention to settle many of the Soviet emigrés in the Occupied Territories and, as Weitz has pointed out, US law as hitherto applied has failed to hold either the WZO or Israel accountable for 'the legal fiction' enabling Israel to transfer US funds to the Occupied Territories. Thus, the envisaged US financial support for the mass emigration of Soviet Jews to Israel combined with the non-reaffirmation of the illegality of the settlements raise the question of the seriousness of American purpose in sponsoring the peace process and constitues a potential death blow of American provenance to the process itself.

The PLO

Even if Washington's bypassing of the PLO in the negotiations were for tactical reasons (which is debatable) and the whole world (except Israel) knows that any Palestinian delegation in Cairo or elsewhere will be but a front for the PLO, the accession on this matter by Washington to Israel's wishes augurs ill for the prospects of peace.

One would have thought that after the extraordinary, courageous moves by the PLO in unconditionally and unilaterally recognizing Israel, and the consequent start of the PLO–US dialogue by the *previous* administration, the new administration would have seen fit to remind Israel of the duty of reciprocity. Instead we get this niggardly reference by Baker to 'evolving Palestinian attitudes',[20] an insistence on more concessions from the Palestinian side, and the charade of ostracizing the PLO from the peace process. Such a punitive attitude to Palestinian moderation devalues moderation itself. It reinforces the impression that the peace process will be determined by Israeli rules alone. It undermines the Palestinian leadership most anxious to deal with Israel and the US. It erodes its ability to withstand the onslaughts of those who warn against placing trust in Washington. And it plays into the hands of those who maintain the inherent bankruptcy of peaceful negotiations.

However different American and Israeli attitudes to the PLO may be, to bypass it is to set a precedent that Israel will insist upon at all subsequent stages of the process. As the process advances and the need for PLO endorsement mounts, the absurdly circuitous route maintained via Cairo behind the threadbare fiction of PLO non-involvement will inevitably collapse to the discredit of both Cairo and Washington. For there is no alternative Palestinian leadership. It is a question of legitimacy: the 'insiders' know that they are one component of a peoplehood, and it is only the PLO leadership that can negotiate in the name of the collective Palestinian rights and hopes, their memories, and their sufferings. By bypassing the PLO, the US is only encouraging Israel's quest of a mirage.

The Palestinian State

Baker describes the 'reasonable middleground' between Israeli annexation and Palestinian statehood to be 'self-government . . . acceptable to Palestinians, Israel and Jordan'. He believes this 'formula provides ample scope for Palestinians to achieve their full political rights [*sic*]. It also provides ample protection for Israel's security.' It is to this end, in his view, that a settlement should be directed.[21]

There is a Victorian proconsular ring to this legislation of a ceiling to Palestinian rights. Surely 'people seek historically that separate and equal status among the powers of the earth to which the laws of nature and nature's God entitle them', to quote the American Declaration of Independence. There is only a spurious symmetry in denying *both* Israeli and Palestinian sovereignty in the Occupied Territories. Denial of Palestinian sovereignty is denial of the minimal turf of survival. It is denial of the territorial imperative that operates even in the animal kingdom. Denial of Israeli sovereignty is denial of triumphalist maximalism. It is denial of the fruits of conquest.

The measure of the 'reasonableness' of a solution to the Palestine problem is the extent to which it relates to the historical context of the genesis and evolution of the conflict no less than to contemporary power realities. Absolute justice is rarely obtained in human affairs, not this side of the grave, but pragmatic justice, by taking cognizance of the losses, the sufferings, and the gains of the two protagonists since the conflict began, as well as of contemporary power realities, can delineate the contours of a historical compromise rooted in the soil of the conflict. Such a compromise is more likely to endure because it is more likely to be perceived by the aggrieved – the Palestinians – to approximate justice. Baker's formula is no such compromise.

Palestinian nationalism is irreversible, like the tide of freedom sweeping Eastern Europe. Palestinian nationalism is irrepressible, like all fully mobilized nationalisms throughout history. Fully mobilized nationalisms end in their 'Final Cause' – the receptacle of statehood. This is as it should be. Not only is Palestinian nationalism one of the most fully mobilized national movements of our time, but the Palestinian people have one of the highest literacy rates outside the advanced industrial countries – certainly the highest in the Arab world. Ironically, the ratio of university students among Palestinians is higher than among their occupiers, the Israelis (18.8 per 1000 as compared to 14 per 1000).[22] The Palestinians cannot be denied a status accorded to some 160 other peoples in this world.

The PLO central leadership has already propounded the kind of state they envisage: a Palestinian state within the 1967 frontiers in peaceful coexistence alongside Israel and in confederation with Jordan.

Arguments from the small size of the state, its economic non-viability, or its inability to absorb all the Palestinian refugees do not stand up to scrutiny. There are at least twenty-five members of the UN that are smaller than the envisaged Palestinian state. Not many states are economically viable, and the Palestinian state would have the most precious asset of all – its high-level human material. Even if the state could not absorb all the Palestinian Diaspora, its positive influence (as in the case of Israel and the Jewish Diaspora) will be felt by those who cannot or do not want to live in it. Confederation will secure the interests of Jordan. But Palestinian sovereignty should precede confederation so that the latter comes about as an act of free choice.

Only such a state will have the psycho-political appeal and symbolism for the Palestinians in the Occupied Territories and the Diaspora to act as balm to their wounds, to give redress for the monumental injustices suffered, and to compensate for the loss of hearth and home and ancestral grave and for the surrender of primaeval historic rights.

Would not such a state constitute a threat to Israeli security? It would not, but the Israeli leadership would never admit this. And it would not be a threat, if only because such a state would be virtually demilitarized and dependent for its security on the peace settlement itself and on the guarantees of the major powers, including Israel.[23] If concern for Israel's security were indeed the reason for Washington's non-support of a Palestinian state along these lines, then let this topic be placed on the top of the agenda in the US–PLO dialogue, unless the start of this dialogue was meant to be a mere empty gesture by Washington.

The Time-Span of the Peace Process

It has been noted that the transitional period in the Shamir Plan, ostensibly five years long, is in effect open ended. The transitional period, it will be remembered, is *preceded* by (a) the dialogue to agree on the basic principles of the initiative; (b) the preparation and implementation of the election process; (c) the elections; and (d) negotiations for the transitional period. Nowhere are there any date-certain provisions indicating when precisely each of these stages would start, how long each would last, and when precisely it would end.

Reinforcing this laxity in scheduling is the total absence of any mechanism to resolve a failure *to agree* at any stage either before or after the beginning of the transitional period. All that one has here is agreement *to try to agree* on a series of issues at loosely designated future times. Should a party have an inherent interest in prolonging the process, it has an inbuilt alibi enabling it to disengage at no cost while continuing (in the case of Israel) to dominate and condition the situation on the ground.

Given Shamir's mind-set and objectives, his most probable strategy is to stretch the period *preceding* the start of the transitional period to the utmost; and since substantive talks on the final settlement can occur only at the end of the third year of the transitional period, to push these talks farthest down the line. Judging by the fact that seven months after the announcement of the Shamir plan in May 1989, the initial dialogue to launch the process has yet to start, it is a safe bet that Shamir intends to stretch out the pre-transitional period alone for some two to three years. Such a time-span (the period both preceding and comprising the transitional period) would carry him well into the second term of this administration, or into the first term of the new administration. Meanwhile, he, or his Likudist successor, will try to mesh in Israeli moves with the intervening US congressional and presidential elections, while bringing the full weight of the mass emigration of Soviet Jews subsidized by the US (Israel's secret weapon) to bear on the situation in the Occupied Territories. There is no dearth of loopholes for Shamir to wriggle out and stay on course.

Conclusion

There is no visceral philo-Zionism or Arabophobia at the White House today, as there was under the Reagan administration. Polls indicate that the American public is well ahead of its political élite in evenhandedness with regard to the Middle East.[24] Freedom is rampant all over the world, and a remarkable constellation of international and regional developments beckons to a courageous leadership to act.

The beginning of wisdom is the realization that the US is as much part of the problem as part of the solution, and that it has moral obligations to the Palestinians no less than to the Israelis. But as Theodore Sorensen recently said describing the Washington scene:

> Too often the sound we hear from Washington is the sound of fear. . . . Fear of the wrath of political donors or the risk of political defeat. . . . The art of political survival today is selecting the right target. . . . Fight drug addiction but not tobacco subsidies. Complain about the intransigence of Arafat but not Shamir. Blame North but not Reagan. . . . Pusillanimity is not confined to any one political party . . . or branch of government.[25]

Is it really a cause of wonder if the glass of Middle East peace does not impress one as being half full?

Notes

1   For the Shamir Plan, see *JPS* 73, pp. 145–48.
2   The use of 'district' in place of the usual 'Strip' may signify that Israel already considers the 'Gaza Strip' no longer exists with its 1967 boundaries.
3   See *JPS* 73, pp. 148–56.
4   This is the figure given by the UN Relief and Works Agency for April 1989 (*Financial Times*, 18 July 1989). The UNRWA figure for the registered refugees in the West Bank and the Gaza Strip are 381,000 and 453,000 respectively, for a total of 834,000.
5   Shabtai Teveth, *Ben Gurion: The Burning Ground 1886–1948*, (London: Robert Hale, 1987), p. 493.
6   See *The Times*, passim, 5 September 1937–3 July 1939 especially 25 July 1938, 26 August 1938, and 26 February 1939.
7   Lenni Brenner, *The Iron Walls*, (London: Zed Books, 1984), p. 193.
8   Brenner, p. 194.
9   Yitzhak Rabin, 'Israel's Peace Initiative and Elections in the Territories', speech to the Washington Institute for Near East Policy, 24 March 1989.
10 *Building for Peace: An American Strategy for the Middle East*, (Washington: Washington Institute for Near East Policy, 1988). The Institute is closely associated with AIPAC. One of the main authors of this report is Dennis Ross, senior aide to Baker.
11 See *JPS* 73, pp. 144–45.
12 See Appendix: *Clarifications and issues for the Israeli Government*: the ten points attached to Note Verbale dated 22 November 1989 from the Permanent Mission of Egypt to UN Secretary General (A/44/796–S/20987).
13 For Baker's five points, see *JPS* 74, pp. 169–70.
14 See *JPS* 70, p. 227.
15 Benjamin Beit-Hallahmi, *The Israeli Connection*, (New York: Pantheon Books, 1987), pp. 192–93.
16 Meron Benvenisti and Shlomo Khayat, *The West Bank and Gaza Atlas,* (Jerusalem: West Bank Data Base Project, 1988), p. 32.
17 Benvenisti and Khayat, p. 59.
18 Benvenisti and Khayat, p. 59.
19 *Moment* magazine (January–February 1987).
20 James Baker, 'Principles and Pragmatism: American Policy Toward the Arab–Israeli Conflict', speech to the American Israel Public Affairs Committee, 22 May 1989, reprinted in *Journal of Palestine Studies* 18, no. 4 (Summer 1989), pp. 172–76.
21 Baker, pp. 172–76.

22 Nili Mandler, 'Palestinian University Students Outnumber Israelis', *Ha'Aretz*, 25 October 1988.

23 Walid Khalidi 'Thinking the Unthinkable: A Sovereign Palestinian State', pp. 82–104, this book; and *At a Critical Juncture*, (Washington: Center for Contemporary Arab Studies, Georgetown University, 1989), pp. 15–19; pp. 140–71, this book.

24 Fouad Moughrabi, 'Public Opinion and the Israeli–Palestinian Conflict', *American–Arab Affairs*, no. 30 (Fall 1989), pp. 40–51.

25 'An America Where Timidity is Cloaked as Caution', *Boston Sunday Globe*, p. A23.

CHAPTER 7

The New Middle East Security Environment*

It would be resoundingly platitudinous to say that most of the major problems destabilizing the Middle East today predate Saddam Hussein's invasion of Kuwait. And yet, the invasion and its horrendous aftermath in Kuwait and Iraq have at once exacerbated old problems, added major new destabilizing ones, and, paradoxically, opened what in the common jargon is termed a window of opportunity, which perhaps for the first time since World War II, affords if resolutely seized a fighting chance of paving the way to a new and relatively more stable order in the Middle East.

On the Eve of the War

Already before the invasion of Kuwait, the major sources of regional tension could be readily identified as being located at either end of the Fertile Crescent: the Palestine problem and the Arab–Israeli conflict on the Mediterranean littoral, and the Iraqi–Iranian conflict on the Arabian Gulf.

To be sure, inter-Arab disputes were legion, with pride of place to be unquestionably accorded to the gratuitous, debilitating fratricidal strife between Hafez al-Assad and Saddam Hussein, to be followed not too far behind by the venomous chemistry tenaciously obtaining between Assad and Yasser

* Essay first published in Occasional Paper no. 8, International Studies Program, The American Academy of Arts and Sciences, Cambridge, MA, 1991.

Arafat. With little effort, the inventory could be swiftly expanded to include tensions at one time or another between King Hussein and Assad, between Arafat and King Hussein, between the Gulf countries among themselves, between North and South Yemen, between Egypt and the Sudan, between Libya and Egypt, between Libya and Tunisia, and between Algeria and Morocco.

And yet, in the decade preceding the invasion of Kuwait, except for the terrible war of proxy (not all of Arab provenance) fought on Lebanese soil, and except for the hamstringing effect on collective Arab diplomatic action of the Arafat–Assad–Saddam triangle of inveterate enmity, none of these enumerated tensions constituted a major source of conflagration even remotely analogous to the Arab–Israeli conflict (with its six regular wars since 1948) or to the Iran–Iraq war (far less deep seated, to be sure, but with its even greater toll of human lives).

At the same time, there seemed during the decade preceding the invasion to be a gathering but countervailing tendency towards inter-Arab reconciliation and cooperation exemplified by the steady rehabilitation of Egypt within the Arab fold, the Arab coalition in support of Iraq against Iran, the new PLO–Jordanian entente, the spontaneous and universal Arab response to the intifada, the Taif agreement on Lebanon, unity between South and North Yemen, Algerian disengagement from the Polisario war, detente between Tunisia and Libya and between Libya and Egypt, greater collective Arab pragmatism towards the Arab–Israeli conflict and the creation of the three sub-League councils – the Gulf Cooperation Council (GCC) in 1981, the Arab Maghreb Union on 18 February 1989, and the Arab Cooperation Council (ACC) grouping Iraq, Egypt, Jordan, and Yemen on 16 February 1989. Of course, many of these developments were tactical in purpose, self-serving in motivation, and even potentially (as regards the sub-League Councils) centrifugal in effect. Nevertheless, cumulatively these developments indicated a definite trend away from the pan-Arab flamboyance of the 1950s and 1960s, and towards greater acceptance of and deference to the separate sovereign components of the Arab states system.

It is true that the backdrop to these tensions and conflicts both major and minor pointed to yet deeper layers of actual and potential instability and tension in the Arab world. The backdrop

common to all the Arab countries might be conceived as being
made up of four, so to speak, superposed 'maps' – a governance
map, a demographic map, a socio-economic map, and a
psychological map.

What a pre-Gulf War governance map would show is that most
Arab regimes belonged to variants of two models: the first, a
doctrinaire, single-party, fundamentally terror-based, autocratic
if not quasi-totalitarian regime led by a more or less self-deified
absolute leader; the second, a monarchical, centralized, patriar-
chal, semi-feudal autocratic regime led by a hardly more self-
effacing dynast. While the purely material needs of the citizenry
were met in all the oil-rich countries, including Iraq and Libya,
the common denominator between the two models is their
aversion to human rights and their committed subscription to the
antithesis of the maxim that 'Man does not live by bread alone'.
The closest approximation to a representative parliamentary
regime was pre-civil war Lebanon, while the leader closest to
having been freely elected was, within the PLO framework,
Yasser Arafat. Nevertheless, rising protest against the monopoly
and abuse of power by rulers forced some governments to move
in the direction of greater power-sharing and accountability. This
trend was most evident in Algeria, Tunisia, and Yemen, and had
gone farthest in Jordan.

The demographic map, which is difficult to separate from the
socio-economic map, would have shown a population explosion.
The 220 million Arabs of today are expected to double in number
by the year 2025.

The socio-economic map would exhibit a striking incongruence
between the distribution of wealth and the distribution of
population in the Arab world. The six oil-rich countries of the
Gulf had a total native population of about 12 million, or 6 per
cent of the 220 million Arabs. The average per capita income in
these countries for the *native* population (that is to say, excluding
the foreign, mainly Arab, workers who in some states outnumber
the nationals) is at least $15,000. Average per capita income in
Algeria (24 million) is $2500, in Morocco (25 million) it is $750,
in Egypt (53 million) $690, and in the Sudan (24 million) $310.

Of course this incongruence was partly offset by the hundreds
of thousands of Egyptians, Palestinians, and Jordanians employed
in the Gulf countries and in Iraq, and of Yemenis in Saudi

Arabia, remittances from whom constituted major sources of hard currency to the countries of origin. It was also partly offset by the Gulf countries' state and private investment in, as well as grants and loans on preferential terms to, the non-oil-rich countries, in addition to special subsidies to the countries bordering on Israel and to the PLO. Nevertheless, the bulk of the oil countries' (surplus) wealth was known to have found its way – however justified this may have been from a strictly financial point of view – into the economies of the Western industrial countries, and particularly into that of the United States.

The high rate of natural increase everywhere in the Arab world, without any correspondingly high rate of economic development and productivity (largely due to low inter-Arab economic cooperation, the diversion of Arab wealth to the West, and excessive defence expenditures) threatened to strain resources to breaking point. Moreover, in the area of Arab–Israeli conflict, this rate of natural increase combined with massive waves of Soviet–Jewish immigrants greatly to increase the psychological and physical pressures on finite land and water resources. But water as a scarce commodity and a fountainhead of conflict loomed also in the relations between Turkey on the one hand and Syria and Iraq on the other.

The psychological map would have registered among wide sectors of mass opinion and of the intelligentsia a striking degree of alienation, both from the ruling circles and from the socio-economic status quo over which these circles were seen to preside. Concurrently this sense of alienation was directed against the major Western powers, particularly the United States. This was partly a product of Islamic cultural defensiveness against the advancing tide of Westernization, and partly a hangover from colonial times, of which the United States was seen as a latter-day representative or symbol. But it also reflected the perception that the Western countries had come to be the true beneficiaries of Arab oil wealth at the expense of the non-oil-rich Arab countries, while acting as the guardians of the hated socio-economic status quo and of the rulers who benefited from it. The fact that the West, and particularly the United States, was seen unconditionally to underwrite Israel's practices in and continued retention of the Occupied Territories did not help to temper this deepening sense of alienation from the West.

As horizontal education extended with hundreds of thousands of university graduates every year joining a mounting multi-million reserve force of unemployed and frustrated young men and women across the Arab world, the calls of radicalism and fundamentalism acquired greater appeal and seductiveness. The depth and ubiquity of this alienation could be gauged from the extent of support for Saddam Hussein in the face of the American build-up. This support was not so much for the occupation of Kuwait *per se* as for what was seen as a deserved blow to the status quo (with all its domestic, political, socio-economic, and international dimensions) which had in the first place given rise to the sense of alienation, and which Kuwait was seen to symbolize irrespective of the merits of its case against Saddam Hussein's claims and grievances.[1]

The Psychological Fallout of the War

Of the four constituents of this backdrop to the two major pre-Gulf crisis sources of tension in the Arab world (the Arab–Israeli and the Iraq–Iran conflicts), perhaps the most crucial for the future of the Middle East is the potential effect of the Gulf War in the psychogical domain.

The Arab world is still in a state of trauma from what has happened. Its present psychological disarray is reminiscent of its state at similar watersheds earlier in this century: the collapse of the Ottoman Empire at the end of World War I and the division of its Arab provinces between Britain and France, the fall of Palestine and the establishment of Israel in 1948 with the attendant Palestinian Exodus and Diaspora, and the Israeli conquest of the rest of Palestine, the Golan and Sinai in 1967.

Ironically, the scale of devastation visited upon the civilian infrastructure of Iraq and the carnage of its military have shifted the focus from Iraq's causative act of blatant aggression against Kuwait to the US motivation in wreaking so much destruction upon Iraq. Already before the start of hostilities in mid January 1991, the extensive support that Saddam Hussein had garnered in the Arab world at both the governmental and popular levels was itself inspired by fear of the motivation of the American response to the crisis since August. The worst of these fears has now been confirmed in the Arab consciousness, at least outside the Gulf countries. And just as the earlier traumas have left indelible marks on the Arab psyche, significantly conditioning the Arab political outlook and behaviour towards the West, the danger, once the full impact of what has happened is absorbed and internalized, and in the absence of countervailing measures, is that this will only serve to compound the sense of alienation from the West and from the ruling circles in the Arab world that are seen to be subservient to it.

The depth of the Arab trauma should not come as a surprise to American readers, considering how powerful until Desert Storm the Vietnam syndrome had been. In comparative American terms, the conservative estimate of 100,000 Iraqi soldiers killed is the equivalent of about 1,380,000 American dead. The United States has fought in nine major wars since its independence – the Revolutionary War, the War of 1812, the Mexican, Civil, and Spanish–American Wars, World War I and World War II, and the Korean and Vietnam Wars. Total American combat deaths sustained in these wars – covering about thirty-seven years of actual fighting spread over more than two centuries – are just under 600,000. It is interesting to note by way of comparison – even given the statistical flaw arising from the varying US population base over time – that the total American combat dead over 200 years is less than half the equivalent Iraqi combat dead sustained inside forty-five days.

More Iraqis were probably killed in the eight-year war with Iran, but never before have so many Arabs been killed in such a short time. Except for the Algerian War of independence, never since the Crusades or the Christian *Reconquista* of Spain have so many Arabs been killed in an encounter with the West in any one battle or war. The number of Iraqis killed exceeds the number of all Arab soldiers killed in all the Arab–Israeli wars since 1948. And, except for the devastation of the Palestinian countryside in 1948–9, when Israel wiped some 400 villages from the map, and that of the Kurdish region at the hands of Saddam Hussein in the late 1970s, there is no precedent in modern times for such systematic destruction of the civilian infrastructure in an Arab country.

Horror in the Arab world (outside the Gulf countries) at these losses does not exclude condemnation of Saddam's brutality against Kuwait. Rather, it reflects regard for the historic and modern standing of Iraq in Arab consciousness as well as sympathy with the plight of the Iraqi people themselves. To millions of Arabs and Muslims, Iraq is not Saddam. Historically Baghdad (founded by the Arabs in AD 762) was the seat of the second major Arab dynasty, the Abbasids, whose reign spanned 500 years until the middle of the thirteenth century. Baghdad was the Athens and Rome of Arab history, the seat at once of imperial power and of a brilliant intellectual and cultural activity. It was under the auspices of the Abbasids that the Greek classics were first translated into Arabic and then transmitted through Latin to the West, contributing thereby to the Renaissance of Europe. Many of the major figures of the Arab Muslim cultural heritage – historians, mathematicians, philosophers, grammarians, theologians, mystics – were born and lived in Baghdad. In modern times the Arab poets of Baghdad are the equivalent of such names in the English-speaking world as Whitman, Auden, Yeats, Eliot and Longfellow. Even so severe a critic of Saddam Hussein and the Baath party as the Iraqi Samir al-Khalil, whose *Republic of Fear* has served as a source book for the anti-Saddam analyses in the West, concedes that the regime 'transformed Iraq's physical infrastructure, its educational system, social relations, and its technology, industry, and science'. The regime 'provided free health and education for everyone, and it also revolutionized transport and electrified virtually every village in the country'. Iraq today has 'a proportionately very large middle class; its intelligentsia is one of the best educated in the Arab world'.[2]

It is such considerations that have driven wide sectors of the Arab intelligentsia to conclude not only that Arab lives are worthless in Western eyes (the ratio of American to Iraqi dead being somewhere on the scale of one to 1000) but also that Saddam Hussein's invasion of Kuwait constituted merely the formal excuse for the United States to exploit the new unipolar post-cold-war configuration of power to achieve certain long-term regional objectives of its own. These included, according to Arab analyses, the tightening of control over the oil resources, the preservation of the political and socio-economic status quo in favour of the oil-rich dynasties, the installation of a protective military umbrella over these dynasties, the elimination of potential Arab deterrence of Israel, the establishment of a threshold of power beyond which no Arab country is permitted to develop, and the consolidation of its own hegemony throughout the region. These reactions may be noted not only in radical but also in centrist generally pro-Western circles. They are summed up by a leading Lebanese scholar of the younger generation who remarked: 'The destruction of the technological and military capacity of Iraq causes every Arab, whatever his current attitude, to feel a greater measure of weakness, powerlessness, and fear.'[3]

These and similar reactions carry the ingredients of a tempestuous popular backlash not only against the West, and principally the United States, but also against the Arab members of the anti-Saddam coalition for having, as perceived, connived with the Western powers at such devastation of Iraq. This backlash would gather momentum from the hardships of the hundreds of thousands of Yemenis, Palestinians and Egyptians uprooted from Saudi Arabia and Kuwait and pauperized through the loss of employment and their life savings. It would be fuelled on a wider scale by the rift between the oil-rich members of the anti-Saddam coalition and the Arab countries that remained outside it. This potentially is the most destructive political and economic legacy of the war.

Indeed, there are indications that the oil-rich countries, and particularly its smaller members, are bent on an economic war against those who sided with Saddam that is virtually Punic in its vindictiveness. This war is taking the form of the interruption of private investment, trade, oil supplies, and of grants (whether from governments or special funds) to these countries. Patently, such a policy will dangerously exacerbate the socio-economic woes of the have-not countries. If persisted in, it might well destroy all hope of tackling the conditions resulting from the incongruence across the Arab world between the distribution of wealth and population. As it is, much of the expected oil income for the immediate and intermediate futures will be spent on war-related costs – post-war reconstruction, environmental damage, purchase of equipment left by Desert Storm, and purchase of new arms to bolster the new Gulf security system (thus lubricating in the bargain the economies of the arms-producing countries). At the same time, above and beyond the war damage, the economies of the Gulf countries will progressively feel the impact of the panicky, massive exodus of funds estimated at between $200 to $300 billion as a result of the war to the safe havens of the West.[4]

Such punitive policies by the oil-rich countries are bound, in addition to attracting new levels of resentment and envy against themselves, to generate indignation against a salient Western presence in the Gulf security system these states envisage as a result of the war. Such a presence would inevitably be seen as the *raison d'être* and the source of protection of the punitive policy itself, and would constitute the lightning rod for an escalating psychological and political counter-movement.

Ironically, it is in the countries outside the Gulf coalition that the process of power-sharing and democratization has gone farthest. In all countries in which this has occurred, fundamentalist groups have made the greatest electoral gains. Most of these, while condemning Saddam's invasion of Kuwait on Islamic moral and religious grounds, have equally strongly condemned the invitation of Western military support. Even in Saudi Arabia, important clerical circles expressed serious reservations about invoking 'Christian' support against Iraq. And during the early stages of the crisis, forty-five prominent Saudi personalities summoned the courage tactfully but firmly to remind King Fahd in a joint petition of his Islamic duty to abide by consultative procedures. It is not unthinkable that the hostile political and psychological campaign against the Gulf countries and the United States would find resonance within opposition and potentially oppositional forces inside the Gulf countries themselves. If Saddam Hussein remains in power, he will try his utmost to turn these conditions to his advantage.

The War's Fallout and the Gulf Region

The Gulf War has already had far-reaching effects on the power relations inside Iraq and between Iraq and its Gulf neighbours, the implications of which continue to emerge by the day. The 'positive' and 'negative' aspects of these effects are essentially in the eyes of the beholder. Even with this reservation, however, some meaningful generalizations are possible using the notion of regional interstate stability and security as a general criterion of evaluation.

Iraq

Inside Iraq, two pivotal issues which the end of the Iraq–Iran war in August 1988 appeared to have buried have resurfaced with a vengeance since the ceasefire between Iraq and the coalition forces in 1991. The first is the issue of the removal from power of Saddam Hussein (an Iranian demand during the Iran–Iraq war, now subscribed to by a chorus of neighbours and others). The second is the territorial integrity of Iraq (threatened by a possible Iranian victory in the war).

Saddam Hussein has only himself to blame for having established such a solid infrastructure of fear, mistrust and animosity towards him in so many countries, and yet there are no signs of his imminent departure. Quite the contrary. In the wake of his army's humiliating defeat at the hands of Schwartzkopf, he seems to have successfully appealed to the ethos of his Sunnite officer class – the backbone of his regime – and with its help he has crushed the rebellions against him, thus apparently ensuring his continued tenure in power for the foreseeable future. This raises the issue of how long he is likely to remain quiescent in the face of the sanctions and reparations regime imposed upon him, and how and with what repercussions he might react to them. But even if he does remain quiescent and meticulously comply with all UN ceasefire provisions, Saddam Hussein's continued presence in Baghdad will cast a dark shadow not only on the Gulf area, but over the entire Middle East. This shadow will remain in place even with a post-Saddam Iraq, unless and until the new regime passes the scrutiny of a severely sceptical jury of regional and extra-regional countries. Indeed, it is difficult to imagine the beginning of a process of normalization in Iraq's relations with the outside world so long as Saddam remains at the helm.

Concerning Iraq's territorial integrity, there seems to be a regional and international consensus (apart from the smaller Gulf countries and Israel) in favour of preserving it, though at first the temptation for many of aiding the Shi'ite and Kurdish rebellions seemed too inviting to resist. With the rebellions crushed – the Iraqi Shi'ite ecclesiastical establishment headed by the paramount Ayotallah al-Khou'i cowed or co-opted, and negotiations inaugurated with the Kurdish leadership – Saddam Hussein now stands more than a good chance to maintain the territorial integrity of his country. A power and oil-revenue sharing formula coupled with administrative decentralization such as Saddam is offering could elicit the acquiescence, however wary, of the Kurdish and Shi'ite leaderships, neither of which appears to see its future in secession or under the permanent protection of foreign parties.

The question nevertheless remains as to whether the arrangements worked out by Saddam with Kurdish and Shi'ite regions would survive his own disappearance from the scene. For the Kurds, this would at least partly depend on the international dimension of the agreement concluded. The chances are that the larger the extra-territorial component of this agreement, the greater its catalytic effect in a post-Saddam Iraq in fuelling the momentum of centrifugal forces in the country.

Concepts of Regional Security

Both the Arab and the non-Arab partners of the anti-Saddam coalition are clearly determined to put in place a Gulf security system to prevent a recurrence of events such as occurred last summer. For the Gulf countries in the coalition, the compulsion to establish such a system with Saddam Hussein still in power is understandably obsessive. But the system is also viewed by them as a bulwark against any post-Saddam recalcitrant or revanchiste Iraqi regime.

Within the Arab members of the coalition, there are three – to put it euphemistically – schools of thought concerning the structure and objectives of such a regional security system: those held by the smaller Gulf states, Egypt and Syria, and Saudi Arabia.

(1) The *smaller Gulf countries*, led by the Kuwaiti ruling establishment, seem motivated by three overriding considerations: fear of Iraq (with or without Saddam); the quest of guaranteed protection of their oil wealth; and, quite simply, sweet revenge, not only against Iraq but also against all those who 'sided' with it. Their slogan would seem to be 'Never Again'.

And if a clean break with the past is what it takes, so be it. From their perspective, just as it was United States military power alone that routed Saddam Hussein from Kuwait, so it is only United States military power that can deter or reverse any future Iraqi aggression. Until the utter harmlessness of a post-Saddam regime is beyond any shadow of doubt (an unlikely and indeed inconceivable eventuality), there is no substitute in their eyes to continued US military presence in the Gulf. In the circumstances, it makes no sense to be coy or sensitive about such a presence. Indeed, the more overt, permanent, and substantial it is on the land, in the sea and in the air, the greater its deterrent value.

Such an approach would necessarily involve a redefinition of the relations between the Gulf area and the rest of the Arab world. But in the Gulf countries' view, such a redefinition is in any case inevitable in the light of the sympathy for Saddam Hussein shown by so much of the Arab world. If such a redefinition does not meet with the approval of their two non-Gulf allies, Syria and Egypt, this would be regrettable; none the less, these countries would still be able to contribute their forces alongside the United States to the Gulf security system. Should they, for whatever reason, be unable to do so, again this would be regrettable, but would not stand in the way of basing the Gulf security system primarily on US military presence.

At the core of the position of the smaller Gulf countries is the concept of a sub-regional group with its own collective identity and interests, as opposed to the concept of individual membership in a larger Arab nation institutionalized in the Arab League. Some such rationale lay implicitly, or at least potentially, in the very formation of the Gulf Cooperation Council (GCC) in 1981, from which Iraq, then embroiled in its war with Iran, was, at Kuwaiti insistence, excluded. Emboldened by the defeat of Iraq and the American military presence, the GCC is increasingly making explicit what had hitherto remained muted.

The 'new' GCC posture gives it more leeway in many areas. Economically, disbursement of funds will no longer be governed by a priori considerations of duty, but by strict *raison d'état*. This will also allow for settling scores with the countries that sided with Saddam Hussein, including the PLO. The new posture will likewise enable the GCC to bypass the Arab League and operate directly as a group on the international scene, e.g., with the

EEC. Diplomatically, it will release the GCC from consensual Arab policies on the Palestine problem and relations with Israel, and facilitate *quid pro quo* deals on this issue with the United States and other countries.

This isolationist trend, if unchecked or untempered, could produce serious instabilities. Already Saudi Arabia, the senior partner in the GCC, is distancing itself from it somewhat. The withdrawal of Egyptian troops from the Gulf is an early harbinger of the deterioration of relations between Egypt and the smaller Gulf countries, particularly Kuwait. The same deterioration is likely to take place in Kuwaiti–Syrian relations. The cutting off of aid to the have-not Arab countries will only exacerbate socio-economic conditions there, and further poison the psychological environment discussed earlier. There are strong opposition forces inside the Gulf countries – the same forces that are demanding more democratization from the ruling families – which are deeply disturbed by this isolationist trend.

Not least of the negative repercussions of an American-based security system is the likely opposition to it by Iran. The Gulf War has produced three windfalls for Iran: (a) the destruction of Iraq's offensive military power; (b) the heaven-sent gift of Iraq's best war planes; and (c) the return of the frontier on Shatt al-Arab to the thalweg, from which Iran was forced to pull back during its war with Iraq.

As early as 12 September 1990, President Rafsanjani outlined his vision of the new security order in the Gulf after the conclusion of the ongoing crisis. From his perspective, the Gulf area would clearly become an Islamic lake under the control of Iran. The main features of the new Iranian system would be a non-aggression pact between the 'Islamic countries' of the Gulf (i.e., Iran) and the countries of the Middle East (i.e., the Arab countries), a Muslim international court of arbitration, the elimination of regional weapons of mass destruction, and the withdrawal of all foreign (i.e., American) troops. It is noteworthy that Syria, Iran's strategic ally on the Mediterranean littoral, has expressed support for this Iranian vision.

The Iranian vision is antithetical to that of the smaller Gulf countries. These countries seem to believe that Iran, which is anxious to mend its fences with the West, would be ultimately reconciled to the envisaged expanded salient American military presence in the Gulf. These countries expect that Iran would see in the new American-based system a counterweight to a resurgent Iraq. They believe that Iran would ultimately acquiesce in the American presence in the Gulf as part of a package deal with the West. There is little to warrant such expectations.

(2) At the other end from the smaller Gulf countries stand their two allies against Saddam Hussein, *Syria and Egypt*. With Iraq having, to say the least, strayed from the path of pan-Arabism, Ba'athist Damascus is now its sole capital. Assad's legitimacy springs from his ostensible championship of the higher interests of the Arab Nation vis-à-vis Israel. And Cairo, after ten years of ostracism from the Arab fold, is now once again the locus of the Arab League, whose new Secretary General will again be an Egyptian. As guardian of the Arab League and its Charter, Egypt is keen to use its newly restored status to refurbish an image badly battered by its 'separate deal' with Israel, universally seen in the Arab world as having been concluded at the expense of the other occupied territories. After their recent 'collusion' with the United States in the destruction of Iraq's offensive military capability, both countries – Syria and Egypt – are anxious to demonstrate that their participation in the anti-Saddam coalition was based on Arab national interest and not subservience to Western behests. After all, it was Saddam who, in invading Kuwait, had betrayed 'the Security of the Arab Nation', the central concept of Al Amn al-Qaumi which lies at the base of the Arab collective security pact endorsed by all members of the Arab League.

The premises of this concept are the imperatives of non-aggression between Arab states and Arab collective security as the responsibility of the Arab states within the framework of the Arab League. Presumably sensing the incipient post-Gulf-crisis separatist proclivities of the smaller Gulf countries, Syria invited its Arab coalition partners to a conference in Damascus to discuss the new Arab order. The result was the Damascus Declaration of 6 March 1991 initialled by the six Gulf countries in addition to Syria and Egypt. The basic idea underlying the Damascus Declaration is that these participants would constitute a group that would closely cooperate in the security, economic and political fields with a view to injecting a 'new life' into Arab collective efforts from which would emanate a new Arab order.

The framework within which the group would operate would be the Arab League and its Collective Security Pact. The League itself should be strengthened. The Egyptian and Syrian troops stationed in the Gulf would constitute the nucleus of an Arab Peace Force in the making to guarantee the security of the Gulf states and of the Arab states in general. These troops would represent 'a model of the efficacy of a comprehensive Arab security defense system'. The group of eight could later be expanded to include the other members of the League. This group is not aimed against any party (i.e., Iran) but 'could become the prelude for a dialogue with Islamic parties (i.e., Iran) . . . that respect the higher interests of the Arab Nation'. Presumably this means that if there were an agreement with Iran, it would be with the Arab League as a group. This does not necessarily conflict with Rafsanjani's vision. At the same time, there is little room in such a system for the salient American military presence in the Gulf as envisaged by the smaller countries of the Gulf, particularly by Kuwait.

(3) *Saudi Arabia*'s position on Gulf security lies somewhere between that of the smaller Gulf states and that of Syria and Egypt, but is almost certainly closer to that of the latter. Saudi Arabia's position is perforce dictated by the fact that Islam rose from its soil and that its king is 'the Servant of the Two Holy Places' (Mecca and Medina). Thus, whereas Kuwait's constituency is some 600,000 Kuwaiti nationals, the constituency of Saudi Arabia is 1 billion Muslims, 1 million of whom annually visit it on pilgrimage. This wider circle of accountability is evidenced by the high percentage of its GNP that Saudi Arabia devotes to foreign aid, mostly to Muslim countries: 2.6 per cent in 1988. This is almost twice as high as the highest percentage for that year among the advanced Western countries (Norway: 1.4 per cent) and more than six times higher than the average for these countries (0.4 per cent). Kuwait's contribution, as well as that of the United States, is as high as this average.

Saudi Arabia's invitation of *Christian* forces to the Peninsula has no precedent in the 1300 years since the rise of Islam. The emotions this has aroused have already been alluded to. Irrespective of whether Saddam Hussein did or did not intend to invade Saudi Arabia, the coalition's war against Iraq could have been launched only from Saudi Arabia and with Saudi consent.

Such consent was, however, conditional upon the withdrawal of the foreign troops after the expulsion of Iraq from Kuwait. In inviting these troops, Saudi Arabia shouldered three monumental moral burdens: responsibility for breaking with a virtually sacrosanct Islamic tradition, 'responsibility' for the carnage and destruction in a fellow Arab and Muslim country, and responsibility for ensuring the departure of foreign troops from the Peninsula.

At the same time, Saudi Arabia is as anxious as all Iraq's neighbours that there be no repetition of the events of August 1990. It is conscious of the instability of the region with or without Saddam and of its own dependence on international and particularly United States military support. Concurrently, however, Saudi Arabia is aware of the region's vulnerability to an over-confident Iran given Rafsanjani's vision of an Islamic new order there. But Saudi Arabia is equally wary of imposing a security regime in the Gulf that goes against the grain in Tehran. Nor is Saudi Arabia averse to settling scores with Saddam or Arafat. But there are lines that it cannot transgress, despite the wholly atypical decision to invite American troops, and it must look at the future and at the security of the Gulf through the prism of the three burdens just mentioned. It is therefore not possible for Saudi Arabia to go as far as Kuwait, and while maintaining its membership and leadership of the GCC, it does not have the option of breaking with either its Arab or Muslim worlds. One thing is certain, however, and that is that Saudi Arabia wants an immensely strengthened military establishment of its own, and prefers an arrangement for expanded American presence or for closer military coordination with the United States, albeit without fanfare and certainly not at the expense of its Arab and Muslim ties.

Oil

The impact of the Gulf war is probably clearest and most 'positive', at least for the immediate and intermediate futures, with regard to oil. The military outcome of the war has prevented the oil resources of Kuwait and those of the other Arab Gulf countries from falling under the control of an adventurist and ruthless ruler in Baghdad. Even if Saddam Hussein had not intended to stay in Kuwait and had voluntarily pulled out of it before the arrival of foreign troops, and even if he had not intended to push on into Saudi Arabia or the other Gulf countries, his invasion of Kuwait, if physically unrepelled and however temporary, would have given him a psychological grip on the decision-making of the other Arab Gulf countries including their oil policies. It is highly unlikely now that any post-Saddam Iraqi regime would tempt fortune by repeating the folly of invading Kuwait.

Given the windfalls Iran has earned from the military humiliation of Saddam Hussein, its own moral stand on the invasion, its quest of detente with the West, and its own vision of the future of the Gulf, it is most unlikely as well that Iran would embark on any such adventure. With the USSR in the wake of its political disintegration and economic collapse trailing the US in the region as a docile but contented and cooperative junior partner, the erstwhile nightmare of a Soviet takeover of the oil states (if it had ever been credible or practicable) has surely now taken its place amidst the archives if not the dustbins of history. In brief, there is no longer an external threat to the oil-rich Gulf countries from direct attack by a regional or extra-regional power.

This leaves as possible threats to the oil of these countries the encouragement of domestic opposition by regional countries, sabotage of oil installations, and a radical takeover by domestic opposition forces. So long as the sanctions against Iraq remain in place, backed by a new security system in the Gulf, particularly one that wins Iranian acquiescence, neither Iraq nor, *a fortiori*, Iran is likely to generate such threats. Even if acts of sabotage are successfully carried out, they would be of Lilliputian significance compared to the raging conflagration of the Kuwaiti wells.

Another major oil-related political result stands out as an additional bonus, especially to the Western and industrialized nations – the 'mood' and new inter-Arab and international orientation of the Arab Gulf states. Indeed, the US role in liberating Kuwait and defending the other Gulf states rules out any use of oil supply as leverage against Western policies on such regional issues as, for example, the Palestine problem and the Arab–Israeli conflict. To all intents and purposes, therefore, it could be said that for the foreseeable future the Gulf war has guaranteed the security of the oil and of access to it, and by the same token that of its production and supply.

It is true that the popular backlash discussed earlier could mesh in with Gulf opposition forces with grave consequences for the stability of the Gulf states. But there is no inevitability in this should prudence guide US policies towards Iraq and Iran, and should American statesmanship show its face at the Mediterranean littoral end of the Fertile Crescent.

The Arab–Israeli Arena and the Issue of Security

Long before the Gulf crisis and indeed almost a decade ago, the major contours of a peaceful settlement of the Palestine problem and the Arab–Israeli conflict acceptable to most Arab countries and to the largest grouping in the PLO led by Yasser Arafat had already become clear. These contours are reflected in the peace plan announced at the Fez Arab Summit of September 1982.

The Fez plan had three main ingredients: (a) Israeli withdrawal to the 1967 frontiers on the West Bank (including East Jerusalem), the Gaza Strip and the Golan; (b) a Palestinian state on the West Bank and in the Gaza Strip, with East Jerusalem as its capital; and (c) a Security Council guarantee of the settlement. There would be guaranteed access to the Holy Places, the Palestinian refugees not wishing to return would be compensated, and the Israeli settlements in the Occupied Territories would be dismantled. The transitional period would not exceed six months. The preamble to the plan referred, though without giving details, to President Bourguiba's peace plan of 1965 which had called for the acceptance of the partition of Palestine as a solution of the Palestine problem. Reference to the Bourguiba plan was a clear indication that the Fez Summit was contemplating a two-state solution, i.e., a Palestinian state alongside and in peaceful coexistence with Israel.

Despite elements of the plan that were unacceptable to Israel, it had many positive features. Its essence was acceptance of the existence of Israel. Such acceptance had hitherto been the principal demand and grievance of Israel against the Arabs. This acceptance was to be guaranteed by the Security Council, which meant that the summit plan was conceived as a permanent settlement. The reference to the compensation of refugees left the door open to only a partial return. And if the return of Palestinian refugees to Israel proper was not explicitly precluded, it was not explicitly demanded either. The plan's provisions for East Jerusalem, the settlements and the frontiers, unacceptable to Israel as they might have been, did not vitiate the plan's acceptance of the existence of Israel itself (albeit within the 1967 frontiers) nor did it derogate from its provisions for guaranteeing this existence. To all intents and purposes, then, the Fez plan had conceded the hitherto traditional core demand and requirement of Israel: *guaranteed acceptance by the Arabs*. Nothing like this plan had appeared before from the Arab side at such a collective authoritative level. The Fez plan was endorsed by all heads of state, including Assad, Saddam Hussein and Arafat. Only Qaddafi did not attend the conference. Substantively, the plan stood the previous Arab collective posture on its head. It was little short of revolutionary.

The compromises contained in the Fez plan were extended and refined by the Palestinians themselves at their historic November 1988 meeting of the Palestine National Council (PNC) in Algiers. It was at that meeting that the PNC as a body accepted for the first time resolutions 242 and 338. It also made more explicit the acceptance of partition (a two-state solution) which had been at the core of the Fez plan. It did so by stating that the UN 1947 partition plan (systematically rejected by the Arab states as a body until 1982) was the source of legitimacy of both the Palestinian state to be *and* of Israel. This went beyond accepting the *existence* of Israel as the Fez Summit had done, to indicating acceptance of Israel's legitimacy *on a par* with that of the Palestinian state. Anyone familiar with Palestinian discourse would be hard pressed to gainsay that this constituted a total break with the past and was indeed in diametric contradiction with the provisions of the Charter of the PLO. The PNC pledged to achieve the settlement with Israel through peaceful negotiations. There was not one single reference to the 'armed struggle' which had figured in the resolutions of all the previous PNCs since the establishment of the PLO in the mid 1960s. Subsequently, Arafat confirmed the purport of the Algiers PNC by explicitly accepting the right of Israel to exist and renouncing terrorism, after which the United States decided to open a 'substantive dialogue' with the PLO. Later still, in a meeting with President Mitterrand, Arafat pronounced the PLO Charter 'caduque', or 'obsolete'.

The PNC resolutions acquired additional weight when later the two Arab summits meeting in Casablanca endorsed them. In particular, they specifically endorsed 242 and 338 which had been accepted by individual states, e.g., Egypt, Jordan and Syria, but never before collectively by an Arab summit. By accepting the PNC 1988 resolutions with their explicit reference to partition, the Arab summits reconfirmed more firmly their commitment to a two-state solution with the Palestinian state living in peaceful coexistence alongside Israel.

To be sure, some of the shortcomings pertaining to the Fez peace plan remained in place. Neither the PNC as a body nor the summit had explicitly and directly recognized Israel or promised normalization. Nevertheless it would be difficult to argue that the predominant trend before the Gulf crisis in the Arab summits and within the PNC had been towards escalating the conflict with Israel, or that the signals being sent to Israel by the PLO and the summits were hostile or provocative.

That much remained to be discussed, fears to be allayed, gaps to be filled, concepts to be refined, assurances to be secured, queries to be made, and clear satisfactory responses to be heard, is hardly surprising. But surely this was at least equally the case, from the Arab point of view, with regard to even the most forthcoming positions elaborated by the Israeli Labour Party. Neither the PNC nor the summit resolutions constituted a complete blue-print. What they did constitute, given the historical context of the genesis and evolution of the Palestine problem, was an unmistakable readiness to compromise and a clear willingness to accommodate the central core values of Israel: survival, existence, acceptance, and recognition, albeit within the 1967 frontiers.

It is no exaggeration to say that there is a well nigh universal recognition, outside Israel and circles of strong support for Israel, that the Arab–Israeli conflict is derivative from the non-resolution of the Palestine problem, and that at the core of the Palestine problem is the issue of the future of the Occupied Territories of East Jerusalem, the West Bank and the Gaza Strip. These territories are all that remains of the Palestinians' ancestral heritage, the only land on which they could under the sun ensure their national core central value of survival, existence, acceptance and recognition. Retention of these territories for this purpose thus represents the core central value for the Palestinians. At the same time, by excluding the whole of pre-1967 Israel (77 per cent of Mandatory Palestine) from their claims, and by restricting their claims to only the Occupied Territories (a necessary corollary to their peace plan as announced in the Algiers PNC), the PLO and the Palestinians made towards Israel a concession of historic proportions in the interests of preserving their central core values of survival, existence, acceptance, and recognition.

Territory, then, is the very crux of any solution to the Palestine problem and the Arab–Israeli conflict. Thus, any negotiations between Israel and the Palestinians, or between Israel and Syria, which ignore or eliminate from the agenda the issue of territory are simply ignoring or even eliminating the source of the conflict and therefore the only possibility of its solution. The same applies to the Golan. Because of Syria's self-image and the pan-Arabist sources of the legitimacy of its regime, the solution of the Palestine problem has to precede or at least be concurrent with the solution of the problem of the Golan. The point to emphasize, however, is that here again we are talking about the exchange of territory for peace.

Yet already before the Gulf crisis, the Likud government had repeatedly, categorically, and unequivocally rejected the land-for-peace concept that lies at the heart of resolution 242. To be sure, there were and are important sectors of Israeli opinion and of its political élite and intelligentsia (Knesset members, retired generals and cabinet ministers, journalists and academics) who see the solution along some such lines as already adumbrated. But that the cornerstone of Likud's policy is the rejection of any territorial concession needs no chapter or verse to demonstrate. This is being daily and cumulatively confirmed, not only by words but also by the relentless escalation of the colonization of the Occupied Territories and their settlement with Soviet Jewish immigrants.

Israeli retention of the Occupied Territories is justified on three grounds: religion, ideology and security. It would be otiose to discuss the religious and ideological grounds, but the security considerations need to be addressed.

Even before the Gulf War it was obvious to some that any Palestinian state in the Occupied Territories would have to be totally demilitarized. This is in the best interests of the state itself. It is not only that a Palestinian state would face formidable reconstruction tasks, and would need to expend all efforts and available funds on tackling such problems. More important, whatever resources it could expend on the military would be wasted: no matter how vast a military force the Palestinian state could assemble, it would be dwarfed by Israel's enormous might. Even if militarization were possible, it would simply sow mistrust and could trigger Israeli preventive action. For these reasons, the strength of the Palestinian state would have to lie precisely in its weakness: its security would not be in its hands but would be wholly dependent on the guarantees of the major powers. Nothing else makes sense; everything else is a recipe for disaster.

To allay Israeli security concerns (all that follows is based on the not easily maintainable assumption that Israel itself would pose no security risk or threat to the Palestinians), the Palestinian state would be bound by its constitution and its treaty with Israel not to enter into any military alliance or arrangement of any kind with any country, Arab or non-Arab. It would be excluded from the provisions of the Arab League Collective Security Pact. It would maintain strong police and security forces armed with equipment specified in quantity and quality in the treaty. It would have no defence installations on its borders with Israel. A multinational force could be stationed in it for ten-year renewable periods: to act as trip-wire along the Jordan River to deter any hostile move from the East, to police the border with Israel against infiltration into Israel, to act as a strategic reserve to help the Palestinian state against radical Palestinian elements, and to move against any Palestinian radical takeover of the state.

Observers from the multinational force would be stationed at all points of access on the Jordan River, at the state's international airports, at the points of access to and from Sinai, and at Gaza harbour. These observers would have the right of unscheduled on-site inspection of any installation or facility that aroused their suspicion.

The treaty between the Palestinian state and Israel would be endorsed by the Arab League and guaranteed by the super-powers. Violation of the treaty would be subject to sanctions and international military collective action if necessary.

The demilitarized regime would be politically reinforced by some federal/confederal arrangement with the moderate monarchical regime in Amman, whose maintenance would be an essential component of the plan. The demilitarized regime would be economically reinforced by economic treaties and arrangements with Israel that could empirically be developed toward some economic association between Israel and the Palestinian/Jordanian federation/confederation.

It is difficult to visualize how the Palestine state outlined above could constitute a security danger to Israel. And there is reason to believe that such a state would be acceptable to the bulk of the Palestinians and to the mainstream factions of the PLO. Even if the latter were not the case, a state with these specifications could be declared by a third party (say, the US) to be the only one that would be envisaged.

It is pertinent to enquire whether some such state has been rendered more or less viable in the post-Gulf war environment. From the Israeli perspective, the Gulf war has had several negative effects. Already before the war the 'geo-political' role of Israel in Washington's eyes vis-à-vis the USSR had been somewhat eroded in the waning of the cold war and the new era of US–Soviet cooperation in the Middle East and elsewhere. The role assigned Israel by the United States in the Gulf crisis – its severest crisis in the Middle East – seemed to be that of 'No Role', which did not serve to enhance the image of Israel's strategic usefulness to the United States in the region.

The arrangements for a Gulf security system, to include pre-positioning of equipment, joint exercises, and the like, had been precisely the role long sought by Israel for itself. From Israel's standpoint, a Gulf security system would consolidate relations between the United States and the Gulf countries, rendering Israel's residual role in the region even more superfluous. It would also expand the arsenals of the Gulf countries and theoretically increase their fighting capacities. Closer US military and economic cooperation with the Gulf countries could be seen as leading to closer political coordination at Israel's expense. The same fear could be entertained as a result of closer US–Soviet relations, as well as closer relations between Syria and the United States and between Syria and Egypt. The increased international and American attentiveness to the Middle East, the new salience of the United Nations and of its resolutions, the precedents being set for sanctions and collective international action, all could potentially generate untoward effects for Israel.

Closer to home, the PLO's alliance with Baghdad and the 'dancing on the roofs' phenomenon (just how many danced on how many roofs and for how long and who counted them, as opposed to how many Israelis cheered Schwartzkopf, will never be known) confirmed in Israeli minds the implacable hostility and utter untrustworthiness of the Palestinians. Last but not least, the Gulf War exposed the vulnerability of Israel to attack by missiles and demonstrated that its deterrence was not foolproof.

Grievously negative for Israel as this list might at first sight appear, closer scrutiny shows that most of these apparent negative factors generated by the Gulf War are multifaceted. Improved relations between the United States and any other country is more an asset for Israel than a liability. The 'geopolitical' role of Israel had always been more rationalization of the massive aid to it than the primary motive power of this aid. The Gulf countries are hardly in a confrontational mood against their erstwhile *de facto* ally, as already shown. Enhanced international deterrence against regional aggression should in theory be welcome to Israel. None of the listed negative effects of the war would seem to reinforce Israel's need on security grounds for the retention of the Occupied Territories. The deepening hatred between Palestinians and Israelis could be argued to be additional cause for separation between the two nationalities. Indeed, the failure of Israeli deterrence (despite the retention of the Occupied Territories) and the demonstration of Israel's vulnerability to missile attack (again despite the retention of these territories) would seem cogently to undermine the relevance of the retention of the Occupied Territories for the security of Israel. Moreover, the prepositioning of US equipment in the Gulf countries is already being 'balanced' by such prepositioning in Israel itself.

If the Gulf War generated some negative effects for Israel, however indeterminate their nature, a longer and far less ambivalent inventory of positive effects could be drawn up. The most far-reaching and significant effect, a *mega*-bonus of undreamed of proportions received at no cost to Israel is the destruction of Iraq's offensive military capability both conventional and unconventional in addition to that of its civilian infrastructure. Already before the war, with Egypt at peace with it and solidly within the American orbit, Israel had a substantial qualitative edge against any practicable Arab military coalition. Not only has Iraq's military capability been destroyed, but the sanctions and reparations regime and its supervisory mechanisms put Iraq under a reincarnated mandate system. Once the Security Council reparations plan is implemented, as much as 25–30 per cent of Iraqi oil revenues[5] would have to be paid as reparations and repayment of debts to foreign governments. Added to this is the vast expenditure needed to summon Iraq back from the Ottoman times into which it was plunged by Schwartzkopf. Even if Saddam remains in office, such predetermined levels of expenditure will ensure his inability to project any significant military power outside his frontiers and particularly against Israel.

To be sure, the arsenals of the Gulf countries will be expanded. But given their isolationist trend, their total absorption in their own priorities, and their newly ingratiating proclivities towards Israel, the likelihood that they would turn these weapons against it are nil. Such a likelihood is rendered even more improbable because of the central role these countries assign the United States in the new Gulf security system.

Nor is Syria in a position to pose a serious military threat to Israel. Syria now finds itself alone facing Israel. If it had illusions about strategic parity in the past, these had already been knocked out by Glasnost Moscow before the Gulf War. To be sure, Syria is using the funds recently received from the Gulf countries to build up its armed forces with Russian, Chinese and North Korean hardware. But it is doing so in strictly defensive mode. It cannot fail to see the pathetically curtailed role of the USSR in the region or to draw the relevant moral from Moscow's acquiescence in the American destruction of its satellite, Iraq. Syria can have no doubt that Moscow cannot help it if it initiates hostilities against Israel. Its strategy during the Gulf crisis was itself an index of its awareness of the sea-change that had occurred in the positions of the superpowers in the region. Relative proximity to the US is itself an insurance policy of Syria against an Israeli attack. It has already given it a freer hand in

Lebanon. Assad in Baghdad would have been an incomparably more formidable adversary. He would have been intellectually and temperamentally incapable of the folly of invading Kuwait. Assad will not subscribe to a peace process that precludes the return of the Occupied Territories and Israeli withdrawal to the 1967 frontiers. He will continue to refurbish his second strike capacity to deter an Israeli first strike. But he also will not sacrifice his vastly strengthened post-Gulf war *political* regional status in a suicidal dash into the Golan.

No security environment is ever ideal. But if the security environment for Israel is less than ideal in the wake of the Gulf war, it is as good as it is likely to be this side of paradise. In fact, a case can be made that Israel stands at the very pinnacle of its military preponderance over the Arabs, more so than at any time since its creation in 1948. The southern front with Egypt is eliminated. The northern front with Syria is quiescent, unless Israel itself wants to stir it up in which case the balance of power, heavily weighted in its favour, would come into play. The incubus of a grand coalition on the Eastern front is dissipated. There is no one who could dispatch out of the blue those rumbling tanks up the eastern slopes of 'Judea'.

Long before the Gulf war, Israel had known what mastery of the skies does to hostile tank formations, however vast, on the defoliated battle fields of the Middle East. It had also known about the devastatingly destructive qualitative edge of smart weapons and high-tech electronic means of communications. The Gulf war could only have reinforced its confidence in its possession of both advantages. It also demonstrated that instantaneous surveillance is possible and is tied to satellites and AWACs, not to isolated lookout posts on solitary hilltops. Even the negative technical military implications of the Gulf War (the demonstration of Israeli vulnerability to missile attack and of the failure of its deterrence) converge with these other considerations to underline the irrelevance of the retention of the Occupied Territories to Israeli security.

Nor do these considerations operate in a vacuum. The perceptions of some Arab countries have been profoundly changed in a manner favourable to Israel. These countries have been shown that aggression can come from an *Arab* country. The war has shown that in certain circumstances at least, a *de facto* alliance can be forged with Israel against an Arab country. The Saladin syndrome has been deflated. Above all, the pernicious outbidding influence of Saddam Hussein on the other Arab capitals has been removed as a major obstacle to the pursuit of a pragmatic strategy for the peaceful resolution of the Arab–Israeli conflict, along the lines of the Fez peace plan.

In addition, the United States now presides as the undisputed and paramount power in the Middle East. It has committed itself to the defence of the international frontiers of the region. Its military presence in the Gulf will add credibility to its deterrent power. It has translated its strategic alliance with Israel into actual participation in the defence of the country. If it is security considerations that inhibit Israel from entering a historic compromise with the Palestinians and the Arabs on the bases of reciprocal recognition of the core values of the two sides, the rationale for these considerations is not instantaneously apparent. On the other hand, it may not be altogether far-fetched to accommodate the thought that perhaps such a favourable constellation of security factors in the wake of the Gulf War might in fact operate as a disincentive for the Israeli leadership to do so. This is less cynical than it sounds given the triumphalist mood of the Israeli leadership long before the devastation of Iraq and even before the perceived neutralization of the Palestinian demographic factor as a result of the massive influx of Soviet Jews.

The Parameters of the Post-War US Peace Initiative

Long before the Gulf War, volatility was characteristic of the two major areas of potential conflagration lying at either end of the Fertile Crescent: The Palestine problem and the Arab–Israeli conflict in the West, and the Arabian Gulf tensions in the East. During the Gulf crisis itself, interaction between the tensions in the two areas (as exemplified, for instance, in the issue of 'linkage') reached threateningly dangerous proportions.

The consequences of the Gulf War have for a shorter or longer period of time put a lid on the volatility of the eastern end of the Fertile Crescent, while offering a breathing space for the tackling of the volatility at its western end. Apart from removing for the duration Iraq's capacity to project its power beyond its borders, the war's outcome has likewise neutralized Baghdad's role in generating outbidding pressures on the other Arab capitals, pressures which in the past had circumscribed their willingness or ability further to develop their pragmatic policies on the Palestine problem and the Arab–Israeli conflict.

The consequences of the Gulf War have also created at the western end of the Fertile Crescent an environment which, as has been argued, could hardly be said to militate against Israeli security and could therefore be seen as propitious for imaginative peace initiatives between Israel on the one hand and the Palestinian people and the Arab countries on the other. In brief, in the wake of the Gulf War, we have the window of opportunity alluded to waiting to be exploited, if not by the regional actors themselves – because of fear, mistrust, self interest, ideology or religious fanaticism – then by a third party with the power, prestige and interest to do so.

The Middle East that has emerged from the Gulf War may not be mere clay in the hands of the American potter, but never since the Ottoman conquest of the sixteenth century and, in more recent times, since imperial Britain at the end of World War I fashioned the political landscape of the region, has any one power so dominated the Middle East as the United States does today. Given this position in which the US finds itself – its leadership of the coalition countries, the principles it invoked in its diplomatic and military campaign against Saddam Hussein, its closer post-war relations with the Arab Gulf countries, its enhanced leverage with the principal actors throughout the Arab and non-Arab Middle East, the deference by the United Nations and all the major powers of the world to its role and wishes in the Middle East, its own repeatedly avowed determination to establish a new order there, as well as the expectations all this has aroused both inside and outside the region – it is transparently obvious that the United States cannot escape the duty of exploring to the full, for the benefit of a more stable and secure Middle East, this window of opportunity proffered by the Gulf hostilities at such an horrendous cost in human lives.

To be sure, the post-war policies pursued by Washington in the Gulf would seem to indicate a strategically percipient approach to that area, inasmuch as the US has rejected the calls for the dismemberment of Iraq or for a salient extra-regional presence to allay minority fears inside Iraq itself. Likewise, the US is apparently opting for a non-salient military presence of its own in the Gulf. It is commendably registering disapproval of Kuwaiti thuggery against non-Kuwaiti nationals, and indicating a readiness to defuse tensions with Iran, while maintaining the sanctions and disarmament regimes against an Iraq ruled by Saddam Hussein.

It is true that despite constraints imposed by other Gulf countries, the United States could do more for the cause of democratization in Kuwait. In the last analysis, a Kuwaiti regime that is popularly accountable is much less vulnerable to a reconstructed but revanchiste post-Saddam Iraq. The US could also probably do more to temper the vindictiveness of the Gulf states towards the have-not Arab countries that did not join the anti-Saddam coalition. Such an American effort makes sense not only for the sake of regional socio-economic stability, but also as a prudential measure to lessen the chances of a popular backlash targeting Washington's Arab wards in the Gulf, no less than American military presence itself in the area, however non-salient. It would also behove the United States to give thought to the process of phasing out the sanctions regime against Iraq in the event of Saddam's disappearance. This, too, as it becomes practicable, would make sense in order to forestall and dissipate to the extent possible any vengeful proclivities in a post-Saddam Iraq vis-à-vis the other Gulf states and to improve the chances of reconciliation with them. Most questionable, perhaps, with regard to American policies in the Gulf area, is Washington's attempt to use these 'peripheral countries' for leverage against the Arab countries neighbouring Israel.

If by and large US post-war policy with regard to the Gulf area is characterized by an apparent long-term view and cognizance of regional conditions, the same cannot be said with regard to US policy on the Palestine problem and the Arab–Israeli conflict. Whereas US policy in the Gulf region seems to be significantly conditioned by the course the war took and its consequences in that region, it appears to be decoupled from such considerations at the Mediterranean end of the Fertile Crescent. Thus, despite President Bush's explicit verbal espousal before Congress of the land for peace principle and Secretary Baker's strenuous diplomatic activity since the end of hostilities, it is difficult to banish the impression that actual US policy in the aftermath of the Gulf war substantively duplicates the pre-Kuwait invasion policy. Indeed, as far as US policy on the Palestine problem and the Arab–Israeli conflict is concerned, it would seem as if the Gulf War to all intents and purposes had not even taken place.

The same assumptions and parameters that guided pre-war policies do so in the aftermath of the war. There had been no cognizance by Washington before the war of the historic compromises of the 1982 Fez and subsequent Arab summits, nor of the 1988 Algiers PNC and the subsequent positions of Arafat. There had been no call to Israel to reciprocate with steps commensurate with those taken by the Arab summits and the PLO mainstream leadership. At best, Washington's posture was one of symmetry of blame, and *both* sides had to start from a *tabula rasa*. To be sure, Washington had started an ostensibly 'substantive dialogue' with the PLO. In fact, out of deference to Israel, the dialogue was not with the PLO nor was it substantive. Washington's assumptions remain the same today, and the 'dialogue' with the PLO has been suspended on the ostensible grounds of the operation by Abul Abbas, no protégé of Arafat. Continued rejection of contact with the PLO is now justified by the PLO's 'alliance' with Saddam Hussein, a consideration which does not however seem to apply to Washington's resumed dialogue with Jordan.

More striking is the increasing evidence that this administration has from the beginning been operating within the parameters set by the Shamir four-point plan of April 1989. Briefly, the plan *first* assigns the three signatories of the Camp David accords (Israel, Egypt, the United States) the leading role in securing the adherence of the other Arab countries to these accords. *Second*, it considers the source of the conflict to be the refusal of the Arab countries to recognize or establish diplomatic relations with Israel. It therefore calls for 'the building of confidence' through a change in the attitude of the Arab countries leading to ending the boycott and normalization of relations by way of bilateral negotiations. *Third*, it considers that the Palestinian refugee problem has been perpetuated by the Arab states and the PLO and that the refugees are principally an international responsibility. Israel itself is meeting its own responsibilities towards Jewish refugees. The Palestine refugee problem is a humanitarian, not a political problem, and must be decoupled from the political process. *Fourth*, it calls for elections in 'Judea, Samaria, and Gaza [*sic*]' to produce a delegation which will negotiate for a self-governing administration to be set up for an interim period to be followed by negotiations for a final settlement.[6]

One does not have to be a clairvoyant to see that Secretary Baker's pre-Gulf war efforts focussed on point four of this plan, formalized by the Shamir government itself (reportedly with guidance from members of the US National Security Council) in May 1989, and that now, in the aftermath of the Gulf War, it is focussing on point two. The whole vocabulary of what Baker calls his 'second track' derives from Shamir's second point: viz. confidence-building, dropping the boycott, normalization and bilateral negotiations.

Nor does one have to be clairvoyant to see that the essence of Shamir's plan as a whole is crafted to avoid and bypass the crux and kernel of the Palestine problem and the Arab–Israeli conflict – the issue of self-determination by the Palestinian people on what is left of their ancestral territory.[7]

That the thrust of Secretary Baker's diplomacy in the new post-Gulf war political and security environment should be point two of the Shamir plan is all the more surprising in view of his pre-war experiences with Shamir over point four, culminating in his public announcement, essentially directed at Shamir, of his telephone number in case serious negotiations were envisaged. But whatever Secretary Baker's compelling considerations today, he seems well set again on a garden path landscaped by Shamir.

At first sight, it could appear sensible to organize a conference to discuss such issues as water, environment and arms control, or the Arab boycott against Israel and normalization with the Arab states. However, it is difficult to see the purpose of such discussions given the yawning gap between Israel on the one hand, the Palestinian people, Jordan and Syria on the other over the core issue of territory and their diametrical, antithetical positions on it. It is more realistic to assume that in the absence of agreement on this core issue, such discussions would remain essentially irrelevant, neither contributing to confidence-building (and more likely exacerbating relations) nor to the resolution of the basic source of conflict.

Seeming US support, under Israeli pressure, of a non-UN-sponsored conference (or a conference involving a meaningless, attenuated UN presence) is in dramatic contrast to the central role assigned the UN by Washington to policy in the Gulf area. The absence of the UN from a conference does not augur well for the role of UN resolutions, particularly Resolution 242 envisaged by the US for the resolution of the Palestine problem and the Arab–Israeli conflict. It further undermines the viability of a conference, regional or international, whose basic function in any case seems to be the implementation of point two of Shamir's plan. It is in such soil that Israeli triumphalism can only become more deeply rooted.

But even if one gave such a conference the benefit of the doubt, it is not clear what it could achieve even within the technical bounds of its agenda items. For example, the most pressing environmental issue in the Middle East today is the raging fires in the Kuwait oil fields and the oil slicks in the Gulf. There is nothing that Kuwait could learn about fighting oil-well fires or oil slicks from Israel, Syria, Jordan or Egypt.

On the water issue, there are no water problems between the Gulf countries and Israel, Jordan, Syria, Egypt or Lebanon. The Gulf countries have solved their water problem through desalinization, a process which is beyond the means of the other countries. Egypt's water problems lie in the classical upstream/downstream context of equitable apportionment with the riparian states of the Nile River, and not with any of the other Arab countries or Israel. The water problems of the Euphrates and the Tigris basin lie within the same context, and involve the three riparian states of Syria, Iraq and Turkey. They cannot be meaningfully discussed in the absence of Iraq or Turkey. The water problems of the Jordan basin (between Israel on the one hand and the Occupied Territories, Jordan, Syria and Lebanon on the other) are structurally and qualitatively different from those of the Gulf countries, or the Nile and the Euphrates/Tigris systems. They are integrally linked to issues of occupation, annexation, colonization and massive extra-regional (Soviet Jewish) immigration. They cannot be seriously discussed *in vacuo* or on a purely quantitative or engineering basis. In short, their discussion cannot precede the discussion of the issue of territory.

Concerning arms control, any discussions by Middle Eastern

countries within or outside the regional conference have to be conducted against the background of the ongoing virtual disarmament (conventional and unconventional) of Iraq and of President Bush's arms control initiative announced in late May. With regard to Iraq, it should be kept in mind that no post-Saddam regime, however benign, is likely to acquiesce in the status of the disarmed guinea-pig of the region. This makes it all the more imperative to put in place in the meantime an arms-control regime acceptable to the other principal regional actors. But an arms-control regime (such as President Bush's) which in essence perpetuates Israel's nuclear monopoly and first-strike capacity (qualitative edge plus anti-missile defences) while eroding or eliminating the second-strike capacity of the Arab countries (unconventional weapons and missiles) does not qualify as such a regionally acceptable regime. When its advocacy is concurrent with the advocacy of a political solution along the lines of Shamir's four-point plan, little incentive is left for the Arab countries to accept. It would in the circumstances seem that the time, political clout and energy to be spent on such an arms-control regime would be better spent on tackling the root causes of the arms race in the Middle East.

To do otherwise is to put the cart before the horse. Man does not fight because he has arms. He has arms because he has to fight in defence or aggrandizement. Looking to the Mediterranean end of the Fertile Cresent, the arms race between Israel and its neighbours where a state of belligerence exists is a function of that state of belligerence, which in turn is a function of the issues of occupation, annexation and colonization. It would seem obvious that as effective an approach to arms control as any for that region would be to address the root cause of the state of belligerence – the non-resolution of the Palestine problem and the Arab–Israeli conflict.

The role most appropriate for the United States, therefore, is to ascertain the exact positions of Israel, on the one hand, and the PLO and the other Arab states, on the other, with regard to the central issue of reciprocal recognition and acceptance of one another. If there are fears to be allayed, gaps to be filled, concepts to be refined, assurances to be secured, queries to be made, and clear satisfactory responses to be heard on this central issue of reciprocal recognition and acceptance of one another, surely this is precisely where US prestige, power and leverage could best be brought to bear in the cause of peace. To do otherwise is merely to seek to give the *impression* of progress. This may well be the objective of the United States, Israel, and the other Arab countries – albeit for different reasons. The impression of progress is not synonymous with actual movement towards peaceful resolution. It could be the opposite.

Time is the most decisive factor affecting the chances of movement towards a more stable Middle East in the aftermath of the Gulf War. The crucial time-span is the immediate future – the next two to five years.

A regional or international conference that bypasses the central territorial issue uses up precious time. If this time is meanwhile used by Israel to bring, with United States support, another one million Soviet Jews into the area, the possibility of a tolerable *modus vivendi* on the Palestine problem and the Arab–Israeli conflict will have been permanently excluded.

Arab perception of the US role in effecting such an outcome will be no asset to the United States or its Arab Gulf allies. The charges of hypocrisy and double standards levelled against Washington will gather momentum. The worst suspicions concerning US motivation in the devastation of Iraq will be confirmed. The factors fuelling the popular backlash in the wings will be reinforced. Iraq cannot be kept in indefinite vassalage. The chances of violent .interaction between the two areas of conflagration at either end of the Fertile Crescent will increase. The post-Gulf War window of opportunity will vanish out of view. The Middle East will ineluctably slide towards its next major catastrophe.

Notes

1   Walid Khalidi, *The Gulf Crisis: Origins and Consequences*, (Washington, D.C.: The Institute for Palestine Studies, 1991).
2   *New York Review of Books*, 11 April 1991, p. 12.
3   Ghassan Salame, *Arabic Journal of Palestine Studies*, winter 1991, issue 5, p. 50.
4   *Al-Hayat*, 30 April 1991.
5   *New York Times*, 15 May 1991.

6   *Jerusalem Post Weekly*, 22 April 1989.
7   See this volume, pp. 174 ff.